LEAD SISTER

LEAD SISTER

The Story of Karen Carpenter

LUCY O'BRIEN

ROWMAN & LITTLEFIELD
Lanham • Boulder • New York • London

Originally published in the English in the UK by Nine Eight Books,
an imprint of Bonnier Books UK

Published by Rowman & Littlefield
An imprint of The Rowman & Littlefield Publishing Group, Inc.
4501 Forbes Boulevard, Suite 200, Lanham, Maryland 20706
www.rowman.com
86-90 Paul Street, London EC2A 4NE

Hardback ISBN: 978-1-5381-8446-2
eBook ISBN: 978-1-5381-8447-9

A CIP catalogue record for this book is available from the British Library.

Every reasonable effort has been made to trace copyright-holders of material
reproduced in this book. If any have been inadvertently overlooked,
the publisher would be glad to hear from them.

∞™ The paper used in this publication meets the minimum requirements of
American National Standard for Information Sciences—Permanence of Paper for
Printed Library Materials, ANSI/NISO Z39.48-1992.

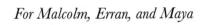

For Malcolm, Erran, and Maya

CONTENTS

INVOCATION

I first became aware of the Carpenters when I was nine years old and "We've Only Just Begun" was drifting across the airwaves. The Carpenters symbolized America, which in 1970 seemed a warm, dreamy, expansive place where the cars were huge, the skyscrapers were tall, and the sun always blazed out of a blue sky. Baudrillard described this vision as "Astral America . . . Star-blasted, horizontally by the car, altitudinally by the plane, electronically by television, geologically by deserts . . . the power museum . . . for the whole world."[1] Britain then was still rebuilding itself after the long shadow of the Second World War and was a society riven by class divisions and the stuffy demarcation of high and low art. American pop culture, by contrast, seemed free and radiant, epitomized in the cool sheen of the Carpenters' sound.

Formed in 1969, sibling duo Richard and Karen Carpenter created lush soundscapes of melodic pop and the Carpenters became one of the biggest-selling acts of the 1970s and early 1980s, with global hits like "Close to You," "Yesterday Once More," "Please Mr. Postman," and "Only Yesterday." Before Karen's tragic death from anorexia in 1983, the duo recorded eight classic albums and had three number-one and five number-two singles on the

1

Billboard *Hot 100. They have sold more than 100 million records worldwide, making them one of the best-selling music acts of all time.*

My memories of growing up are infused with Carpenters songs—in the 1970s they were everywhere. I used to tape the top twenty every Sunday night on my Philips cassette recorder and write down the weekly charts in an exercise book and the Carpenters were a permanent fixture. Despite their wholesome image (the first time I saw them on TV Karen wore a long starched faux-Victorian dress and Richard looked awkward in a pink shirt and crisp white suit), their music morphed and moved in surprising ways. I remember singing "Top of the World" and "Sing" at the top of my voice in the primary school choir, but then one night "Goodbye to Love" debuted on Top of the Pops. *The video showed a woman gazing from the window as a car pulled away, while Karen Carpenter's soulful voice trailed into an astounding choral break followed by Tony Peluso's passionate, extended, shredding guitar solo. It was a sound so dramatic, so desolate, that the next day at school it was all we could talk about.*

Aged thirteen, I remember going to the fairground with my friend Catherine, both of us wearing long multicolored stripey socks with platform shoes, flirting with the fairground boys and being spun in circles on the Waltzer to the joyful girl group-style blast of "Please Mr. Postman." Even though I discovered punk rock at fifteen, I was still drawn into the Carpenters' world with the off-kilter resonance of "Calling Occupants of Interplanetary Craft," where Karen's voice echoed into a distant, electronic ether. I formed an all-girl punk band and for a few years was listening to different, more urgent, DIY post-punk sounds, but the Carpenters still played in the back of my mind as an example of the perfection against which punk rebelled. They became a symbol of pop kitsch that everybody loved.

2

THE STORY OF KAREN CARPENTER

The news of Karen's early death in 1983 was shocking. I was at university in Leeds at the time, and research into eating disorders and anorexia was in its early stages. Her illness was undoubtedly influenced by the slimming culture of our generation. Along with my friends I remember counting calories and religiously checking my weight on the scales every morning, fretting if I gained 1 or 2 pounds. We self-policed our bodies, trying to eradicate any excess, because signs of extra weight or cellulite meant that you were out of control and undesirable. As young women in the 1970s and '80s we were bombarded with messages that we had to say No to extra calories, No to unwanted attention, No to predatory men—we had to set the boundaries; this was all within our jurisdiction. We had to be liberated and free and sexual, while at the same time suppressing ourselves.

I gained a new understanding of Karen Carpenter when Todd Haynes's film Superstar *came out in 1987, an artful low-budget animation of her life story and her struggle with anorexia. His film showed the dark undercurrent beneath the surface of that shiny, glossy American pop. This was followed in 1990 by Sonic Youth's "Tunic (Song for Karen)." Written by their iconic bassist Kim Gordon, it was a blistering, evocative tribute from one female musician to another. And then in 1993, when I was researching Karen's story for my book* She Bop, *a history of women in popular music, I listened again to "Rainy Days and Mondays" and heard a deeply felt suburban blues. For me, this was the beginning of reframing her story as a feminist heroine—someone who with her brother made beautiful, heart-wrenching music despite her eating disorder and despite feeling restricted by the expectations of her family and her record company. Her life was an example of how the music industry—in its relentless promotion of women as saleable commodities—made female performers sick.*

3

Returning to her story now, I am aware how Karen's legacy and influence has grown and, though her death was unutterably sad, what survives is a sense of her unique chutzpah and precise focus—not just as a singer, but also a drummer, vocal arranger, and producer. Like all significant artists, what is fascinating is the way her voice has permeated pop culture. Once I played "Goodbye to Love," in full, to a seminar class of young music technology students. They have little patience with music that's inauthentic or superficial or beyond their millennial reference points. But while I played the track they listened, rapt, and sat in silence after the closing chords. "Wow," said one. "That was in the 1970s? That was something special."

When the Carpenters first toured Japan, a translation error in a magazine meant that Karen was mistakenly referred to as "lead sister" of the band. The term stuck and Karen liked it so much she had a T-shirt custom-made with the slogan and wore it while she played drums on the band's 1976 world tour. The term sums up Karen's life as a pioneering woman with her own agency and vision. In the teen press of the 1970s much was made of the Carpenters as talented siblings—with Karen portrayed as a cool girl who could sing and play drums. To a generation of female fans she was like an older sister, our lead sister.

With this book I want to capture what was special about Karen, the lead sister. She was self-effacing about her talent and disinclined to talk about it, and this, coupled with the sexism of the 1960s and '70s, meant that her words and her contribution were downplayed, almost buried. In order to tease out who Karen was as an artist and musician, there is detective work to be done: not just interviewing friends and musicians who worked with her, but digging through radio and media archives to find her words—what she said about herself and the process, what she communicated in song and how she saw the world.

Now, forty years after her death, we can still hear in her voice a deep understanding of the power and pain of love. Paul McCartney once described it as the "best female voice in the world: melodic, tuneful, distinctive." She has inspired generations of singers across music genres, from Madonna to k. d. lang to My Chemical Romance's Gerard Way and transgender dream pop artist Ethel Cain. Karen is now recognized—along with Frank Sinatra, Aretha Franklin, and Dusty Springfield—as one of the greatest singers in popular music. This is her story.

PROLOGUE

It was 1979; this was her chance. Karen loved the studio session recorded two years previously for the song "B'wana She No Home," in which she plays a wealthy recluse with a swanky car and a sassy servant. Everyone had been in the studio that day—all the musicians, technicians, and engineers—for a jazz fusion jam. Pete Jolly played that syncopated piano and Tom Scott riffed with his sax. She had a blast, singing with a different voice, one that was lighter, sly, wry, and funky. She'd always been a jazz drummer and loved the swing in the song, the touch of Brazilian samba.

That was the first time someone other than her brother Richard had composed the vocal arrangement. Gene Puerling, who'd led jazz vocal groups like the Hi-Lo's and the Manhattan Transfer, scored the vocals and had Karen singing in a playful style, refreshingly different from the Carpenters' trademark lachrymose ballads.

Now she was about to cut her solo album and she knew she wanted to explore more of that sound. Sales of Carpenters records had been falling off and it was time to bring in a new audience. Disco had revolutionized the scene, and they were moving into the 1980s. Her best friend Olivia Newton-John had reinvented herself with *Grease*, so why shouldn't Karen? Only she wasn't going to do it with a character like Sandy, chewing gum and doing '50s moves in black Spandex pants. No, Karen liked wearing tailored suits; she was going to re-vision herself in a way that was cooler and more androgynous, more like her mentor, A&M Records boss Herb Alpert. The elegant trumpeter had dominated the 1960s and early '70s with the Tijuana Brass and classy but corny easy-listening songs like "This Guy's in Love with You." But then in 1979 he came out with "Rise," an electric finger-snapping piece of jazz funk. If he could reinvent himself like that, so could she.

From twenty-two floors up in her Century City apartment, Karen had an exhilarating view of Los Angeles, the Hollywood Hills, and Santa Monica. It was time to sound less suburban, more uptown. Phil Ramone was already on board as producer and she would be working with some hip arrangers—Rod Temperton, the architect of disco smash "Boogie Nights," and Bob James, whose piano break on "Nautilus" would later be sampled on a million hip hop tunes.

Karen had the team and she was excited. But there was the problem of her anorexia, which haunted and drained and dogged her at every turn. She'd been in hospital and got her weight back up. She had been on the phone with Cherry Boone O'Neill, eldest sister of the singing Boone family, who had also suffered from anorexia. During their blunt, direct conversation

Cherry told Karen that the only thing that cured her was giving up showbusiness and moving far away to a quiet life in the northwest. But Karen didn't have time for that. She was usually the family problem, but ironically it was Richard who was in a rehab treatment center. While he was far away in Kansas, she had the space to explore a new side of herself. With this record she could help reposition the Carpenters and bring them into the 1980s. Karen wanted to disprove the naysayers, those who'd written off the group as too sugary and white-bread. She was no longer the tag-along sister; she would prove that she wasn't Richard's puppet, just the voice for his production. Her time was now.

BOOK 1
Offering

CHAPTER 1

1950–1963

For a long time my parents had been waiting for a daughter. Finally, on March 2, 1950, my mother gave birth to a girl, that, of course being me. I was born in Grace New Haven Hospital located in New Haven, Connecticut . . . The fun in my life began when I began to walk . . . I opened my mouth, which never closed since, and said my first words, those being "bye-bye" and "stop it."[1]

So begins Karen Carpenter's autobiography, written for a school project in precise, elegant, cursive handwriting on three sheets of paper, at the age of thirteen. It was June 1963 and the Carpenter family were about to move three thousand miles away to Los Angeles and leave New Haven behind. The town is like its name—christened the "Elm City," New Haven's calm, green tree-lined streets border the wild beauty of East Shore and the Long Island Sound. Karen grew up in a modest three-bedroom house in a neighborhood of Italian immigrant families.

She was a tomboy who loved playing softball and baseball, and whenever her sensitive older brother Richard was bullied by local boys she would fight to protect him. "She was different, an iconoclast," Richard said. Right from the start, Karen's energy and enthusiasm were infectious.

Even though she was not seen as the musical one in the family, Karen took ballet and tap lessons from the age of four and when she and Richard devoured piles of records in marathon listening sessions, Karen was always drumming her fingers to the beat of the tracks. According to her family script Richard was the one destined for greatness—"He is a talented pianist," she wrote in her autobiography, whereas "my hobbies are popular dancing, collecting records and drawing. I like them all very much although I never get much chance to do them." Over time, the popular dancing and collecting records developed into drumming and singing and intense musical creativity. Karen's initial path to success was a series of accidents, of trying and failing and experimenting until she arrived at the identity the world came to know.

At fifteen, when most girls of her age had pictures of pop stars on their bedroom walls, Karen's idols were middle-aged jazz drummers. Their bebop parlance and rhythmic approach to the world hold clues as to what drove her, as do the other influences— divas she studied such as Barbra Streisand, Dusty Springfield, and Ella Fitzgerald. Like so many female artists before her, Karen was driven by an instinctive rhythmic and musical passion and thought outside what was expected of her as a girl. "I've never been one that likes being told what to do . . . I'm kinda hard-headed . . . so I find other routes," she once said.[2] A restless spirit, her life became a quest to find her place as a musician, a sister and a woman in the world.

*

Karen's father, the gentle, kindly Harold Carpenter, had an unsettled childhood of broken attachments and frequent disruption. He was born in 1908 in Wuzhou, southern China, the son of a British father and an American mother. Karen and Richard's paternal grandfather, George Bertram Carpenter, was an enterprising London boy who went to Glasgow to find work at a forge company constructing castings for battleships. He befriended a Scotsman who sailed to America to start a new life, and George followed him, arriving in New York in 1900. There he became a missionary and met fellow religious training student Nellie Jane Lynn, a red-haired woman with a strong singing voice who became his wife. She and George moved to China to carry out missionary work but soon abandoned it when they started a family, ending up in Hong Kong, where George worked as a harbor engineer. They were a sociable couple and keen pianists, playing at their formal Hong Kong dinner parties. They had high hopes for Harold and organized piano lessons, but he showed more interest in listening to music rather than playing an instrument.

Those days of genteel parties and playing the piano soon ended when George found work in a large merchant firm in Yunnan province, nearly 800 miles away. Nellie baulked at this and for the sake of their children's education she decided to take Harold and his siblings Esther and Richard to England, leaving their father behind. Harold was nine years old when they made the long, tortuous journey by land, sea and Trans-Siberian Railway to England. It was 1917, so they were traveling through Russia at the time of the revolution and in the middle of the First World War. Not long after they arrived Harold and his siblings were deposited at boarding school. He spent holidays with a foster mother in London watching German Zeppelin bombing raids, while Nellie went back to China, where younger sisters Geraldine and Guinevere were born.

Harold had to wait four years before seeing his parents again, when in 1921 George and Nellie reunited the family in England. Relations between them were strained, however, because they parted again and Nellie took the children to live with her family in Wellsville, New York. Fourteen-year-old Harold attended Wellsville High School, dropping out two years later when his mother fell sick with a lung ailment.

There was pressure on young Harold to provide for the family, so he moved to Middletown, Ohio, where his uncle Frank Stoddard found him a job working at a cardboard box company. He moved several times with his relations before they settled in Catonsville, Maryland, just west of Baltimore, and he secured work in a printing firm. It was there that he met Karen's mother, Agnes Reuwer Tatum, an athlete and a capable seamstress who went to the oldest girls' state school in Baltimore. The second eldest of four sisters, Agnes had a bustling, pragmatic energy— once she focused on a goal she could be very single-minded. So when she met easy-going, good-looking Harold through a family friend, her interest was piqued. Sixteen-year-old Agnes was even more impressed when he saw her a few weeks later standing at a bus stop with younger sisters Audrey and Bernice and gave them a lift in his Chevrolet.

So began a four-year courtship that led to their wedding in April 1935, in the middle of the Great Depression. Although Agnes's father, George Tatum, ran a wholesale underwear business, money was short, so she and Harold had no wedding cake, no honeymoon and the only wedding gift was an electric iron from her uncle.

As newlyweds Agnes and Harold rented a $5-a-week apartment and as soon as they moved in she scrubbed it clean until the three rooms and shared bathroom they had were immaculate. Then she proceeded to wash the whole house. In their next furnished apartment, she cleaned that too, including all the dusty decoration plates their landlady had placed on the narrow wall ledge in the living room. Not long after Agnes and Harold were married, her elder sister Jenny Tyrell separated from her husband. Being a single mother in the late 1930s would have invited social disapproval, so Agnes and Harold took in Jenny's eighteen-month-old daughter Joanie and raised her as if she was their own child.

With baby Joanie in tow, Agnes and Harold relocated to Mechanicsville, Virginia, for five years before moving once more to an apartment in New Haven, Connecticut. Jenny joined them and was reunited with her daughter for a while, living with the family until 1943. Agnes and Harold began to build up a little capital—he operated the printing equipment at the New Haven Pulp and Board Company, while she worked eight-hour shifts six days a week at the local defense plant, Mettler Brothers Manufacturing, keeping three thread grinders running. To make additional money Harold and Agnes washed cars at weekends with their own pick-up and delivery service.

The Carpenters were a prime example of a proud, practical working-class American family made good. After grafting and saving during the war years, in 1945 they had enough money to put down a deposit on a new house being built as part of a post-war development at 55 Hall Street, in the suburban East Shore Annex area near New Haven harbor. In the tenth year of their marriage Agnes became pregnant and their son Richard Lynn (named after Harold's brother) was born on October 15, 1946, two months after they moved into the house on Hall Street.

From an early age Richard showed a fascination with music. As a toddler he took an avid interest in his father's copious collection of 78s and at the age of three requested his own record, a copy of the cowboy song "Mule Train," quickly followed by "How Much Is That Doggie in the Window?" by pop country singer Patti Page. Soon he had someone to share that musical enthusiasm. Agnes became pregnant again and on March 2, 1950, Richard's sister Karen Anne arrived. The Carpenters' compact three-bedroom house was now crammed full with five people, including Joanie, who was now a teenager.

Agnes kept the house meticulously and ferociously clean, made sure the lawn was neatly manicured and shined the car in the front yard until it was gleaming. Karen's close childhood friend Frank Bonito remembered Agnes as "functioning at a very high anxiety level," polishing other people's windows as well as her own.[3] The Carpenters continued their car-washing service to earn extra money. Doing all the cooking, housework and childcare, as well as scrubbing all the neighborhood cars (and windows), meant that Agnes didn't get much time to rest.

Karen inherited her parents' busy, down-to-earth work ethic and her mother's strong-willed determination. Richard was thin and sensitive and although she was three years younger, Karen took on all the hoodlums if he was bullied at school. A self-declared tomboy, she loved baseball and was a devoted Yankees fan, displaying a prodigious talent for memorizing batting averages. She enjoyed wrestling and acrobatics and preferred toy guns to dolls. Karen was also one of the few girls in the area to do a daily paper round, zipping round on her bike delivering the *New Haven Register*. "While Richard was listening to music the whole time—we had a basement and he never left it—I was out playing baseball and football and playing with my machine gun. Very tomboyish," recalled Karen.[4] She expressed her love of music in dancing and was delightfully unselfconscious, practising steps and performing on the sidewalk outside their house in her tap shoes and sequinned costume.

Karen was a popular girl, making friends with children who lived on the street, many of whom came from Italian immigrant families. She became particularly close to Debbie Vaiuso, daughter of Carl and Theresa, who lived at number 77. Debbie and her brother Joe would spend time with Karen and Richard rollerskating or playing ball games or hula-hooping or snowballing in winter and every afternoon they would watch *The Mickey Mouse Club* on TV. Karen's love of Mickey Mouse stemmed from those idyllic days when the children were constantly in and out of each other's houses. She was a thoughtful friend—one summer Joe broke his arm and she visited him every day to keep him company. Another companion was Frank Bonito, who lived at number 83 and who, like Karen, attended Nathan Hale Elementary School just round the corner from Hall Street. Every day they walked to and from school together, picking up other friends as they went along.

The parents became friends too, sharing hardworking aspirant American values. Theresa Vaiuso, for instance, was close to Agnes, remembering her as a direct woman and a disciplinarian, but also ready to help her neighbors. Karen and Richard were accepted and welcomed as part of the Vaiuso family in an effusive warm-hearted way that was typical of the Italian community. Cathy Capozzi, a musician who grew up near New Haven in the 1960s, recalls these connections as very important. "My own family were hardcore Italian, it's a super-tight community. Karen would have been considered family if she was a friend. 'Yo, you want to have food? You come to our house!' All the Italian families were very similar," she says.[5] Music was also a key part of the culture, particularly romantic crooners. Capozzi remembers how much her grandparents loved Frank Sinatra, Perry Como, Guy Lombardo, Louis Prima—singers who transplanted the romantic embellishments of Italian folk to American popular music.

Karen's velvety singing style echoed some of those Italian crooners. "The money's in the basement," she once said, with reference to the deep tone of her voice. Her musical world did indeed develop in a basement. When the children were small Harold converted the cellar into a play area, hanging swings from the rafters. It was also where he stored his vast record collection, shelves of 78s and 45s that were carefully curated and arranged, spanning every music genre from classical Russian romantics like Rachmaninov and Tchaikovsky to Dixieland jazz, western swing and Spike Jones, the 1930s and '40s bandleader who played spoof arrangements of popular songs.

The basement became a haven and an escape from the rooms upstairs where Agnes might be busy cooking or cleaning. Karen idolized her brother, spending hours with him dancing and listening to records, singing along to melodies and dissecting the arrangements. Pretending it was a record shop, Richard fashioned a sign for the space which spelled out in big, bright letters "RICHIE'S MUSIC CORNER." One of Richard's first toys was a Bing Crosby Junior Juke, a tiny record player for shellac 78s that lit up when it played. After that he was glued to a Zenith radio console, regularly tuning in to Alan Freed's top-forty show coming out of WINS in New York. Freed was the pioneering DJ who in the 1950s helped to break down racial segregation in music by promoting African-American R&B sounds under the moniker of rock 'n' roll. With a manic style and jive chat, he championed original records by black artists, accusing other DJs of prejudice when they chose to play cover versions by white artists. From a young age, Richard listened to WINS and took note of the *Billboard* charts and the sounds of the singles that made the top ten. "I idolised Richard so much and we were so close, even though we were three years apart, I did everything he did," said Karen. "Thus every record we've ever listened to is embedded in my mind. And we listened to a lot of different types of music because my father had a varied record collection."[6]

This was the beginning of Karen's musical education, where she absorbed all her formative influences. And the basement den was something that the Carpenters replicated later on with the recording studio, creating for themselves a similarly closed, magical musical world. It was a while before Karen showed any inclination to play an instrument, but Richard gravitated toward the piano at the age of eight, when cousin Joanie bought one for the household and he began lessons with a local teacher, Mrs. Florence June. She was a hard taskmistress, however, and her rigorous approach took all the fun out of piano-playing. Richard gave up lessons, but kept improvising on the keys until, three years later, his parents found a new teacher, a pleasant, keen music student at the University of Hartford called Henry Will. By the age of fourteen Richard was making such progress that Agnes and Harold bought a new piano, a black Baldwin Acrosonic with a bright, powerful tone, and positioned it in the center of the dining room. Richard progressed rapidly on the piano until he outgrew Will and, at the latter's recommendation, began studying at Yale Music School under the tutelage of Professor Seymour Fink. Will stayed in the family—having taken a shine to Joanie, he began dating her and later they got married.

Richard was the family prodigy and, despite her enthusiasm for music, Karen's gift wasn't acknowledged and she was relegated to little sister, following in his shadow. But she was an active listener, absorbing every melody she heard. Later, music critics would write that Karen's smooth vocal style was at odds with the raw rock of her contemporaries, that she was one of a kind. However, there are antecedents for her sound. Karen's influences can be traced back to early songbirds of the air, 1930s and '40s radio singers like Harriet Lee and Annette Hanshaw who pioneered an intimate, close-mic style. Called "the heavy-voiced crooner" by *Variety* magazine, during the 1930s Lee was the best-known and highest-paid singer on US network radio and audiences assumed she was a man because she had such a deep voice. However, the introduction in 1934 of the Hays Code, the industry guidelines for self-censorship applied to motion pictures by major Hollywood studios, had a knock-on effect on radio broadcasting and led to a decline in employment for Lee. Her low-pitched voice was too "mannish" and unacceptable for mainstream audiences. It didn't conform to code standards because there was an assumption that women should sing in higher octaves. Even in the 1970s, Karen's deep singing voice was considered highly unusual, setting her apart from most female artists who sang in higher registers.

Antecedents to Karen's style can also be heard in the sound of 1950s crooners like Patsy Cline and Patti Page, who drew inspiration from country and jazz. And most influential of all was Mary Ford, who recorded layered harmonies with her husband Les Paul. Their rockabilly version of jazz standard "How High the Moon," with its long vowels and laid-back delivery, became the Carpenters' template. Ford sang close to the mic in a way that emphasized the low frequencies in her voice—a method that Karen was to use years later. With their innovative arrangements and leading-edge overdub technology, Paul and Ford were one of the most successful pop couples of the 1950s. A major source of inspiration for Richard and Karen, they were two music geeks who bought a woodland retreat in northern New Jersey and turned it into a recording studio, carving an echo chamber out of the mountain.

While Karen went to Nathan Hale Elementary, Richard attended Wilbur Cross High—the school that produced doo-wop group the Five Satins, whose song "In the Still of the Night" was one of the biggest hits of the decade. Alan Freed played it continually. As founder member and songwriter Fred Parris recalled, despite being recorded on basic equipment in the basement of St. Bernadette's Catholic School, New Haven, the song was a hit three times between 1956 and 1961. The Five Satins were at the epicentre of a vibrant scene, with acts like the Nutmegs, the Desires and the bluesy, rhythmic Chestnuts dominating the R&B charts. They also had strong links outside the local area. The Five Satins and the Nutmegs were signed to Herald/Ember, a small but prolific independent label in New York run by Al Silver, an entrepreneur with an ear for R&B vocal groups.

Doo-wop was a staple of 1950s and early '60s rock 'n' roll—a scene driven by young, inexperienced amateur singers who couldn't afford musicians, so they used vocal rhythm and four-part harmony instead of instruments. In New Haven, teenagers would form a cappella groups and sing near the jazz clubs along Dixwell Avenue, or dance on *Connecticut Bandstand*, a music show broadcast on local TV. "We had a blast and it was so much fun dancing and watching the performers singing on the show. Every once in a while we would take a quick peek at the monitor and see ourselves dancing," recalled New Haven girl Paula Renzoni Crean.[7]

The doo-wop influence can be heard in the Carpenters' sound, in the way vocal harmonies are syncopated and foreground the lead melody. It was also a major influence on Frank Zappa, an artist whose arrangements Richard much admired. Even though the Carpenters' smooth vibe seems diametrically opposed to Zappa's playful avant garde dissonance, Richard would have appreciated his use of overdubbing, the jazz influences and his inventive deconstruction of easy listening and surf pop in songs such as "Who Are the Brain Police?" or "You Didn't Try to Call Me." An even more direct link is *Cruising with Ruben & the Jets*, a Mothers of Invention album Zappa recorded in 1968 that is a satirical homage to doo-wop. He later said that the album was inspired by Stravinsky's work in his neo-classical period: "If he could take the forms and cliches of the classical era and pervert them, why not do the same . . . to doo-wop in the '50s?"[8]

There was a lot of cross-pollination of young bands on the New Haven scene, so fifteen-year-old Richard found it easy to form his own musical group at Wilbur Cross High and he gained a reputation as a skilled piano player. Richard was underage, but his height and his slicked-back hair made him look older and his natural talent as an arranger gave him authority. As a result he was recruited by neighborhood bands and got his first gig playing with older musicians at a rough venue on Boston Post Road called Patti's Pizza. Karen once sarcastically referred to the place as "a class joint." Fights would often break out and after one particularly violent altercation on the dancefloor, Agnes and Harold told Richard to give up playing gigs until he was older.

Richard focused on his own band the Sceptres, practicing at home with the drummer Jim Squeglia, an extrovert friend from school. Karen would sit in on their rehearsals and laugh and joke with Squeglia. "Now I see that she was watching how I played. All the time," he recalled.[9] Those informal sessions were the beginning of her lifelong interest in playing the drums. "I was absolutely fascinated with drums, I don't know why," Karen said later.[10]

*

The rumbustious gigs and fights on the dancefloor were symptoms of a city in transition. New Haven was an area that benefited from rapid postwar expansion, with major employers like the Winchester firearms factory attracting Italian, African American, and Puerto Rican families in increasing numbers. By 1960, 75 percent of the Dixwell neighborhood (where the Winchester factory stood) was African American. This precipitated the "white flight" of middle-class families to other areas of greater New Haven and beyond. "You'd hear people saying that the neighborhood was going downhill," recalls Cathy Capozzi. At this point Agnes and Harold decided to migrate to the West Coast. Harold hated the harsh Connecticut winters and had long nursed a desire to relocate to the California sunshine and, now that Richard's talent as a pianist and arranger was emerging, there would be more opportunities for his son to work as a musician. "My parents are very hip," Richard noted later.[11]

In the summer of 1960, while ten-year-old Karen stayed in Baltimore with her Aunt Bernice and Uncle Paul, Harold took Agnes and Richard for a drive across country to scope out opportunities and places to live. After they came back, Agnes worked hard to save money and became a top machine operator at Edal Industries, an electric parts supplier in East Haven. In 1962, Harold was offered a job by his former boss at the Container Corporation of America, a firm that produced corrugated cardboard boxes in Vernon, south of Los Angeles, and announced to the family that they would finally be moving. Richard was overjoyed. That same year he got a taste of studio work when New Haven doo-wop group the Barries asked him and Jim Squeglia to back them on a recording session for Ember Records in New York. They cut a single, "Why Don't You Write Me," which features rich harmonies and Richard performing a Jerry Lee Lewis–style embellishment on the keyboard. Thrilled when he heard the single played on local radio, that session fired up his enthusiasm for Los Angeles, a city with even more studios and where surf music—from Link Wray to the Beach Boys—was just taking off.

By contrast, Karen had just won a scholarship to a local private school and felt anxious, reluctant to uproot herself and leave behind all her friends. When the day came for the Carpenters to leave, Debbie Vaiuso went round to say goodbye to Karen, deeply upset that she was losing her best friend. It is testament to the strength of their friendship that Karen never lost touch with her and in later years visited her in Connecticut whenever she got the chance. "I cannot be certain on the outlook of my future," Karen wrote in her 1963 school autobiography. "In June I know for certain we are moving to California."

CHAPTER 2
1963–1966

When I took up the drums, both the drums and the voice started to come together. Everybody looked at me funny, but I didn't really care.[1]

When the family moved to Downey, a suburban commuter town south of Los Angeles in Orange County, Karen was thirteen years old. She missed her friends and the friendly neighborhood on the East Coast, and there were signs that the move was disruptive for her. Karen snacked on junk food like waffles and candy and retreated from the sports activities she had pursued back home. Unlike the outgoing child who tap-danced on the sidewalks of New Haven in full spangly regalia, just for the sheer joy of it, after the move Karen grew into an awkward teenager reluctant to participate in school. Her previous obsession with sports and ball games waned and she went from being a dedicated scholarship student to achieving lackluster grades and flunking classes. Her government studies teacher Jim Allgood remembered Karen as "a plump little girl, rather quiet, who did not excel academically."[2]

Moving long distance is a stressful life event leading to a severance of social ties in the old community and the need to build new ones. For teenagers at a time of psychological turbulence, when they are building self-identity separately from their parents, this can be challenging. A 2006 study of adolescent health found that movers found it hard to join friendship groups and being "the new kid in town" led to reduced academic performance and emotional problems.[3] Girls can be more adversely affected because they often rely on their intimate, affectionate friendships for support. It is notable that Karen had many close companions in New Haven, including her best friend Debbie Vaiuso, but she was more isolated after the move to California. "She didn't have a lot of girlfriends," observed Leslie Johnston, who later sang with Karen in the college choir.[4]

Seventeen-year-old Richard coped better because his experience gigging with older musicians meant he already had a life outside school. He had been bullied as a boy in New Haven so was less invested in those kinds of friendship networks and had identified a clear way out through music. And, crucially, Karen and Richard had been told repeatedly by their parents that the move was to further his music career. Favoritism toward Richard was cemented in the family dynamic, leading to problems that were to surface later in profound and complicated ways.

But these undercurrents weren't considered in 1963, when Agnes and Harold packed up their car and headed out with the children to California and their big adventure. Dubbed a "gateway city," Downey was one of the towns at the center of California's postwar boom. In the early 1960s newcomers were arriving in the state at the rate of 500,000 a year and in Downey alone the population had increased in twenty years from 12,000 to 86,000. With a touch of hyperbole, state governor Pat Brown called it "the greatest mass migration in the history of the world." Hailed as the builder of modern California, Brown was a liberal Democrat with an ambitious masterplan for expanding state services, which included free higher education. Described as "the boom-boom governor for a boom-boom time," he commemorated the moment it became the nation's most populous state with the ringing of church bells and a four-day celebration.[5] The Carpenters moved west at a time of buoyant optimism. As cultural essayist Joan Didion wrote in *Where I Was From*: "For most of my life California felt rich to me: that was the point of it, that was the promise, the reward for having left the past."[6] Downey was home of the oldest McDonald's restaurant in the world and North American Aviation (NAA), the town's largest employer, was the birthplace of systems for the Apollo space program. After their move Agnes quickly found a job in the NAA stockroom and Harold started work as a lithograph printer in a box factory in nearby Vernon.

On paper the move represented sun-filled freedom and opportunity, but in reality the family's first year was at times stressful. After they first arrived in Downey the Carpenters lived in cramped conditions at the Shoji Apartments, 12020 Downey Avenue. Agnes and Harold were financially strapped, juggling rent for the apartment with mortgage payments on the New Haven house, which hadn't yet been sold. Unlike the lush, tree-lined roads of Connecticut, this part of Downey was located at a busy intersection, surrounded by auto-part shops and cheap malls. "There's a street in Downey that's both north and south of the tracks. We were south of the tracks (the wrong side)," Karen said later.[7] The upheaval of the move and forging a life in a strange town meant that the Carpenters protected themselves as a separate, self-contained family unit. This later contributed to the impression from others who interacted with them that, although polite and sociable, the family were also self-reliant and impervious to outsiders.

Enrolled at the local South Junior High School, Karen took a while to make new friends and adapt to the change. The junior high fed into Downey High School, a sprawling building fronted by a vast concrete car park. In contrast to her cosy school in New Haven, Karen had to get used to a completely different environment, with several thousand students streaming into Downey High every day from the wider district.

After eight months of hard work and thrifty budgeting, Agnes and Harold sold the New Haven house and the family relocated to 13024 Fidler Avenue, a small, three-bedroom property that was still the wrong side of the Downey railtrack. However, by then Richard's musicianship was getting attention and he was spotted at a talent show in Furman Park by Vance Hayes, music director at Downey Methodist Church. Richard began playing the organ at weddings and entertaining the congregation by improvising Beatles riffs with the hymns. Methodism has a rich musical tradition and this experience of sacred hymnody would later feed into the Carpenters' vocal arrangements.

Karen and Richard joined the Methodist youth group, which in the 1960s organized hiking trips, charity events, and retreats. As part of this group, they would have been taught key principles of Methodism, such as imparted righteousness—striving for holiness and sanctification—and works of piety like prayer and fasting. The ultimate goal, according to the religion's founder, John Wesley, is Christian perfection. Although they left the church as they grew older, saying, "We believe what we want to believe," that goal of perfection and purity still resonates through the Carpenters' music. "Perfection is just about impossible," Karen said later, "but we really try."[8] That perfectionism led to their success, but the pressure to be a good girl and cultivate piety and modesty also contributed to a spiritual aesthetic that was about denying the body and suppressing one's desires and appetites. Writer Naomi Kooker is the daughter of Reverend Frank Kooker, a Methodist minister who was director of New England camps and conferences in the 1960s and '70s. "They were educational programs for the youth. We would go on sleepaway camps and do car washes to raise money for charity," she remembers. "Mission work is a large part of Methodism and a striving for godliness with works of piety."[9] For the Carpenters, the link with Methodism goes back to the early 1900s, when Karen's grandparents George and Nellie were carrying out missionary work in China.

Kooker says that there is an aspect of denial in Methodist teaching. "I think of messages my mother received, like it was bad to look in the mirror, because that was vanity," she says.

There was also a strong message about depriving oneself in order to take care of others. "My mother tells a story of when she was five and having a birthday party. Instead of friends bringing gifts, her father made her go out and buy gifts for the children coming to her party." That Methodist message of selflessness would have added to Karen's innate sense that she had to put others before herself, which meant that later on she found it hard to ask for help when she needed it, even denying that she required help at all. "There's a lot of pressure to be careful, do good works and do the right thing," says Kooker.

*

At Downey High School Richard accepted a new opportunity when music teacher Bruce Gifford encouraged him to join the school band and brought him into their jazz group. Keen to play music like her brother, Karen tried flute and accordion lessons, but these instruments didn't hold her attention and after a while she abandoned them. Then she realized that if she joined the school marching band she wouldn't have to do gym or field sports. "They wanted me to run around a track and get into a swimming pool at eight o'clock in the morning. I just couldn't see that," she said.[10] While Richard's musical ambition was steadily progressing, Karen was struggling to find her feet, recalling later that "junior high was a waste and I didn't do much of anything in music until I was sixteen."[11]

Karen was allowed to join the high school marching band, at first given a position banging a mallet on the glockenspiel. She didn't care for that, however, showing an almost extreme sensory sensitivity to the instrument. "I thought they were awkward, cold, stupid. They looked ugly and they smelled funny." She also rejected the more feminine roles of majorette or cheerleader, uninterested in twirling batons or dancing in a short skirt. Before long she wangled her way upfront to where the real power lay, becoming the only girl in the drum line. "It hit me that I could play drums as good as nine-tenths of those boys," she said. "When I got into the marching band I immediately fell in love with the drums and I was the first female drummer. The band thought I was crazy, but luckily I took to them right away."[12]

Spurred on by this brand-new enthusiasm, Karen persuaded Agnes and Harold to buy her a bargain Ludwig drum kit—the preferred kit of two of her heroes, Joe Morello in the Dave Brubeck Quartet and the Beatles' Ringo Starr. In contrast to her lukewarm response to the flute and accordion, Karen became obsessed with the drums, practicing "Take Five" over and over for hours until she had mastered the rhythm.

Finding the drums was, for Karen, a liberation. "Two months in I wanted a show set! I wanted silver sparkle double floor tom-toms, the whole thing." It was a visceral outlet for those difficult teenage feelings, a way to fully express herself and carve out her own identity. She had the sense of being, as she described it, "safe and lost" while marching on the football field, tuning out any thoughts of fear or anxiety by engrossing herself in the music. Until then Richard was the one who had ideas about what he wanted to do and knew exactly where he wanted to go. "When I took up the drums, both the drums and the voice started to come together," said Karen. "Everybody looked at me funny, but I didn't really care."[13]

In 1964, the drums were seen as a masculine instrument and there were very few female role models, apart from Viola Smith, a rapid-fire swing drummer who made her name in the 1930s, and British beat-girl drummers like Honey Lantree of the Honeycombs and Sylvia Saunders in the Liverbirds. Despite Smith's assertion that "we girls have as much stamina as men [and] are not the helpless creatures of earlier generations," the work of female drummers was overlooked or, in Bobbye Hall's case when she started out in Motown, uncredited.[14] The dynamic female drummers of the late 1960s and '70s rock years, such as Moe Tucker in the Velvet Underground, Brie Howard in Fanny, and Ruth Underwood from the Mothers of Invention, hadn't yet hit the limelight.

When she was at Downey High School, all Karen's role models were male. Amie McBye, a UK drummer and producer of Girls and Women Can Drum! workshops, says that playing the drums can give women their voice. "Yet it feels forbidden, that there's these strictures around it. There are expectations and conditioning that say women are fragile, or don't have the physical strength. Or if they get something wrong they will be ridiculed or criticised."[15]

The fact that fourteen-year-old Karen forged ahead in the drum line shows a remarkable instinct and lack of fear. She hung out with classmate Frankie Chavez, who was in charge of writing drum patterns for the group, and went from playing the hated glockenspiel to the cymbals, the tenor drum and, finally, the glorious snare drum—leading the way beside Chavez during parades and football games. In marching at the front of the band she resurrected that unselfconscious little girl who tap-danced on the sidewalk in New Haven, communicating through music and rhythm, asserting herself in the world. "A lot of women are very good at dancing, so they have drumming rhythm," says McBye. "Drumming is an empowering thing and a great skill. I've always felt as a drummer that the best thing is being able to make people move. So if I see people dancing to the beat I've achieved the main goal."

Karen and Chavez developed a strong friendship, which led to her dropping by his house after school to enthuse about drums and listen to jazz music. With her experience of the marching band Karen found a tribe of friends and became more settled at Downey High. She was confident enough to think about dating, indulging in an unrequited crush on Chavez. Eventually she started seeing a clarinet player called Jerry Vance and he became her steady high-school boyfriend. But even though they went to school proms and dances, Karen was more excited by drum practice and being in a band than pursuing a romantic relationship. Drummers like Buddy Rich and Louie Bellson were her pop idols, larger-than-life band-leaders who pioneered speed and virtuoso technique. Also a fan of Joe Morello's cymbal-playing in the Dave Brubeck band, Karen practiced at home for days with plasters on her sore fingers, until she perfected a similar style. In the 1950s Brubeck's mix of cool jazz and classical led to the creation of "third stream," a genre which was a source of inspiration for both Karen and Richard in their early days.

Playing the drums brought out her independent tomboy side. "I taught myself and did most of the things that experienced drummers could do," she once said proudly.[16] Chavez recommended she have drum lessons at Studio City on Santa Monica Boulevard, to learn what she didn't know. Co-founders Roy Harte and Remo Belli ran the Studio City store like a family home for drummers, holding competitions, dishing out advice and contacts for good teachers. "Drummers are like hockey goalies; nobody knows how to talk to them except another drummer," said Harte.[17] His business partner also saw drums as life-enhancing. "The drum is so accessible to so many different environments. It's one of the very few things you can do in a group immediately," he said in 2010.[18] Most weekends the store was packed with men buying kit, but this didn't deter Karen from hanging out there and swapping notes with other players. Because of her experience in the marching band and the working relationship with her brother, she was comfortable in this male-dominated music environment.

Through Studio City she began having drum lessons with a well-known jazz musician in Hollywood called Bill Douglass and cultivated her own eccentric lingo, with a penchant for talking like a zany beatnik jazz player. For instance, in a school yearbook message to Frankie Chavez, Karen wrote, "Listen man . . . it's been a gas in every sense of the word. I can honestly say that it wouldn't have been near as crazy without ya . . ."[19] Later on she would abbreviate key words in her own style, calling parents "rents" and shortening people's names with nicknames, like "Chard" for Richard, "Frenny" for Frenda Leffler and ONJ (pronounced "Ahhnj") for Olivia Newton-John.

Karen wanted to try singing. Her high-school friend Corey Christensen had a band called Knights of the Sun who were looking for a vocalist, so she auditioned. She didn't get the job and was told that she couldn't sing. The sweet irony of that was not lost on Christensen when, five years later, the Carpenters became famous.[20] However, in the mid-1960s, she had yet to discover her deeper voice. "I used to sing in this upper voice and I didn't like it," she said. "I was uncomfortable."

Deciding to stick to the drums, she joined an all-girl surf band called Two Plus One, with school friends Linda Stewart and Eileen Matthews playing guitar. The girls would cart their guitars and amps to the Carpenters' house every week to rehearse and were joined on bass by Nancy Roubal, a friend from the Downey High marching band. Karen contributed many ideas, including a version of the Beatles' "Ticket to Ride" (a song that later ended up on the Carpenters' debut album). She also suggested Richard join the band, but was outvoted, because Stewart was intent on keeping it a girl group. After some intense rehearsals, Two Plus One (and one more) were booked to play a local party, but Matthews's mother refused to let her daughter attend and Stewart broke up the band out of disappointment. One can speculate on how Karen's identity as a performer might have developed had the all-girl band stayed together, but once Two Plus One imploded, she gravitated back toward Richard. Her older brother was already out there forging a path and she recognized his strengths. "He has a rich, inborn talent . . . he's damn good," she said.[21]

By then Richard had enrolled as a music major at California State University in Long Beach, where he met Wes Jacobs, a fellow student who played double bass and tuba. The two struck up a friendship and Richard suggested they form a jazz trio with Karen on drums. All that summer of 1965 they squeezed into the Fidler Avenue living room, practicing covers of Duke Ellington, Henry Mancini, and a ballad version of the Beatles' "I Want to Hold Your Hand." Jacobs remembered both Karen and Richard having "a tremendous driving force," aided by concrete support and encouragement from their mother Agnes. It wasn't long before the Richard Carpenter Trio were playing at clubs and weddings and hotel events. Because Karen at that point was focused on drums, Margaret Shanor from the Downey Methodist Church was recruited as a featured vocalist.

Although Shanor was a strong singer, Richard sensed that Karen's softer vocal style would fit more seamlessly into his arrangements and he introduced her to his Cal State choir director Frank Pooler, a creative visionary who took Karen on for Saturday morning voice lessons. He became a key influence in helping Karen find her voice. To paraphrase John Steinbeck's 1955 poem "Like Captured Fireflies," behind every great artist there is the unsigned manuscript of a great teacher, and Frank Pooler was that teacher.[22] "I do think Frank was a strong mentor to Karen—everybody who sang with him felt that same sense of mentorship," says musician Stan DeWitt, who studied under Pooler at Cal State. "He was both terrifying and nurturing in a way that was very frank, honest and very, very forthright. If you were doing something wrong, he would tell you and if you're doing something right, he would tell you as well. You always knew where you stood with Frank, he had a really good eye for what people's strengths were and their inner motivations."[23]

On those Saturday mornings, Pooler taught Karen classical lieder songs by Beethoven and Schumann and also let her sing pop, encouraging her to expand her range. As she became more vocally confident, Richard called on Shanor less and coaxed Karen to sing lead at the same time as playing the drums. Many assume that Karen's voice emerged fully formed, but DeWitt can see Pooler's influence in the Carpenters' tone. "In terms of choral music, he liked a tone that was straight, didn't have a lot of vibrato and was in tune to the point of being on the high side of the pitch. He even said one time that he didn't mind if we were a little sharp; he said, 'Being sharp is a little bit arrogant,'" he recalls. "Frank also liked a really bright sound. So he would do warm-ups where he would sing, just, for example, an 'e' vowel. And he would want that 'e' vowel to be really bright and that would inform the tone for the whole choir. So when you listen to the Carpenters' background vocals, you hear that brightness in the tone? That, more than anything else, came from Frank." Pooler himself analyzed the Carpenters' high-voltage singing in a 1973 article for the *Choral Journal*, praising their "knife-edged, razor sharp" vowel pronunciation, arguing that such vocal control created "an absolutely unified sound . . . from a soft to a dynamic level."[24]

Restlessly ambitious, Richard was constantly looking for opportunities for their voices to be heard. Early in 1966 his friend Dan Friberg from the university choir secured an audition with producer and bass player Joe Osborn, asking Richard to accompany him on piano. Sensing this could be their big break, Richard jumped at the chance and made sure Karen tagged along, too. At that point, Osborn was twenty-eight years old and part of the Wrecking Crew, a collective of Los Angeles-based session players who had featured on dozens of top-forty hits. The Wrecking Crew were so called because, according to drummer Hal Blaine, the old guard of more formal "jacket and tie" players thought that these young rock 'n' rollers were going to "wreck" the industry. Along with the Nashville A-Team, the Memphis Boys, and the Funk Brothers in Detroit, the Wrecking Crew were identified with their city and known as players who could record in the fewest possible takes. Studio recording then was a very expensive process, so the more skilled and adaptable the player, the more they were in demand. The Wrecking Crew and all the top Los Angeles players were later to become a key element of the Carpenters' sound.

Having cut his teeth working with rock 'n' roll stars like Rick Nelson, Johnny Rivers, and Brenda Lee, Osborn had a distinctive rhythmic bass style. Although his roots were in rockabilly, he was infinitely adaptable—and he, drummer Hal Blaine and keyboardist Larry Knechtel become known as the Hollywood Golden Trio. By 1966, they had played with massively successful acts such as Jan & Dean and the Mamas & the Papas. Keen to run his own company, Osborn had just cofounded with Don Zacklin the indie record label Magic Lamp. He built a four-track studio in his North Hollywood garage, soundproofed it with egg boxes and began producing artists there in his down time—usually after midnight when most regular studio sessions had ended. Osborn had been working with Johnny Burnette, a brash rockabilly singer trying to revive his ailing 1950s career and also doing sessions with Dean Torrence, the chiseled blond skateboarder in Jan & Dean. When Richard and Karen walked into his studio that night in April 1966, he had no idea of their potential.

Referring to them as "the Kids," Osborn didn't take to Richard at first, considering him impatient and cocky. He also thought they were a little gauche. Only Dan Friberg had rehearsed for the audition, but Osborn assumed that Karen was doing one too and asked her to sing. Nervous and unprepared, she sang "Ebb Tide," a calypso lounge ballad made famous by the Righteous Brothers. Osborn was rendered speechless. "She stood up there in my garage, sixteen years old . . . and sang 'Ebb Tide'—not an easy song. She sang that song and that voice was there. The way she sang was there, she was born with that," Osborn said.[25] Karen had a different, more critical memory of that night. "I was in tune, but there was no vibrato and I sang very hard," she later recalled.

Over the next few weeks Osborn worked with the band to develop their sound. Though Richard showed a knack for arranging and composition, Osborn was primarily interested in Karen, signing her as a solo artist to Magic Lamp. Because she was a minor, her parents checked the contract, particularly Agnes, who pored over the small print. Agnes and Harold took an active interest at every stage in the process and remained involved as the duo's career developed. Their support and encouragement, however, bordered on overprotective, a micromanaging that led to an odd combination of overconfidence and fear of making mistakes. Over time, Karen in particular grew to see imperfection as failure, rather than an integral part of the creative process. From the very first audition she exercised her stringent inner critic.

Richard and Karen recorded two of their own songs as a double-A-sided single, taking inspiration from the Beach Boys' "Good Vibrations." Though taped on a rudimentary four-track, "Looking for Love" is a striking slice of psych pop driven by Karen's frenetic drumming and loud, confident vocals. The lyrics echo a theme that was to recur again and again in Carpenters songs: searching for an elusive love that is always just beyond reach. The other side, "I'll Be Yours," was just as strong, with its clearly defined girl-group garage sound. With the right promotion the single could have been a local hit, but only 500 copies were pressed and with no proper distribution the single disappeared. One year later, the Magic Lamp label folded, too.

Richard and Karen focused instead on their jazz trio, perfecting a short set that included "Ice Tea," an instrumental that featured Karen's drumming and Jacobs' tuba. They also played an intricate version of "The Girl from Ipanema," the bossa nova jazz classic made famous by Stan Getz and Astrud Gilberto. On June 24, after a few weeks of practice, the Richard Carpenter Trio entered the Battle of the Bands amateur talent contest at the Hollywood Bowl. The band name shows that they started off with Richard as the frontperson and at that point Karen deferred to him and was happy for him to take the lead. He was three years older, he had taken her to that first audition in Joe Osborn's studio, and, most importantly, he was the one designated by

Agnes to be the musical genius in the family. During the contest the trio played with panache—"Ice Tea" and "The Girl from Ipanema" went down well, prompting a roar of applause from the judges as well as the crowd. Richard won Outstanding Instrumentalist and the trio was awarded not only Best Combo but also the sweepstake trophy for the highest score in the contest.

On their way into the car park afterward, Richard was approached by a man asking if they would like to record a few demos. Cocksure and elated, Richard said they already had a record deal, thank you. "Give me a call if things change," said the man, passing Richard his business card. The man was Neely Plumb, key West Coast A&R for the major label RCA Victor. Realizing that he had been a bit hasty, Richard quickly told Plumb that the deal was a solo record with his sister, not him.

Within three months RCA had signed the trio, keen to develop a jazz sound with Wes Jacobs's cool tuba at the center. They went into the studio and recorded eleven instrumentals, including the easy-listening song "Strangers in the Night" and Richard's pop Bach-style composition "Flat Baroque" (that later ended up on the Carpenters' 1970 album *A Song for You*). Although it was a snappy collection, the trio were swimming against the tide and they failed to make an impact on the charts. Richard said later that the Battle of the Bands win had made him smug and a little brash. Their live jazz set had gone down well in the Hollywood Bowl on a sunny afternoon, but cracking the singles chart required a different focus and an awareness of what was hot, hip, and popular.

Psychedelic rock was in the ascendant, and RCA couldn't see the sales potential in novelty jazz, so the trio were dropped from the label. Richard found himself back on campus at Cal State, trying to compose new tunes with limited equipment. At that point it felt like everything was a struggle. "When we were trying to make a go of our music our parents bought everything they could afford for us," said Richard, but that wasn't enough. He and Karen possessed a drum set and a piano but couldn't afford to buy amplifiers, or an electric piano, or mic stands. "When we wanted to buy a tape recorder, to make demos of this first group . . . Dad wanted to get it for me, but we just couldn't swing it."[26] The family had to save for months before being able to make a down payment on a Sony recorder.

He and Karen needed commercial success and for that they had to find a sound that chimed with the times. They were to find inspiration from within Frank Pooler's choir—the place where it all started.

BOOK 2
Sing

CHAPTER 3

1967–1968

Choir director Frank Pooler is a genius with vocals . . .
There are certain choirs where you have eighty people and
it sounds like eighty people yelling. That's one school. But
Pooler's thing is to make eighty sound like one. I tried to
do that.[1]

Frank Pooler had a gift, not just for identifying talent but also
for bringing people together. It was in his choir that Richard
met John Bettis, a political science major at Cal State with long
fair hair and a wayward hippie style. Rebelling against his middle-class upbringing, Bettis rejected his parents' plans for him to
become an attorney and was keen to move into showbusiness,
but unsure about the route. He had been playing for a while
in a duo with Maury Manseau on the California folk circuit,
when one day they heard Simon & Garfunkel's "The Sound of
Silence" on the radio. "When we heard that we looked at each
other, we knew we'd never be that good. We broke up right

there that minute," he said.[2] Manseau went off and started a psychedelic folk group called the Sunshine Company and Bettis ended up at Cal State, joining Pooler's choir as a non-compulsory elective course.

Soon after joining the choir Bettis showed a talent for writing lyrics, song fragments that were poetic, observant, and satirical. Though he appeared slightly arrogant, he was insecure about performing solo and tried to avoid it by composing a jokey cantata called "Acapella Music," a piece "that ridiculed everything about being in a choir." Pooler called his bluff, telling Bettis he would like him to perform it—so Bettis found himself rehearsing a 45-voice choir, struggling to form vocal arrangements with just a guitar for accompaniment. Sensing his discomfort, Richard offered to help. As they worked together on the piece, they chatted about cars and girls and realized they shared an irreverent sense of humor. Despite contrasting musical tastes in folk and jazz, they both appreciated a good tune and approached songs from an angle, so there was an immediate creative fusion.

Bettis's background was rooted in the southern California folk scene, which in the mid-1960s was focused on venues such as the Golden Bear and the Cosmos. Located in Huntington Beach ("Surf City"), the Golden Bear was where Buffalo Springfield and David Crosby started, while the Cosmos featured folk rock acts like singer-songwriter Hoyt Axton and bluegrass band the Dillards. Bettis loved Bob Dylan, Phil Ochs, and Richard Farina, lyric-heavy folk artists, but was also attracted to the bright vibrancy of Rodgers and Hammerstein musical theater classics such as *Oklahoma!* and *South Pacific*. His love of poetic lyrics and unvar-

nished melody chimed well with Karen and Richard's aesthetic.
By then Wes Jacobs had left Los Angeles to study music at the
Juilliard School in New York, so Richard disbanded the jazz trio
to launch his vision for a new kind of choral pop. "I've got a sister
who sings great and plays drums," he said to Bettis. "Let's put a
group together and make a band."

Bettis was invited to the Carpenters' house on Fidler Avenue,
where he met sixteen-year-old Karen. "She sang that way when
she was sixteen. She later gained some breath control and gained
some taste and she could control it better," recalled Bettis. "But
in terms of just the instrument itself, no, man, it was that. Wow.
Did I appreciate it the way I oughta have? Probably not. [Then]
it was all about me."[3] Karen, Richard, and Bettis began regular practice sessions, writing and arranging songs in a harmonic
choral style. At first Agnes Carpenter wasn't sure about Bettis's
long hair and dissolute image, but she soon became aware that
the group had distinctive vocal flair. She would bustle into the
living room where they rehearsed with trays of lemonade and
iced tea, offering words of approval and encouragement. For
Karen there was no question about making music with anyone
else, or teaming up again with former school bandmate Nancy
Roubal. This was to be the winning musical triumvirate.

Richard and Bettis cemented their musical friendship with a
summer job performing at Disneyland, wearing straw hats and
shiny brocade waistcoats, playing ragtime piano and banjo on
Main Street, USA. A little too irreverent for the management,
they were fired after a few months and set down the experience in what became the satirical song "Mr. Guder." Karen,

meanwhile, graduated from high school, saying goodbye to the marching band and Frankie Chavez in particular. She won the school John Philip Sousa Band Award for outstanding musicianship, a prize that showed how much her confidence and ability were growing.

Her attention was now wholly absorbed in the new group, which was augmented by folk singer/guitarist Gary Sims, a science major at Cal State, plus his friend Danny Woodhams on bass and Leslie Johnston, a young woman from the college choir whose voice blended in well with Karen's. Starting out as the Summerchimes, the group morphed into Spectra and finally vocal harmony band Spectrum. The sextet rehearsed five evenings a week in a church in Orange County, where Woodhams was employed as choral director. Johnston struck up a friendship with Karen, remembering her as caustically funny and totally focused on her music. "She was so serious about her music I don't think she had time for other things," she said.[4]

With high school over, Karen followed Richard to Cal State to study music, enrolling in the autumn of 1967. One of the main reasons she went there was Frank Pooler's inspired tuition. Though not particularly interested in the college units she had to study, Karen was enthralled by his choir, soaking up whatever he had to teach. "Frank Pooler is a genius with vocals, just a genius. There are certain choirs where you have eighty people and it sounds like eighty people yelling . . . but Pooler's thing is to make eighty sound like one," she once said. She enjoyed his experimental approach, describing him as a "far out" character. "In the music department he's like a thorn, he's different, he's not one to be stepped on. He does what he feels like. He doesn't always do strait-laced stuff. He brings in tape recorders and plays them backwards while you set them on fire."[5]

The choir sang at festivals, sometimes accompanied by Karen on drums. Once they performed a piece about the Holocaust, an avant garde vocal depiction of mass execution in a Second World War concentration camp. Much of it was improvised in a way that Karen found riveting. "This thing was so wild . . . no notes [just] whispering and controlled yelling," she enthused. "It's got tom-toms and at the end I do a great snare drum roll to sound like machine guns. When we got done the director of the next choir was in tears. She [said], 'I'm not going on after that.' Oh, it was wild!"

At Cal State Karen's exuberant creativity was to the fore, with a willingness to experiment that was different from Richard's more commercial pragmatism. Less interested in the scholarly aspects of music, Karen had little patience for academic study and was happy to cut classes to go to auditions with her brother. Her university work suffered. Her attendance was so low that in the spring of 1968 she was suspended— much to Agnes and Harold's dismay. "What good is biology going to do me? On the stage it's of no use," she declared.[6] Frank Pooler became Karen's advocate, lobbying the university authorities on her behalf, arguing that she had a natural talent that shouldn't be penalized. The suspension was lifted, but a year later the Carpenters' career took off and she left university. However, Karen retained what she had learned from Pooler—the varied repertoire, the precise pitching, the complex harmonics and the strength of the voice as pure expression, an elemental force. While this classical rigor was later modified and toned down in commercial pop singles, that period at Cal State from 1967 to 1968 was a formative time for Karen. Even though she didn't complete her degree, she learned and understood the concept of being an artist.

While they took classes at Cal State, Richard and Karen worked on material with Spectrum, hoping to get a record deal. The group recorded some tapes at Joe Osborn's studio and found an ally in Ed Sulzer, a local singer Richard had worked with back in 1963. Looking to expand into the music business, Sulzer offered to book Spectrum some dates and secured them a slot at the Whisky a Go Go. Although they were booked for three nights, the management fired Spectrum after the first show because their cerebral harmonizing didn't encourage people to dance or buy drinks. Then Spectrum opened for raw rock group Steppenwolf at the Blue Law in Torrance, where the crowd watched them with blank incomprehension. "We thought we were going to get killed," Karen said. They also played open-mic spots at the Troubadour's Hoot Nights, hoicking drum kit and keyboards through a tightly packed audience for a rapid twenty-minute set. Spectrum's jazzy textures didn't click with the young folk or rock crowds, but they fared better at Ledbetter's on Westwood Boulevard, a night promoted by Randy Sparks of the New Christy Minstrels. Here they went down well as a leftfield lounge act, a sort of supercharged easy listening.

Leslie Johnston later remarked that Spectrum should have just been a recording group, but even their demo failed to attract interest. Recorded at United Audio in Santa Ana, it included an original track, "All I Can Do," which featured Karen's bold lead vocal against a background of punchy harmonies. This, combined with Richard's florid keyboard breaks and her quickfire drumming, created a sound that was edgily sophisticated but not smooth.

It has been argued that the band didn't secure a deal because their preppy look was considered too square. However, it is more likely that the music and Karen's voice had not yet crystallized into an immediately identifiable style. Spectrum were hard to categorize and record companies had no idea how to market them. The group were rejected by every label in Los Angeles and sometimes in ways that John Bettis described as "stunningly aggressive." He remembered going into meetings and grown men castigating him and Richard, two young twenty-year-olds, saying that their music and their wardrobe were hopelessly uncool. "We were white middle-class American kids, so of course we sounded like white middle-class American kids," he said.[7] At some point during this process, Karen decided (or it was suggested to her) that to attract the pop crowd and the attention of major-label A&Rs, she needed to do some work on her image.

*

Much has been written about Karen being "overweight" in her teens, described variously as chubby, pudgy, plump, bulky, and rotund. Richard (admittedly when he was a teenager) called her "Fatso" and their mother Agnes summed her up as "hefty round the butt." It is now known that name-calling plays havoc with young women's self-image, research pointing to the fact that the impact is worse when the weight stigma comes from family members. UCLA psychologist Jeffrey Hunger said in 2018, "Labeling young girls as 'too fat' will never spur positive health behaviours; it is simply going to result in poor body image, unhealthy weight control practices and disordered eating."[8] Back in 1967, though, there was much less awareness about the effect of harsh words and the phrase "body-shaming" didn't exist. Agnes—an unsophisticated woman who spoke plainly—took Karen to the doctor for weight-loss advice. He recommended the Stillman water diet, a high-protein, low-carbohydrate craze that was popular in the late 1960s, but has since been discredited as a fad diet. Karen was "prescribed" a daily dose of vitamin supplements, eight glasses of water, and zero fatty foods.

She hated the diet, suffering long evenings after rehearsals watching the members of Spectrum wolf down burgers and fries while she sat there sipping iced tea. But, despite temptation, she avoided the fast food she had once loved, losing 25 pounds over six months. This was the start of a calorie-counting and fat-burning routine that became an integral and dominant part of her everyday life. The irony is that, according to NHS metrics in the UK and the Centers for Disease Control & Prevention in the US, at 5 feet 4 inches and weighing 145 pounds, Karen had a healthy BMI. A glance at high-school photos shows a girl who was athletic and assured, not dumpy. Maybe the "chubby" epithets were a subconscious strategy to rein in tomboy Karen and make her more feminine and malleable.

Karen had an ambivalent approach toward hair and beauty culture and wasn't interested in just looking decorative. "At college she was a Levi's person, not particularly caring whether she was real feminine," recalled Leslie Johnston. And Agnes was typical of many mothers in her 1950s generation in that she gave Karen mixed messages, encouraging her to be strong and forge a career, while at the same time urging her to regulate her weight to attain a slim, docile feminine ideal. Internalizing any social judgment that came her way, Karen said later, "I was heavier, about 20 pounds heavier. I was just tired of being fat so I went on a diet . . . I don't know how I ever got through a door."

When Twiggy graced the cover of *Vogue* in 1967 with her slender frame, she launched a youthquake. This girl from Neasden, north-west London, with large eyes, cropped hair, and spider lashes became the first international supermodel, photographed by Richard Avedon and feted by the New York fashion elite. The summer that Karen consulted the doctor about her diet, America went Twiggy crazy, with stores across the country selling Twiggy pens, lunchboxes (very small ones, presumably), lashes, and cosmetics. Overnight, it seemed, the voluptuous Marilyn Monroe-style glamour of the 1950s had become outdated and the newly defined beauty ideal was stick-thin. "I wasn't trying to be that thin, I was perfectly healthy, but . . . that look is a total impossibility for women over the age of twenty," Twiggy said later. "Fashion has a lot to answer for, doesn't it?"[9]

For Karen, who had naturally curvy hips, the straight-up-and-down Twiggy silhouette was frustratingly out of reach. Gary Sims, Spectrum's gentle guitarist, remarked that Karen was insecure about her appearance and was "always trying to get rid of the hips."[10] This obviously was not a problem for him because soon after she stopped dating Jerry Vance, he and Karen started having a relationship. Although she was self-conscious about her weight, Karen had a natural, easygoing manner and shy smile that Sims found enchanting. They would spend days at the beach, go to the movies, and, under the watchful eye of Agnes and Harold, hang out at home. Like his predecessor, the fervent feelings were more on Sims's side than Karen's. Their steady romance was to last two years before he went into the army and she abruptly called it to a halt.

*

In a bid to cultivate a more sophisticated image, Richard too paid more attention to his appearance, wearing Sta-Prest trousers and Chelsea boots and ditching his geeky horn-rimmed glasses for contact lenses. As Spectrum developed a stronger sound and stage presence, they finally attracted record company interest. Uni Records had a varied roster of artists, from Neil Diamond's dramatic pop to the acid rock of Strawberry Alarm Clock to Jamaican artists Desmond Dekker and Dave & Ansell Collins. And White Whale's biggest act was the Turtles, whose sunshine pop single "Happy Together" was a huge number-one hit in 1967. Richard plumped for White Whale, but they wanted a large chunk of the group's potential revenue and after some discussions he and Karen rejected an offer that felt too exploitative. By then Uni had lost interest.

Despite Ed Sulzer's best efforts to secure a deal, nothing else was forthcoming and Bettis and Johnston drifted away from Spectrum. Karen and Richard decided to try recording songs as a duo and went back to Joe Osborn's garage studio. Osborn liked Karen and wanted to help her by providing some free studio time at weekends, or at night after his regular sessions ended. By this point gigging experience had enriched their sound and Karen's rhythmic drive on drums helped her phrasing as a singer. Richard studied the way vocal parts were stacked on songs like the Beach Boys' "Good Vibrations" and the Beatles' "Eleanor Rigby." Because they couldn't afford session singers, Karen and Richard produced and recorded themselves, overdubbing their vocals to find an effortless blend in tone. The Beach Boys provided a precise model for bridging surf pop with a choral concept, so along with elements of third stream jazz (the 1950s fusion of jazz and classical they loved in Dave Brubeck), the Carpenters arrived at their sound.

Once their voices were overdubbed the siblings discovered that the purity of their sound could be magnified multiple times. As Karen remarked, "a 10-ton thing was born." In Osborn's garage they recorded "Don't Be Afraid," a song by Richard eulogizing the joys of love. The lyric is simplistic and the demo a little rough around the edges, but Karen's voice animates the words with a brisk energy. Also recorded were two songs Richard had written with Bettis—the satirical sunshine pop track "Your Wonderful Parade" and "Invocation," a graceful hymn sung a cappella that has its own mystical power. Now that Spectrum had imploded it was clear that the way forward was as a duo. This required a name change, so Richard and Karen decided on "Carpenters' without the prefix and a clear focus on them as a sibling act. Realizing that his sister's voice and his arrangements were now at the center of their sound, it was no longer the Richard Carpenter Trio. Richard felt that the bold, plain name "Carpenters" would give them a strong identity that was more in tune with the pop charts. Although it became the official name on their album covers and merchandise, for ease of reference the band were mostly mentioned with the determiner. "It was just a matter of the right song and we were getting close," he said later.[11]

The Carpenters needed to get some exposure, particularly via the growing mass medium of TV. *Your All-American College Show* was a national program that sent talent scouts to campuses across America. That summer of 1968 Karen and Richard teamed up with bassist Bill Sissoyev to audition at the Hollywood Video Center. The trio were selected and featured on the show over the next eighteen months. Most memorable is their version of "Dancing in the Street," a 1964 hit for Motown group Martha & the Vandellas that went on to become a radical anthem for the civil rights movement and a pop soul classic. The Carpenters' supercharged rendition had eighteen-year-old Karen in white mod boots and a Nehru jacket executing a full-throttle virtuoso drum solo while singing with a joyful shout. Promoted as the lead and star attraction, her name displayed in giant cursive script across the bass drum, Karen very much owned the spot. The show's presenter, Dennis James, could hardly contain himself, saying that Karen used to hear Richard play and "she'd get so filled with rhythm on the kitchen chairs and the table that finally she decided 'I'd better get some drums!'" That footage has survived, and by the 2010s Karen's ebullient performance became one of the most popular videos on YouTube.[12]

That valuable TV exposure on *Your All-American College Show* led to $3,500 in prize money and some high-profile offers. The program's executive producer, Wendell Niles, talked about representing them, and actor John Wayne, a celebrity judge on the show, wanted Karen to audition for the role of feisty farm girl Mattie Ross in his new western movie *True Grit*. The part eventually went to Kim Darby, but it was flattering for Karen to be asked. The best opportunity arose when John Bahler saw the Carpenters on *Your All-American College Show* and alerted his brother Tom. The Bahlers were prolific composer-producers who had their own band, the Love Generation. They were also jingle writers and had been commissioned by advertising agency J Walter Thompson to provide the music for a campaign for a new Ford car called the Maverick.

In the late 1960s, the two dominant US car manufacturers were General Motors and Ford, with Chrysler in third place in terms of sales. "Ford were trying to get a larger slice of that pie," says Tom Bahler. "Ford did not have a reputation for making a bad product. But General Motors in the '60s was passing them up with style and Ford was becoming an old man's car."[13] Henry Ford II decided to make a radical change and sent a memo to everybody in the company, from the management to the car park attendant, saying, "You can sell a young man's car to an old man. You can't sell an old man's car to a young man. I want a young face on this company."

The "Going Thing" campaign for the Ford Maverick was an important one. Two hundred acts were auditioned in New York and a further 200 at Sunset Sound in Hollywood. "We were looking for young, good-looking people, a cross-section of America, but more to the point we wanted musicianship," recalls Bahler. After he saw the Carpenters on TV, his brother John called *Your All-American College Show*'s producers, saying, "I want to get their number."

"We don't give out numbers."

"This is for the Ford Motor Company."

"Ah well, in that case . . ."

Karen and Richard were called and invited to audition. Before they started playing Tom Bahler was a little skeptical. "Karen happened to be beautiful and Richard was very good-looking. At first I thought, *A chick drummer. Yeah, sure!* But she did an excellent job and of course her voice was amazing."

Impressed with the duo's tight playing and musicianship and Karen's mellifluous voice, the Bahlers offered them the job. Thrilled to get this chance for more exposure, the Carpenters signed an advertising deal that was worth $50,000 each, with a free Mustang thrown in. For the first time in their career they were about to earn serious money. Their vibrantly commercial sound was finally being recognized, so a "legit" recording contract must surely be just around the corner.

CHAPTER 4

1969

I remember thinking, *If we don't have a hit record by the time I'm twenty, I'm going to have to kill myself!* We just made it because when I turned the record went to number one. And I'm glad it did, because I didn't want to go anywhere . . .[1]

Karen was a young woman in a hurry. *Your All-American College Show* and the Ford contract gave her a glimpse of what could be achieved and she was impatient for success. The Carpenters' demo tape attracted interest from Reprise Records signing Kenny Rogers & the First Edition, a hot, versatile country rock band who had a top-five hit in 1968 with the psychedelic single "Just Dropped In (To See What Condition My Condition Was In)." They were looking for a new female singer, so Richard encouraged Karen to audition, confident she would get the job. He was prepared to scupper his own chance of success because he could see how gifted she was as a singer. "I was more interested in Karen's future as an artist than my own," he claimed.[2] At that point the concept of the Carpenters was still in its precarious early stages. As yet there had been no concrete interest from a record label, so if a gig with the First Edition meant raising their profile Richard was happy to let her go. It was only later when so much was invested in the Carpenters as a band and a product that the idea of Karen going solo would become problematic.

However, Karen was fated to stay with her brother. After the audition, she was rejected in favor of country pop singer Mary Arnold and later that year the First Edition had global success with "Ruby, Don't Take Your Love to Town," a song about a disabled war veteran who comes home traumatized after battle. Karen had a sonorous voice, but she was still naive and a little reserved. She hadn't been on a tour and had yet to develop a live stage presence forceful enough for that late '60s rock scene.

"Ruby, Don't Take Your Love to Town" was a timely record. Men as young as eighteen were being drafted and sent to fight in the Vietnam War against the communist Viet Cong and by the end of 1968, 30,000 American troops had died. A mass anti-war movement propelled student rioting on campuses and civil unrest on the streets. Thousands of young men avoided the draft by college deferment, feigning mental illness or homosexuality (gay people were excluded from the military), or fleeing across the border to Canada. Many publicly burned their draft cards in protest. The counterculture had grown from beatnik poetry and pop art to a politically charged movement driven by activism, music and a transcendental consciousness. The Beatles embodied this shift, going from the bouncy beat pop of "She Loves You" to referencing the *Tibetan Book of the Dead* in "Tomorrow Never Knows" and avant garde *musique concrète* for "Revolution 9." As did the Beach Boys, turning good-time surf pop into the art psychedelia of *Pet Sounds*. Despite their upbringing in quiet suburban Downey, the Carpenters absorbed echoes from the counterculture and they emerged in a tentative form in songs like "This Wonderful Parade," a stab at the conservative hypocrisy of the parent generation.

Karen was disappointed not to get the First Edition gig, but that rejection meant she was free when a much better offer for the Carpenters came along, from someone whose aesthetic matched theirs. Herb Alpert was from east Los Angeles, the son of eastern European Jewish immigrants. He learned to play the trumpet, performing with dance bands as a teenager and, like Karen, he had played in a marching band, was briefly signed to RCA and made his first solo recordings in a garage.

In 1962, he started the independent Carnival label with budding music promoter Jerry Moss to release his own music and that of artists he admired. When they realized the name was already copyrighted, they took their initials and rechristened the new company A&M. At the same time, Alpert was frustrated with a song he was writing and, looking for inspiration, he took a break in Tijuana, Mexico, where he found himself at a bullfight. Entranced by the sound of the fanfare that heralded the arrival of each bull, Alpert overdubbed his trumpet with ambient sounds of the crowd to create the track "The Lonely Bull," and the band the Tijuana Brass was born. The track became a hit, leading to the album of the same name, the first LP release on A&M.

Within four years Alpert and Moss had moved out of the garage to the grounds of the old Charlie Chaplin studios, located at 1416 North La Brea Avenue, just off Sunset Boulevard, building a roster of sophisticated pop artists like Sergio Mendes, Burt Bacharach, and folk rock group the Sandpipers. Alpert's approach in the Tijuana Brass was subtly tuned into new trends. He had an astute, instinctive commercial aesthetic—in 1965, for instance, the Tijuana Brass sold 6 million copies of *Whipped Cream*, smooth and sensual soundtrack music that oozed out of tracks like "Ladyfinger," "Butterball," and "A Taste of Honey." The Tijuana Brass dominated the album charts and in 1966, Alpert recordings outsold the Beatles.

When the Carpenters' demo arrived in Alpert's office early in 1969, there was a quality in Karen's voice that made him pause. "She had something really magic. When her voice came out the speaker it felt like [it] was sitting right next to me. It had that much volume," recalled Alpert.[3] The demo tape arrived by a circuitous route via Jack Daugherty, a musician who worked with Agnes Carpenter at North American Aviation, who passed it on to Alpert's guitarist, John Pisano.

A&M was one of the finest independent labels in Los Angeles. Called "the white Motown" by Chicago radio legend Dick Biondi, by then A&M had grown into an artist-driven company with a roster that spanned everything from adult pop to hip folk rock. The Carpenters were an unusual signing for a label with bands like the Flying Burrito Brothers, Procol Harum, and Humble Pie, plus influential acts secured through Island Records in the UK such as Fairport Convention, Jimmy Cliff, and Free. But it was Karen's voice—expressive, clear and utterly distinctive—that made Alpert the group's defender and champion. "Her voice touched me. It had nothing to do with what was happening in the market . . . but that's what touched me even more," he said. "I felt like it was time."

At first Jerry Moss was not convinced and the Carpenters were required to play a set for the label executives. Thad Maxwell, who later recorded a studio session with the Carpenters, was at that point the guitarist in A&M space rock band Tarantula. He remembers seeing the audition. "We used to rehearse every day in the Charlie Chaplin soundstage—a great barn of a room. One day they told us we had to cut our rehearsal because they were auditioning this band from Orange County, south of LA, called Karen Carpenter & the Carpenters. We said, '*Really*?' And they said, 'Yeah. The lead singer is a her and she's a drummer.' We kinda raised our eyebrows a little bit. That was unusual."[4]

While the stage was set for Karen, Richard and accompanying musicians, Tarantula lurked at the back on a balcony so they could see the whole thing. Alpert, Moss, Chuck Kaye (president of A&M's publishers Almo/Irving and Rondor Music), and other executives all sat in a row and folded their arms as if to say, "Let's see whatcha got." "We were up in the rafters doing the same thing—let's see whatcha got," recalls Maxwell.

It must have been intimidating playing to a row of executives. "That's a lot of pressure, when you're performing not for an audience or applause or fans. Just those guys who've got your future in their hands." Nineteen-year-old Karen was unfazed, playing and singing with panache. "She seemed young, but quite comfortable," says Maxwell. "She had the long hair and she wore a long dress, which was appropriate since she was sitting there straddling a drum set while singing. She had an aplomb, no doubt. Karen was very competent—she wasn't a basher or thrasher like Keith Moon, but the music didn't call for that. Her voice was smooth and polished, with a mellow, deep tone. She had it right then. We were all super-impressed."

With just a few songs, Karen and Richard won over the room. "Chuck Kaye used to say he knew an act had it when he scratched his arm tattoo. Once he found himself scratching his tattoo that day he knew they had it," says Maxwell.

The Carpenters were offered a record deal. The duo were jubilant, but they had already signed a major contract for the Ford campaign and were afraid that would jeopardize their chances with A&M, their dream company. Just before the first Ford rehearsal the Bahler brothers got a call from Karen and Richard.

"We really want to thank you for picking us," said Karen, sounding chagrined.

"Well, you already thanked us for that, what's going on?"

The Carpenters didn't say they wanted out of the Ford contract, but carefully explained their plight. "You've offered us a ton of money and Herb Alpert has offered us a lot less money. But he's offered us the label that we want to be on and the people that we want to be with."

The Bahlers were young and ambitious like the Carpenters and understood their predicament. They often worked with A&M artists and knew Herb Alpert. They were also taken with

Karen and Richard ("they were both such darling people"), so they called Ford asking for the duo to be released from their contract. The president said, "I'll let them go when you bring me somebody I like as good or better." Tom Bahler promptly recruited a dynamic frontwoman from their pool of Love Generation musicians and took over Richard's duties on piano. Then he rang the Carpenters. "I said, 'Hey, you guys are done. Go! Go out there and conquer the world.'"

That savvy decision cemented a special friendship that would last and a strong connection for Karen and Tom Bahler that would later turn into love.

*

On April 22, 1969, Richard and Karen signed a contract for a standard $10,000 advance with 7 percent royalty. Jack Daugherty was responsible for the production of their first record. As a fan of Herb Alpert & the Tijuana Brass, Karen was particularly interested in A&M. Thad Maxwell elucidates: "Don't forget, A&M nurtured a variety of styles and genres. Oftentimes record labels in those days were headed up by business guys, by number crunchers, but Herb Alpert was a musician. The thing with the Carpenters was not to improve their craft so much as get it to the right people—those who could see the potential and put it together into a presentation that records well."

Alpert was protective of Richard and Karen from the start. "We signed directly to Herb, so he said, 'Do what you want.' He gave us everything we wanted and nobody pushed us," Karen recalled. As soon as the deal was signed the Carpenters went into the studio on the A&M lot and recorded most of their existing Spectrum repertoire, including songs based on demos cut in Joe Osborn's garage. Karen couldn't believe their luck. "There are really sensational studios," she said. "Herb's built mix-down rooms in the back and there's a basketball court. The A&M lot is like a great big country club, because nobody bothers you and you can go in anytime you feel like it. Like a great big home."[5]

With Osborn on bass and their old Spectrum bandmate Gary Sims on guitar, the Carpenters painstakingly worked all day and into the night, layering vocals and experimenting with arrangements. Their debut album, *Offering* (later called *Ticket to Ride*), is a mini-oratorio that starts with the choral religiosity of "Invocation" and the marching band snare of "Your Wonderful Parade," before moving through flowing psych pop, touches of jazz, and a coolly dramatic version of the Beatles' "Ticket to Ride" (which later became the title track when the album was renamed). There is a gender role reversal in the way Karen sings the deeper tones, harmonizing with Richard's sweet, almost feminine, tenor. From the first song to the closing choral "Benediction," Karen plays drums on every track. Most songs were written by Richard and John Bettis, though included are Chet Powers's antiwar song "Get Together," first recorded in 1964 by the Kingston Trio, at the height of the early civil rights movement and Neil Young's "Nowadays Clancy Can't Even Sing," here given a folk pop treatment. One of the stand-out tracks, "All I Can Do," features full-power harmonies and Karen's funky avant-jazz snare. She also plays bass on "Eve," a dramatic (if a little strained) song that was inspired by an episode of British horror series *Journey to the Unknown*, where Dennis Waterman's sales clerk falls in love with a creepy shop mannequin. Though primarily a drummer, Karen was adept at the guitar and quick to pick up other instruments— to her, music was primarily a means of channeling ideas and emotion whatever the method.

Offering's album cover, featuring Karen clutching a vivid bunch of sunflowers, firmly positioned the band in flower power folk pop territory. After its release in October 1969, the album made a moderately successful climb to number fifty-four on the *Billboard* chart and stayed in the chart for twelve weeks. To many people at the label this wasn't good enough and there were mutterings that the Carpenters should be dropped. Alpert stood by them, arguing that the band needed one more chance. In order to broaden their appeal, he and Moss made the canny decision to have them perform at key film premieres that autumn, the first of which was a musical remake of *Goodbye, Mr Chips*, a war love story starring Peter O'Toole and Petula Clark.

Best known for 1960s hits like "Downtown" and "My Love," British singer and film actress Petula Clark was then a major Grammy-winning artist in the US. *Goodbye, Mr Chips* had already created a buzz and over a thousand people attended the film premiere, including Sammy Davis Jr. and Steve McQueen. Richard and Karen were the cabaret group booked to play the after-show party. Even though she was the star of the evening, Clark took a keen interest in the young band. "It was a big do, an all-star thing with a dinner," she recalls. "I usually don't like music during dinner—if it's bad it puts me off my food. But this was good. I thought, I have to see who this is."[6]

Clark went to the side of the stage, which was on a raised dais in the middle of the room. "There they were, just the two of them, Richard at electric piano and Karen on drums. A very unusual blend of voices and harmonies. I was the only one watching and listening." After they finished the set Clark said hello. Karen recognized her and beamed.

"Hey, man," she said to Clark, "hey, man, you're great!"

"Why, thank you so much." Clark then turned to Herb Alpert, who was sitting at the next table and said, "You gotta listen to these people." Later that night she found out the Carpenters were already signed to A&M.

Clark remembers the duo as being "pretty inexperienced as people. But they sounded so sophisticated musically. Karen was a bit gawky and uncomfortable in her skin, yet also lovely and charming. I adored her." After that first meeting they stayed in touch and, though eighteen years her senior, Clark became Karen's close friend and mentor and a valuable source of support as her career grew.

Karen's charm was noticed at the party that night by other key Hollywood people, like *Goodbye, Mr Chips*'s soundtrack composer, Leslie Bricusse, who praised her "God-given voice." It was clear that the Carpenters resonated with an older, influential supper club crowd, so they were booked a few weeks later for the premiere of *Hello, Dolly!*, a romantic musical comedy starring Barbra Streisand. This was momentous for Karen, who already looked up to Streisand as an inspirational performer. Through their connections, Alpert and Moss introduced the Carpenters to an easy-listening audience, hoping this would prove more successful for them than the eclectic folk pop of their debut album. When the iconic Burt Bacharach told Jerry Moss that he liked the Carpenters' version of "Ticket to Ride," Moss quickly responded that he, Bacharach, was one of their favorite composers, suggesting the duo could open a benefit show he was doing in February with a medley of his songs. The event was for the Reiss-Davis Child Study Center, an organization offering high-quality mental health therapy to low-income children and adolescents.

Ecstatic at the thought of playing before their idol, Karen and Richard drew up a shortlist of six Bacharach songs they loved and began industrious rehearsals on the A&M soundstage. One of the songs that Alpert was keen on them recording was a little-known track which had been tucked away on Dionne Warwick's 1964 album *Make Way for Dionne Warwick*. "Herb's the type that doesn't like to do the 'San Jose's. We love "em, but he wanted to pull out stuff that nobody had heard of," recalled Karen.[7] As she and Richard sifted through piles of songs, Alpert walked into the studio.

"Have you heard of a tune 'They Long to Be Close to You'?" he asked.

"No."

"Well, I'll sing it to you." He sat at the piano and crooned a few elegant bars. "That's your record. I don't want you to do it the way Burt did with Dionne, I just want you to take the lead sheet and do what you want."

71

Richard dutifully worked on an arrangement, but thought the song was a little corny and left it out of the medley. Alpert, however, instinctively felt that the song was right for the Carpenters and asked them to record it as a possible single. This might be the one to convince naysayers within A&M, those who were ready to give up on the band. Karen and Richard obliged but their first version was too light, so in order to beef up the sound a little, Alpert brought drummer Hal Blaine and keyboardist Larry Knechtel into the studio, along with trumpeter Chuck Findley. Blaine had played on records by the Beach Boys, the Ronettes and Neil Diamond and was a seasoned rock 'n' roll drummer, one of Los Angeles' Wrecking Crew. When he first met Richard and Karen he was struck by their naiveté. "Here's this girl and this guy, both wearing little leather fringe jackets, almost country types. I remember them being a couple of chubby kids. They weren't fat or anything, but they were kind of chubby," he said. "Of course they made it—they did a 180 and became Hollywood, but [at that point] A&M were about to drop them."[8]

Much to Blaine's annoyance, Agnes Carpenter attended the recording sessions and bristled at the thought of another drummer supplanting her daughter. "I've seen many drummers on television and Karen is as good as any of them," she declared. It was explained to Agnes that Karen was great but, according to Blaine, "she just didn't have the studio chops, the studio experience for the records and that's when they brought me in." It wasn't necessarily about tougher playing but creating a sonic mood, sometimes doing gentle brushwork or, if the song demanded it, a definitive beat with the thick end of the drumstick. Blaine likened it to driving a small car or an articulated lorry: "each one has different rules for maneuvering." Session playing, he argued, improves only through being in the studio listening to what works. Blaine's reasoning sounds logical, but it is significant that no one offered to help Karen develop her drumming and that she was so quickly usurped as a drummer. This was the first undermining of her talent and what she saw as her role in the band.

In those sessions Blaine did notice a strange family dynamic, an intimation of future conflict. "Her mother kept saying, 'But Richard is the star, Karen is just the drummer.' I think part of that stuff pushed Karen over the edge eventually. The poor thing was playing her buns off on the drums trying to do the right thing." Blaine saw Karen's drumming as a form of compensation, a way of gaining acceptance and pleasing her parents. But to Karen, drumming was much more than that—it was an instrument that allowed her to express herself and be heard, an integral part of her musical identity and her style. Those early A&M recording sessions were fraught because, although Agnes defended Karen's right to play the drums, she made it clear that it was a secondary role, that she was there to back Richard. Just at the point that she could have affirmed Karen as an artist, Agnes crushed that emerging self by insisting that Richard was the star, the one in the family with the original talent.

As he sat there in the studio watching this all play out, Blaine also picked up on tension in the band over their future direction. This recording was a pivotal moment as the Carpenters desperately needed "Close to You" to be a hit, otherwise their luck was over.

BOOK 3
Superstar

CHAPTER 5

1970

We came out right in the middle of hard rock. But we were ready to make our music, y'know? We were the first. And we didn't plan it. When it hit, boy . . . it just exploded. And we were sitting there goin," "What happened?"[1]

During the recording of "(They Long to Be) Close to You" in March 1970, people kept poking their heads round the door of Studio B, even when the red light was on. A buzz was slowly spreading round the building. These young kids from Downey were recording something special. Larry Knechtel's riffs had been a little too heavy-handed on the first take, so Richard was back on the piano, punctuating the arrangement with cheeky, sparkling quintuplet notes, and Hal Blaine's gentle rhythm added subtle flavor in the right places. "My drumsticks are my paint-brushes. I was painting a picture, with certain colors coming in and going out," he said.[2] Meanwhile producer Jack Daugherty asked Chuck Findley to stay behind at the end of the session and play the flugelhorn solo that adds such exhilarating definition to the song. "It was the hardest thing to dip the note out, very difficult to do . . . but I got there in two takes," he remembered.[3]

What also stands out in this luxuriant arrangement is the heady rush of Karen and Richard's harmonies. It was Karen who insisted on the extra attack of their last "Whaaaaaaa!," deliberately overemphasizing the lavish vowel sounds. Many people at A&M loved the track, including Alpert. He was cautious, however, concerned that because it was so soft and slow the record might not appeal to a broad audience, particularly teenagers used to beat-driven rock, and it would either be a smash hit or a complete failure.

When the song was released in June 1970 it entered the *Billboard* charts at number fifty-six and began to climb steadily. Radio DJs enjoyed the rich, sensual harmonies and playlisted the song. By July 22 "(They Long to Be) Close to You" had hit number one and sold a million.

"Close to You" was the longest-running number-one single that summer in the US. It also went to number one in Australia and Canada and made the top ten in the UK, Ireland, and New Zealand, so for now the band's career was safe. "I was glad because I didn't want to go anywhere," said Karen. "[Success] was just out of the blue. Our first record, *Ticket to Ride*, was a half-hit, half-flop. In some places it was ashtray material. Then lo and behold, "Close to You" was given to us by Herb Alpert and within six weeks it was number one."[4] Alpert was so delighted that on the day they reached the top of the *Billboard* charts he wrote in delirious scribble on A&M paper to Richard and Karen, "We're no. 1. Weeeeeeeeeee Congratulations + Love, HA." As Chuck Findley noted, "With that unbelievable huge success the Carpenters and the A&M record label were back on the map again."

The Carpenters needed to consolidate their success as quickly as possible, so Jerry Moss called Daugherty with a message for Richard: "We need an album, like, now." Richard and Karen had already begun recording their next album and they picked up the pace, finishing off what was to become their second mega-hit single, written by two aspiring young songwriters signed to A&M. Pianist/composer Roger Nichols initially started out as a solo artist, collaborating with Randy Newman, Melissa MacLeod, and soundtrack composer Van Dyke Parks on his 1968 debut album, *Roger Nichols and a Small Circle of Friends*. The record's vocal harmonies and elements of chanson show Nichols's ear for strong melody. When he met Paul Williams, a pithy, evocative lyricist, the pair continually sparked off each other, but their songwriting career was slow to take off.

"We were getting some album cuts, but nothing like a big hit," Nichols said later. "And then along came the Carpenters, who were looking for material."[5] Shortly before that Williams and Nichols had been approached with a request to write a song for a bank commercial. Crocker Citizens Bank wanted to attract parents and newlyweds, so Williams and Nichols wrote two verses to accompany short scenes of a young couple on their wedding day, his first day at a new job, then moving into a home with their first child. "You've got a long way to go," read the strapline. "We'd like to help you get there." Richard saw the advert on TV and even though the visuals were corny, the tune resonated with him and he thought it would be the perfect song for Karen. Recognizing Williams' voice on the soundtrack, he assumed it was a Williams and Nichols composition. In the meantime Crocker Citizens Bank requested a full song for their clients, so the songwriters completed it with a bridge and last verse. "When Richard called us, I said, 'We have a full song,'" recalled Nichols.

In the studio the Carpenters transformed a saccharine commercial into a song with long-lasting depth and pathos. Williams assumed that because songs like Iron Butterfly's hard rock opus "In-A-Gadda-Da-Vida" were in vogue there was no way in the world that "We've Only Just Begun" would be a hit. "But then Karen Carpenter sang it . . . an angel sang it."[6] Karen's interpretation lifted the lyrics from the level of a trite jingle to a meaningful optimism. "Let's be honest, it was the Carpenters that really launched our career," recalled Nichols. "Richard to this day says that 'We've Only Just Begun' was their theme song."

Released on August 21, 1970, their single sped up the *Billboard* charts to number two and sold over a million copies in the US. Their second album, *Close to You*, was released at the same time and also landed at number two, staying on the chart for eighty-seven weeks. With its swathes of ripe harmonies, *Close to You* had a distinctive swagger, pioneering soft rock—a new genre that spawned groups such as Fleetwood Mac, Bread, and the Eagles. The Carpenters stood out because of the intricacy of their arrangements and Karen's voice, which had the purity of plainsong. Mixing a swing rhythm with plaintive oboe and triple vocal overdubs, "We've Only Just Begun" became the soundtrack to a million weddings—and in its evocation of the future ("So much of life ahead"), it heralded the promise of the new decade.

With its touches of jazz and baroque, the album *Close to You* has an air of experimentation and a deliberate reframing of past records. Take the way Karen sings Burt Bacharach's song "Baby It's You" with a quiet, loaded focus that is opposite to the teen innocence of the Shirelles' 1961 original, or the impatient urgency she adds to "I'll Never Fall in Love Again." Dionne Warwick had already scored a hit with the song in 1969, but Karen was careful to sing in a way that was different to her measured style. At first Warwick was ruffled by her labelmate singing songs that she had already recorded. Toward the end of her working relationship with Bacharach he asked, "Who will be the voice of my songs now?"

"Karen Carpenter," she drily retorted.

However, Karen was so unguarded in her admiration of Warwick that the two of them became friends and remained close throughout Karen's life. "She was a dream with a magical voice, purely magical. She was fun to be around and a good friend. She'd often say to me, 'I'm gonna sing this song and I'll try not to sing it like you, but it's very difficult not to sing it like you!'" recalls Warwick.[7]

Also included on *Close to You* were Spectrum songs from their early repertoire like the jaunty "Mr. Guder" and "Another Song," a quirky baroque number that dissolves into Karen's trancelike drumming. On this album they were trying out imaginative ideas, like Karen's reading of the Beatles' song "Help," overriding the

bouncy flow of the original to create a sense of desperate, con-
flicted drama. Her mournful treatment of the song is an eerie
foreshadowing of the personal anguish that was to come later.
Even then Karen was insecure about her talent and her place in
the world, communicating through the song an emotional reality
and vulnerability that may have been unconscious at that point,
but that was nevertheless still there, buried deep.

That summer of 1970, the band went out on their first tour
with a core line-up that included former Spectrum bassist Dan
Woodhams, saxophonist Bob Messenger, their college friend
Doug Strawn on reed instruments and guitarist Gary Sims,
who joined them once he had finished his stint in the Army
Reserve. John Bettis signed with Almo Publishing as one of
the Carpenters' key writers, spending six days a week on the
A&M lot. Before they went on the road, the group rehearsed
for weeks on the soundstage, making sure that harmonies were
meticulous and that the live sound was as near as possible to
what had been captured on record.

Karen became a driving force in the band and she assumed a
kind of management role, contacting musicians, keeping a date-
book, and being punctual and precise with logistics and pick-up
times. "We worked our thing off to run that first album. When
the pre-orders outsold in one hour what the other record sold in
a month, that's stupid," she recalled. Personable and competitive,
she did most of the talking in record company meetings, made
swift decisions and wasn't afraid to be confrontational. This
contrasted with Richard, who was seen as more introverted and
anxious, described by A&M president Gil Friesen as "a very

intense young man."[8] Some A&M staff looked down on the Carpenters as being unhip, but Karen didn't let that faze her. With their best-selling album, people from top agencies were starting to circle and the Carpenters signed to Creative Management Associates, with Dan Cleary as their booking agent. Cleary hinted that now that they were in demand across America the Carpenters needed a more experienced manager than Ed Sulzer.

Richard baulked at the idea of letting Sulzer go. Although Karen was loyal, once a decision was made she could be assertive and she urged Richard to act. Even though Richard made decisions on arrangements and song selection, when it came to the day-to-day running of the group Karen often took the lead, displaying an astute business sense. At critical moments like this in choosing personnel and the team around the band, Karen could be very persuasive. The pair of them had a meeting with Sulzer, saying that it was time for a change, but as compensation Richard offered Sulzer a new role as tour manager. He refused and quit immediately. Not wanting A&M's new prize band to become rudderless, Herb Alpert quickly stepped in, recommending the Tijuana Brass's manager, Sherwin Bash, a slick, sharp operator who took over their affairs for the next five years.

Bash began his career in music publishing in New York, before forming BNB Management in 1950 with songwriter Mace Neufeld (who would go on to produce films including *The Omen* and *The Hunt for Red October*). In 1959, Bash moved to California to open a West Coast office and BNB expanded their clientele with Alpert, Petula Clark, and Randy Newman. When they signed the Carpenters, BNB were also expanding into film and TV production and had plans to steer the band into the music stratosphere. The approach was simple—get them on the road and on TV and radio as much as possible. In that first year, for instance, the Carpenters appeared on all the big TV shows such as *The David Frost Show*, *The Ed Sullivan Show*, and *The Tonight Show Starring Johnny Carson*, and their records were a staple of mainstream radio.

At a time when the Vietnam War divided the country and the entrancing energy of 1967's summer of love had dissipated into a darker period of violence and protest—from riots in Detroit to the murder of a fan at the Rolling Stones' Altamont Speedway concert in 1969—the Carpenters' mellifluous sound was a panacea. "We came out right in the middle of hard rock everywhere. It was such a turnaround, I guess a lot of people were waiting for something in that vein," Karen said later. "We were the first. Around that time it was Carpenters and Bread, then later James Taylor, Carole King. But we were really the first . . . We were the first brother-sister team since Fred and Adele Astaire and that's a long time."[9]

Their 1970 tour itinerary began by supporting Burt Bacharach at Westbury Music Fair on Long Island, followed by a three-week engagement in Nevada at the King's Castle in Lake Tahoe, an eleven-story hotel and casino with a neo-Tudor structure and mock medieval battlements. Lake Tahoe was a prime destination for wedding venues and honeymooners, so the Carpenters' set, with "We've Only Just Begun" at its heart, was in the perfect location. That summer tour also included August dates at Harrah's hotel in Reno and, when they had a night off, Petula Clark went with Karen to see Elvis Presley in nearby Las Vegas.

Presley was then thirty-five years old and at the peak of his career, playing two shows a night at the International Hotel. "Sinatra was a show. Elvis was a happening," says Joe Guercio, the musical director for his Vegas shows. "It was another world."[10] The International was a mega-resort with a mammoth showroom that had opened the previous year. Construction of the resort on the site of the old Las Vegas speedway had been completed in record time and Barbra Streisand and Presley were hired for its grand opening in 1969. That year Presley did fifty-seven consecutive performances and then returned every February and August for the next six years. After a decade of bad B movies and declining record sales, the International was where Presley relaunched his career.

The stage was 60 feet wide, with a heavy gold-lamé curtain and fussy decor that featured crystal chandeliers and figurines of angels. In contrast to the glitzy showbiz surroundings, Presley would start each show with an acoustic guitar and barrel through '50s hits like "Hound Dog" and "Blue Suede Shoes" with a burning intensity that rocked the crowd. Accompanied by a dynamic band that included rockabilly guitarist James Burton and gospel groups the Imperials and the Sweet Inspirations, the high point was a charged seven-minute rendition of "Suspicious Minds," where with a blues wail and sophisticated soul, he painted a world of paranoia, heartbreak, and betrayal.

The night that Petula Clark and Karen saw the show they were recognized by the doormen and given the full VIP treatment. "He was on form, wearing his white jumpsuit. He looked beautiful and the place was jumping," says Clark.[11] Karen, too, was blown away by his performance. "That face! We worshipped Elvis. We'd gone as guests . . . I couldn't have cared less about our gig, I just wanted to go see Elvis. He walked out and my heart stopped. I've been watching him for as long as I can remember. He was not only gorgeous, his voice was beautiful and his talent immense," she recalled.[12]

At the end of the show the maitre d' came over to Karen and Clark saying, "Mr. Presley would like to see you." They were led backstage through the dressing room to an area where Presley's entourage, a collection of guys known as his Memphis Mafia, were lounging and having a drink. "Elvis had been in a big changing room getting out of his jumpsuit. Then he walked in, absolutely gorgeous," says Clark. "We were looking at him and he was looking at us. He seemed thrilled. Someone gave a signal and suddenly all those Nashville guys went." Presley could be an edgy presence. As Joanie Shoofey, wife of International Hotel president Alex Shoofey and a former Miss Nevada, remembered, "He used to mess up his suite so bad. We had to redo it every time he was there. They all dyed their hair and [there was] black dye all over the walls. And one time he shot the TV with a gun. I mean he was wild, he was not nice in a room."[13]

The night he met Karen and Clark, however, Presley came across as the perfect Southern gentleman, chatting with them and drinking wine. "He was coming on to both of us. Karen was a pretty naive twenty-year-old, but I was a married woman living in Paris. I could tell he was keen on both of us at the same time and he started to get a little too flirty," says Clark.

She remembers standing up decisively. "Well, Karen, you've got your thing in the morning."

"What thing? No one has things in the morning in Las Vegas."

Presley glanced at Clark as if to say, "Okay, I get it." As they left he stood at the door and threw her a look.

According to Clark they scampered out "like a pair of frightened rabbits. I don't think Karen knew what was going on!" Maybe Karen wasn't as innocent as Clark imagined and she saw something in Presley that fired up her sense of adventure. "The first time I met him I thought I was going to drop dead in my tracks. I was just beside myself," she later said in glowing terms.[14] Most importantly, it was the elemental force of Presley's performance that impressed Karen and inspired her as a singer. With his dyed black hair, pouty lips, and dark eyeliner, Presley felt free to express his feminine side as well as belt out rock 'n' roll, while Karen loved to sing in a deep voice and play drums like a tomboy. Both of them were unusual artists with a certain androgynous appeal.

*

As the Carpenters became more successful and the royalty checks started rolling in, the family decided it was time to move from their modest home on Fidler Street. Both Karen and Richard wanted a big house with a swimming pool, so their mother, Agnes, went with family friend Evelyn Wallace and estate agent Beverly Nogawski to look at properties in the residential, more upmarket north-east part of Downey (the "right" side of the railroad track). They found a five-bedroom split-level ranch house in a quiet cul-de-sac and moved in on Thanksgiving. From that day, 9828 Newville Avenue became the family home and, in the years ahead, a source of both comfort and claustrophobia, a place to which Karen would always return.

At the same time as the family move, Karen was going through changes in her personal life. While on tour she finished her romance with Gary Sims by letter and she began a new relationship with the band's road manager, Jerry Luby. This liaison was the first in what would become a pattern of Karen dating men from within the Carpenters' entourage, people known to the family and therefore "safe." There was a feeling of camaraderie on that 1970 tour, driving together in cars rather than taking the luxury Learjet of later tours.

One night the band made the long drive home from Boise, Idaho, to Los Angeles. Doug Strawn drove with his girlfriend Carol in one car, Jerry Luby and Karen were together in another, and Richard steered his Plymouth 'Cuda, blasting out the radio and having a good time. "We stopped in the middle of the night for some petrol . . . and Doug said he was hallucinating. He was so tired," Richard said.[15] As they crossed the Los Angeles city limits, they heard "We've Only Just Begun" for the first time on the radio, giddy and excited at everything that was to come.

CHAPTER 6

1971

"Superstar." . . still upsets me when I sing it. That and "Rainy Days and Mondays," tear me to shreds. It just gets to me . . . and I go into a different world.[1]

One day in January 1971, harmonica player Tommy Morgan was booked into a session at the A&M studio, not knowing who he would be working for that day. "A tall, good-looking guy walked in and said, 'Hi, I'm Richard . . . you wanna hear the track?'" recalls Morgan. Richard played a new song that had been written by Roger Nichols and Paul Williams, called "Rainy Days and Mondays." Karen then appeared, looking quiet and subdued. "In walks this girl, doesn't introduce herself, a very shy, private person. Not outgoing."[2]

For this session Richard was in control. "I know what I want you to play," he said, sketching out a tune on the piano. Morgan transcribed his part for the harmonica with a solo at the beginning and a counterline. "In the middle there was a modulation, so I took what Richard played on A and transposed a step," says Morgan. The Carpenters were lucky to have such expertise—his signature harmonica sound embellished pop tunes like the Beach Boys' "Good Vibrations" and albums by Randy Newman, Carly Simon, and Neil Diamond and can now be heard on hundreds of TV shows and feature films, from *The Rockford Files* to *Dances with Wolves*. "The harmonica was an instrument that found me. It's very strange. In my early days I didn't particularly like my sound and I developed it over the years, trying to improve it," Morgan says. "Most people blow into it with no control or shaping of sound." A choir director for many years, he took cues from vocal music, which explains why his phrasing was so *simpatico* with Karen's singing. "I went in, put on the headset and started the take. Six bars into the intro there was a note jam. I cleared the instrument and started at the top again. I hadn't played the piece before, I was reading the pencil part I'd written. We did it in one take and nailed it."

Richard said he was happy, so Morgan filled out a form for the A&M payroll and glanced at his watch. "The total time had taken twenty minutes, from start to finish, with no rehearsal. That's the way we did it then, that's the way you work," says Morgan. Karen was present the whole time, listening but not saying a word. "Like Dolly Parton, she only spoke when she had something to say." After the session Morgan walked out and didn't give it much thought. "When you do a session you never know what's going to survive and I didn't know who they were. Richard didn't give me his last name."

Then three months later he heard "Rainy Days and Mondays" played everywhere, on the radio, in stores, and in bars, for months.

"It's an absolute classic piece and it survives. My sound from then on was associated with that record. I even listen to it today and would change nothing in the way I played. It was made in that moment and lived in that moment," says Morgan. The plaintive, flowing quality of the harmonica combined with Karen's soulful voice made this a Carpenters classic. It showed a new side to the band, its mood chiming with another female singer, Carole King, who was recording her new album *Tapestry* in A&M's Studio B, with the support of Joni Mitchell and James Taylor. After its release, *Tapestry* became one of the biggest albums of 1971, spending fifteen weeks at number one.

As a key writer with her husband, Jerry Goffin, King started out penning Brill Building hits for girl groups like the Chiffons and the Shirelles, and she showed an ability to encapsulate what women were thinking. In 1960s New York, she was young, happily married, and riding high on the R&B explosion, but by the 1970s she was divorced, bringing up two children as a single mother in Los Angeles, and her songwriting became more introspective. Combining the streetwise girl group sound with a laid-back hippy mindset, King created an album that perfectly captured an era when women were exploring independence and re-evaluating their relationships. Many women found themselves relegated to a lonely, disconnected existence as adjuncts to their husbands, seeking escape with lunchtime sherry or prescription medication. Karen's moody vocals on "Rainy Days and Mondays" became part of that zeitgeist, conjuring a world of Valium-fueled suburban blues. Even though she was only twenty-one at the time, Karen expressed a drifting malaise and alienation beyond her years.

"Rainy Days and Mondays" was recorded at a point when the Carpenters were gaining artistic recognition. At the 1971 Grammy Awards, they won Best New Artist and Best Pop Vocal for "Close to You," which by then had been a worldwide hit. To capitalize on this the Carpenters' debut album, *Offering*, was repackaged with a new streamlined cover shot, taken on a sailing boat on Lake Tahoe. Renamed *Ticket to Ride*, it included "Close to You" as one of the featured tracks. After four years of trying, they had finally arrived.

Sessions for the Carpenters' third album took place between tour dates, as during 1971 the band toured in earnest. Regular gigs had honed their sound, so that when musicians from the live band like Doug Strawn and Bob Messenger were in the studio they slipped into a groove. From those sessions emerged "For All We Know," a reflective song about a troubled relationship, which features Earle Dumler's rich oboe and Karen's voice, clear and powerful over a tinkling piano. Richard first heard the song on the soundtrack to the film *Lovers and Other Strangers* and thought it would be perfect for the Carpenters. Released in advance of the album in January 1971, it became their third hit, closely followed by "Rainy Days and Mondays," which went to number two.

Now they were on a roll. Richard noted another song that he thought would suit Karen's vocal, a chilling ballad about a groupie who falls for a rock star. Written by Leon Russell and Ronnie Bramlett, "Superstar" is one of the first songs about celebrity stalking, showing how heartbreak can turn into dark obsession. Richard heard Bette Midler sing it on *The Tonight*

Show and persuaded Karen to record it. In the rock 'n' roll world of the 1970s, female musicians were rarely taken seriously as creators, so women often experienced music through their boyfriend's record collection or by having relationships with male musicians. The groupie was a relatively new concept, a figure often portrayed as a user or a victim. At first Karen was unconvinced by "Superstar" but, swayed by the melody and the lyric's bruising intensity, she gave a profound performance in one perfect take, as if exorcising a repressed spirit. After its release in May, "Superstar" became the song of the summer.

Apart from Richard and John Bettis's oddball track "Druscilla Penny" (another mocking song about groupies), the Carpenters' new album was an assured collection, including a lilting Bacharach–David medley as well as the hit singles. Many acts use an eponymous title for their debut album, but the Carpenters did this for their third. Otherwise known as "The Tan Album" by fans, it was the first to prominently display their logo, signaling the birth of the group as a brand.

The new logo was designed by Craig Braun, who had previously worked with Andy Warhol on the banana peel cover of *The Velvet Underground & Nico* and created the tongue for the final version of the Rolling Stones' logo. His West Coast design studio revolutionized album art and packaging, creating indelible images that linked music and pop art. Together with illustrator Walter Velez, for the Carpenters he came up with a vintage typeface that was reminiscent of early twentieth-century Americana, symbolizing pioneer family values. Symmetrical in design, Braun described the logo as evoking "two people, two sides."[3] With this logo the Carpenters became one of the most successful musical brands in the pop industry.

According to award-winning graphic designer and author Jon Wozencroft, the logo "is quite schizophrenic because it uses a well-established visual trope of the ascending and descending, denoting balance and movement. But, at the same time, it's like a suspension bridge between two worlds. The world, the Carpenters subliminally suggest, is going from the chaos of Vietnam protest and insurrection over to the other side of the river, to calmness, love, peace and harmony." There is duality in the way that letters join and connect, so there is both flow and interruption. "In the visual mode of instant recognition the viewer harmonises all those things without realising it, hence its epic nature," says Wozencroft. "It's a bullet to the brain."[4]

Also evoking the visual iconography of 1950s vintage cars, the logo had immediate appeal for Richard. He and Karen were so pleased with it they decided to put the logo on everything—all aspects of their merchandising, from album covers to belt buckles, key rings, and patches on jeans. It became one of the most enduring logos of the 1970s and marked a shift in gear for the band in terms of their image. Until that point most photos of Karen and Richard were staged and gawky, with hit-and-miss styling. On the cover of *Close to You*, for example, Karen looks uncomfortable in her chunky white maxi dress and leg-of-mutton sleeves and Richard doesn't know what to do with his bulky cashmere jacket. Both are also clearly having a bad hair day. Karen was most comfortable in jeans and a T-shirt and as the band became more successful she cultivated a more casual look for videos and photo shoots, keeping the unwieldy gowns as stagewear.

For their first interviews the Carpenters were excited to talk about their lives, giving open and honest answers and inviting journalists to their home in Newville Avenue. Karen in particular had a girl-next-door appeal and liked to joke and clown around. She was very adaptable, one day showing *Teen* magazine her black fur bedspread and stuffed animal collection. "They all have names. That's Gru-pig and there's Marshfield," she said, pointing to a checkered pig and a large pink dog.[5] Though she could be childlike in a way that was engaging, she also showed awareness of current issues. She and Richard told radio presenter Dick Biondi, for instance, that they were against the Vietnam War, believed in sex before marriage, and were in favor of legalizing marijuana. The PR department at A&M reacted with horror, telling Karen and Richard to tone down the interviews in case they offended their growing mainstream audience. "We were told . . . don't say anything bad, don't say you dislike anything. Everything is groovy, everything is terrific," Richard later told *Melody Maker*.[6] From then on Richard and Karen felt awkward about expressing controversial opinions, so they started to dilute their responses. The band became pigeon-holed as bland and conservative, a stereotype that would later come to haunt them.

*

By the summer of 1971, the Carpenters had their own logo, top-flight management, and a hectic touring schedule and the self-titled "Tan Album" had gone platinum. Now there was a combined effort to coax Karen away from the drums. During a long drive across country to see family in Baltimore and New Haven, Richard told Karen that it was time to step out from behind the drums and front the group. From the start, Karen's role as the drummer in the band had been the subject of discussion. As Hal Blaine said, when he first met the band, "There's nothing wrong with female drummers . . . but to me Karen always looked like a little high-school kid sitting behind the drums."[7] The bigger the band became, the more Richard, their manager Sherwin Bash and the record company put pressure on Karen to just focus on lead vocals. "I knew damned well that people did not want to see her singing these great love songs from behind this big drum set," said Richard.[8]

Karen, however, was deeply reluctant to abandon the drums; they were part of her persona, her primary means of expression as a musician. This is illustrated by two videos of the band performing in the Desert Inn, a Las Vegas nightclub. The "Rainy Days and Mondays" video features Karen drumming, positioned at the center of the band. She is dressed casually, comfortable both singing and playing and clearly taking a creative role in the music. The band came across as progressive and intelligent, with Karen communicating a powerful message—I'm lonely and I have the blues, but it's my loneliness and my blues. "Superstar," by contrast, is in a more formal and traditional setting, with Karen standing motionless in a long supper club gown, singing a song about powerlessness and obsession. She delivers it looking down with her head bowed as the song fades.

John Bettis said that pulling Karen out from behind the drums was "a big deal, very hard for Karen."[9] He maintained that she was loud and physical and hitting the drums gave her a sense of independence, that it was something she was born to do. Once in an interview, Karen laid out her priorities: "I was always part of the gang. On tour I packed my own drums and helped pack the trunk. Then I'd go into the dressing room and set my hair."[10] On stage, she sang and played drums with ease and precision, comfortable as an instrumentalist. However, now the Carpenters were dominating the charts, A&M felt it necessary to foreground their hit voice. Karen's vocals were referred to as a commodity, her tones translated into cash. Composer and easy-listening icon Henry Mancini noted, for instance, that "in the low end was the money part of her voice."

Music historian George McKay argues that Karen's drummer-singer style was her own striking innovation—yet she was discouraged from pursuing this mode of performance.[11] In reviews at the time, some critics added to the trivialization of Karen as a player, questioning whether it was ladylike to sit with a drum kit. "Rarely do you see a fetching brunette seat herself at the drums and flail away so perfectly," commented the *Cleveland Press*. Lester Bangs in *Rolling Stone* acknowledged that Karen was "pretty damn good" on the drums "but singing from behind that massive set she doesn't give you much to look at." Others, however, saw it as an intrinsic part of the show. "Once the novelty of seeing Karen on drums had worn off, the audience began to enjoy a neat arrangement of 'Help,'" reported Richard Green for the *New Musical Express*. And *Variety* noted that Karen "manages to be seen and heard to very good advantage."

After long-drawn-out discussion with Richard and Sherwin Bash, Karen made a deal to play drums on some songs and front the band during the ballads. Richard recruited a second drummer for the live shows, his old New Haven friend Jim Squeglia, who had played with Richard in their high-school band, the Sceptres. "Singing and playing drums was the most comfortable thing. Finally I had to get up. Petrified. You have no idea. The fear! There was nothing to hold onto," Karen said later.[12] Standing upfront made her feel utterly exposed. Without the drums she was untethered and insecure. For many musicians facing an audience can feel precipitous. Even those with sturdy mental health and self-belief can be daunted looking at a large crowd of faces gazing back at them. Karen's admission that she felt petrified would not have helped her later issues with body image and the need to control her environment.

The underlying message to someone so proud and committed to drumming was that she was no longer rated as an instrumentalist. In losing her drums Karen was deskilled, navigated into the role of decorative frontwoman. "I didn't start playing just to be a gimmick," she said. "I took a lot of pride knowing how to play my instrument. It hurt me that I had to . . . be upfront."[13] Martin Slattery, a top producer who has worked with musicians in a range of genres, maintains that Karen was a gifted drummer. "To drum and sing at the same time and keep perfect pitch and time, requires such intelligence. It's unique. It also suggests a real sensitivity and fragility," he says.[14] Karen had to sublimate her fears and her feelings for the greater good of the band. Musician and drum historian Amie McBye says, "Whenever I get off the drum kit, I feel like something is missing. When you're [an] instrumentalist the instrument is part of you, so I can see for Karen how taking something away from her like that would have been pretty dreadful. Women should be able to do what they want and have it respected, rather than adhere to a male blueprint of female performance."[15]

Richard was to complain bitterly during interviews about the fact that critics dismissed the Carpenters as square and uncool. Ironically, if Karen had kept her place behind the drums, the band would have been seen as braver and more distinctive. Feminist writer and anthropologist Wendy Fonarow remembers that shift in Karen Carpenter's image. "The first time I saw her on TV in the '70s she was behind the drums. As a child, you're not thinking in terms of gender, you're just thinking, *Super cool band.* I was watching a cool drummer singing. Then at some point I thought, *Oh, why are they making her do less? Why is she doing less when the other part was so cool?*"[16] In the 1990s and 2000s artists like the White Stripes' Meg White and Lori Barbero from Babes in Toyland proved that female drummers could be a focal point and still achieve massive success. But in the early 1970s that was too quirky and marginal by far.

Foregrounding Karen as the lead singer also complicated her relationship with Richard. At the beginning of their career he was considered the special one. Interestingly, their mother Agnes was keen for Karen to stay on the drums because she saw Richard as the gifted family prodigy. When the writer from *Teen* magazine came to Downey, for instance, Agnes announced in hallowed tones: "We're having another room added to the house this year so that Richard can have someplace to write and not be disturbed. He wants to get a grand piano—a larger one."[17] Being pushed to the front presented Karen with a paradox—sell the song and take the limelight, but don't take credit for your own success. This made it difficult for her to fulfill her potential as an artist and musician. Tension began to surface and show in unguarded moments, like the July day they rehearsed with an orchestra and chorus in the sound studio before playing their biggest concert that night at the Hollywood Bowl. Karen sang beautifully when it was her turn to test the mic, but sat bored and restless while Richard scolded the chorus and brass section into playing with the precision he wanted.

During a break their publicist tried to clear a few minutes for a chat with *Chicago Tribune* reporter Ken Michaels, but Richard just shook the journalist's hand and scooted off, leaving Karen to do the interview. Her silent frown and noncommittal answers showed her exasperation. When the publicist told Michaels his minute was up, Karen said, "Good," and stalked away.[18] Even though the concert that evening went well, with 18,000 fans giving a standing ovation, at the after-show party Karen sat slumped in a chair, frowning, while Richard stood in the bar talking to the press.

At twenty-one years old, experiencing such sudden and unexpected fame, Karen hadn't yet learned the art of being gracious with everyone. But she was also feeling a little isolated and trapped as the only woman on tour with ten men.

"Sometimes I feel as if I've got to have another girl to talk to," she said. "The guys are all very protective toward me. It's wild. I can't make a move."[19] It's not surprising that Karen valued and made connections with other female singers, like Petula Clark and Dionne Warwick, who could understand the issues of being a woman in the spotlight.

Then in September 1971 she met someone who would become one of her closest female friends. The Carpenters flew over to Europe to play their first London date, supporting singer-songwriter Labi Siffre at the Royal Albert Hall. After the show Karen went to Annabel's, a members-only nightclub in Berkeley Square, where she met a sparky Australian girl called Olivia Newton-John. Newton-John was twenty-three and living in London at the time, just starting out in her career and recording her debut album, *If Not for You*, at Abbey Road. The two struck up an immediate rapport and shared understanding and kept in touch. A few months later when Newton-John's country pop version of the album's title track, a Bob Dylan song, became a major US hit, Karen was one of the first to congratulate her.

That night at Annabel's also gave Karen a taste of the high life. Opened in 1963 by society entrepreneur Mark Birley as a place he declared "must smell of exclusivity and sex," it was frequented by everyone from the Beatles and Mick Jagger to the Shah of Iran.[20] Frank Sinatra became an early member (like Karen, going there after a concert at the Royal Albert Hall), and Ella Fitzgerald played there in January 1971. The red lacquered walls and crystal chandeliers made Karen feel special, that she had "arrived." That was the beginning of an internal tug between the down-home Downey girl who talked drum talk and loved life on the road and the aspiring "uptown" girl who relished success and status. She wanted to explore whatever life had to offer, but at the same time needed to feel anchored by family and her duty to the band. This duality was apparent to Frenda Leffler, the elegant, poised wife of Ed Leffler, who was managing the Carpenters with Sherwin Bash. When she first met Karen after a concert Leffler found her gauche and brattish, someone who sang with a heavenly voice but who, as the only girl in the band, was "rough around the edges."[21] As she got to know Karen, however, Leffler discovered behind the guarded demeanour a trusting, funny, and constant friend.

Back in the US after the London trip, Karen was challenged by a power struggle at the heart of the tour. She had finished with her boyfriend Jerry Luby and begun a relationship with Paul White, the new road manager. Thirteen years her senior, he took on the role of a protective mentor. He and Karen often traveled separately in the truck and he would give her advice about her performance and band politics, feeling that she was underappreciated and that others took her talent for granted. Bash became aware of this and, impatient with White's influence, engineered his dismissal in one short, sharp meeting. Bash must have felt he was acting in Karen's interest, but Karen was understandably upset. The swiftness of his action meant there was no opportunity for discussion, no time for her to reflect and come to her own decision about White's behavior, and in this way her power in the band was undermined.

She was so distressed by the dismissal of White (which precipitated the end of their relationship) that the family bought
her a new Mercedes 350SL to help her forget him. Karen loved
cars, so why not buy off the recalcitrant daughter with material
things? This would be compensation to soften the blow. Little by
little the family and management were gradually taking control.

CHAPTER 7

1972

It's just the way that I feel. I've never copied anybody or styled myself after anybody. The way my voice showed up was a kind of accident in the first place.[1]

Karen may have felt frustrated in her personal life, but one thing she knew she could rely on was her voice—it was always there, pitch perfect when she opened her mouth to sing and, as the hit singles proved, audiences loved it. She threw herself into promotion because healthy record sales and success were a panacea for the loss of her on-the-road relationship with Paul White. At this point she was fiercely motivated by her career. "When I met them, they were two fresh California kids who wanted to be stars," recalls Harold Childs, then senior vice president of promotion and sales at A&M. "I went to their house in Downey. It was a small town, an average middle-class family with [a] nice house, nice people."[2]

He was impressed by Richard and Karen's dedication. "They were so smart and knowledgeable of the market and they knew the history of music in America. They knew musical arrangements that the layman didn't know." He was particularly struck by Karen's inquisitiveness, the way she spoke up in meetings and her astute analysis of the industry. "She was very questing, wanting to know why particular radio stations played their records and how the record was selling in different parts of the country." The Carpenters approached promotion with the same meticulous attention to detail as they had in the studio. "You couldn't bullshit them, they *knew* what was going on. You had to tell them the truth about things," says Childs. "A&M had thirty reps around the country and the Carpenters had dealings with all of them. Also, on the A&M lot they would go to people's offices and talk to everybody—they were really on top of their career." Karen also kept a keen eye on what other artists were doing. "There's not a day goes by that we're not buried in the charts of the music papers. The competition is unbelievable. We keep watching what we're up against," she said.[3]

By the end of 1971, Carpentermania had exploded and it was no longer cars ferrying them from gig to gig, but a private jet. One day John Bettis joined the band in Nashville to do some songwriting on the road and was surprised to see over 2,000 fans waiting outside the War Memorial Auditorium. He realized the fan mania had shot to another level. He was even more thrilled when the band got into a Learjet to travel to the next date on the itinerary. "Richard kinda grinned at me because he knew that I wasn't expecting that. I'd never been in a Learjet before. Those planes built up a lot of speed and had to take off nearly straight up, so there's a lot of g-forces," he later recalled. Looking over at

Richard, feeling the g-force, Bettis said, "Well, we're on the top of the world now, aren't we?"

When they next met, Richard had composed a country pop song that captured that vertiginous, jubilant feeling. "Top of the World" also conveys the precarity of that emotion, because no matter how dazzling things are today, tomorrow happiness may be gone. Originally recorded as an album track, the song was picked up by radio programmers and took on a life of its own, becoming popular right around the country. Lynn Anderson recorded a version that went to number two in the country charts, so the Carpenters finally released it as a single in 1973 and had a number-one *Billboard* hit. "'Top of the World' was a country song and country radio normally wouldn't play the Carpenters, but they fell in love with the song and went crazy for it. That gave us another market place. We had every kind of major radio force in the country," says Harold Childs.

"Top of the World" was the second track on their next album, *A Song for You*, which was to be their biggest yet. Despite an intense schedule throughout 1972 with 174 concerts and six television appearances, the Carpenters carved out studio time while they were on a high and as a result the album is infused with a fresh, focused energy. Early albums were a mixture of styles, spanning Spectrum songs, jazz instrumentals, and easy-listening pop. By contrast *A Song for You* had a unified sound and was presented as a concept album from start to finish. The title track was written by Leon Russell, the Southern showman and piano maestro who also cowrote "Superstar" with Bonnie Bramlett. Its combination of intimacy and passion was perfect for Karen, her voice nesting amid the fluid sax, fulsome strings and Hal Blaine's intuitive drumming. This is song as testimony, the Carpenters' manifesto.

The musicians on *A Song for You* felt they were cocreating something special. Harpist Gayle Levant, for instance, looked forward to the studio sessions. "Everyone loved being with Karen and Richard on those sessions. We had a magical nucleus of fantastic musicians," she says. "Richard understood the importance of an arrangement is to surround the singer and not get in the way and let the phrasing happen. He was a master at that. And, of course, the musicians knew that we were being given a gift beyond the sessions. I never wanted them to end."[4]

Currently president of ASMAC (American Society of Music Arrangers and Composers), Levant's graceful harp can be heard on countless soundtracks, from *Titanic* and *Grease* to the opening credits of *The Simpsons* and on albums by artists as varied as Judy Garland, Michael Jackson, and Lana Del Rey. Her father, Mark Levant, was an experienced concertmaster for the film studios, and although Gayle studied classical piano he encouraged her to take up the harp. "At thirteen I wanted to follow in his footsteps. He told me, 'Gayle, if you would like to have a career in our industry, there will be many great pianists available. But there won't be that many harpists.'"

With her cascading blonde hair, golden harp, and a Great Dane called Doheny sitting quietly beside her in the studio, Levant cut a memorable figure during those *Song for You* sessions. She enjoyed the close collaboration of studio work, the sense of creating something new—a feeling she shared with Karen.

"When I go into the studio I always tell everybody, my heart walks in five feet ahead of me, I just can't wait to get connected. I hear 360 degrees what's going on around me. I think, *How can I express the emotion in the lyrics and help make it even better?*"

Levant felt a bond with Karen, right from when she accompanied the Carpenters on their first Lake Tahoe dates in 1970. "Karen always had a joy about her and the kind of voice that no matter if you couldn't sing, you felt like singing with her, she made it so comfortable. She and I connected on a level that was beyond the session. We became friends, we would sit and talk. The joy that she had seeing the musicians come in and being able to hear what Richard had created come to life—I felt exactly the same way. So maybe that was the invisible thread that pulled us together. We were obviously on the same page."

The invisible thread connecting all the tracks on *A Song for You* is a powerful theme—that music can evaporate one's troubles and offer salvation. Each track has a personal reflection on music, from the Williams and Nichols song "I Won't Last a Day Without You" to Randy Edelman's "Piano Picker." The latter was Richard's story—how years of practice indoors on the piano keys while the other boys were out playing football led to his success. During recording, Karen's input was constant, and she showed a penchant for pushing vocal extremes. While listening back to the sixteen-track vocal overdubs of the song "Hurting Each Other," for instance, she said, "I want to make the 'We ares' huge."

"They are huge," said Richard.

"I want to make them huger."[5]

At the same time as the Carpenters were working on *A Song for You*, Carole King was in the next studio recording *Music*, her follow-up to *Tapestry*. They heard "It's Going to Take Some Time" and loved it so much they recorded it. King commented that the Carpenters' version was so lavish it made hers sound like a demo. For this album the Carpenters also branched out into film work with "Bless the Beasts and Children," which was on the soundtrack to Stanley Kramer's 1971 movie and earned them an Oscar nomination.

The stand-out track on *A Song for You*, though, was one that would revolutionize the pop ballad. When they were in London the previous year Richard had been watching a late night Hollywood movie, *Rhythm on the River*, in which Bing Crosby plays a jobbing ghostwriter working for a composer. Crosby's character keeps mentioning his greatest song, "Goodbye to Love," a fictional number that is never actually heard in the film. This title stayed in Richard's mind, so he started sketching out a melody and lyrics. The next time he and John Bettis met they worked to perfect the song, a melancholy "death" ballad that ends with a heavenly chorale and a guitar solo. At that point Richard, Bettis, and Karen were all in their twenties and struggling to find love, so the song matched their mood. As time went on, the lyric would gain greater poignancy for Karen, and Bettis admits that, like so many of the songs he cowrote for the Carpenters, he was tuning into her emotions and writing with her in mind.

Just before the Carpenters recorded the track, Richard looked for someone to play the solo and remembered Tony Peluso, a rock guitarist with long hair who had played with one of their support bands, Instant Joy. Both he and Karen had been struck by the wild, unhinged virtuosity of his style. Karen was the one who rang him and brought him to the studio, a fact that shows how centrally she was involved in all the recording sessions. "At first I didn't believe that it was actually Karen Carpenter on the phone but she repeated her name again . . . it was at this point that I realized it was really her and that I was speaking to one of my idols," Peluso said later.[6]

The night the Carpenters recorded the song everyone was relaxed and buzzing. Fueled by several glasses of house wine at Martoni's, their favorite restaurant and record industry hang-out, Karen launched straight in with a "cold opening," that is, with no musical introduction. The deep intake of breath that kept her voice flowing through some tough, difficult phrasing adds to the song's tension and soulful immediacy. When it came to the guitar solo at the end, Peluso improvised a gentle riff on his vintage Gibson, but Richard told him to do it again, this time burning it up. Everyone cheered on as Peluso executed an aggressive, piledriving solo through the fuzzbox. Afterward he was mortified, thinking he had spoiled the Carpenters' track, but Richard said that was exactly the effect he wanted.

When "Goodbye to Love" was released the song was a hit worldwide, charting in the US, Canada, UK, Ireland, Australia, and Japan. Some Carpenters fans hated it, thinking the band had sold out and gone "hard rock," but its innovative collision of torch song and guitar barrage pioneered the power ballad and it has since become a 1970s pop classic. After that recording session Peluso joined the touring band and became an integral part of the Carpenters' sound, both live and in the studio.

Released in June 1972 in the middle of a tour, *A Song for You* yielded six hit singles during its first year. The recording sessions had been inspired. Gayle Levant recalls that after a Carpenters day she would get into her car and leave the radio off. "I wanted to hold onto what I had been experiencing for the previous three or six hours, or I'd lose it. I wanted to keep it with me." *A Song for You*'s melodic rapture established a fresh direction for A&M. Harold Childs says, "A&M led the way in creating a new kind of radio sound. Karen was such a unique singer and with the Carpenters made it the A&M sound for the whole country. It took a while to get established, but once they did, the band hit like wildfire. The Carpenters moved all those MOR radio artists like Perry Como, Vic Damone, Eddie Fisher into the background." The Carpenters spearheaded a new easy-listening genre that radio programmers dubbed "adult contemporary." "A&M and the Carpenters were *the* adult contemporary act," says Childs. Now the band had grown so big they caught the attention of the US president.

That year Karen became youth chairperson of the American National Cancer Society and the Carpenters donated $100,000 in concert profits toward cancer research. This compounded President Richard Nixon's view that the Carpenters, with their dulcet sound and wholesome image, represented "young America at its very best."[7] In September 1972 they were invited to the White House, where Nixon gave Richard a set of golf balls and cufflinks and Karen a gold powder compact—all stamped with the presidential seal. The meeting took place two years before "Tricky Dicky" was engulfed by the Watergate corruption scandal that led to his downfall, so Richard and Karen didn't anticipate it might play against them. Posing with the Republican Nixon in the Oval Office and being vague about their political allegiance, however, did little to dispel the duo's "Goody Four Shoes" image. "We think the world's a bit of a mess, but we couldn't seriously get into politics now because we're too busy," Richard said. That photo opportunity compounded the tendency for the Carpenters to be misinterpreted or misunderstood by many 1970s critics and musical peers. And the fact that Karen and Richard still lived with their parents added to their aura of innocent naiveté, a throwback to a past era.

CHAPTER 8

1973

I don't have a beau at the moment because I'm too busy. He'll have to be in the same business. Who knows what's going to happen? I prefer someone into music, otherwise you'd be in a lot of trouble.[1]

With its restless, continuous movement, the Carpenters' song "Road Ode" perfectly captures the full-tilt energy of those early years. Written by two guys from the touring band, Gary Sims and Dan Woodward, this insider song affects world-weariness in its catalog of endless roads and bland motel rooms, but Karen's breezy delivery tells another story—one of excitement and volition. She was moving at breakneck pace, building her career, while at the same time bucking a trend.

In the early 1970s, the median age of marriage for women in America was twenty-one and the women's movement was still young.[2] Equality legislation had just been passed in Britain with the 1970 Equal Pay Act, while in 1972 the Equal Rights

Amendment was approved by the US Senate, but at the time of writing it has still not been ratified by all fifty states. Women could not get a bank loan or hire a television without a male signatory and newspapers had separate pages advertising "Men's Jobs" and "Women's Jobs." At the point she was expected to become a full-time mother and homemaker, Karen was averse to settling down and hitching herself to one man. "I'm a bulldozer in relationships," Karen said once, "I don't think I've ever been in love."

A sensual woman, she dated a number of men on tour—so Jerry Luby and Paul White were followed by their trumpeter and sound man David Alley. She was touring in a highly protected environment, in a hermetically sealed world of hotel rooms, Learjets, and backstage spaces, so it was difficult to meet anyone outside the entourage. Alley was a reassuring, stable influence, but as with previous boyfriends, he was more enamored of Karen than she was of him. When the Carpenters were playing the Riviera in Las Vegas during September 1972 she also dated Alan Osmond, one of the Osmond brothers, but once that residency ended in early October so did the fling. They kept in touch via telephone for a while afterward, but busy schedules kept them apart, as did the fact that home for his family was Salt Lake City, Utah, nearly 700 miles from hers in Downey.

Boyfriends complained that Karen wouldn't make time for dates and that she was always in the studio. Although a deep romantic, she was ambivalent about having a settled relationship. In many accounts, this has been pathologized, but Karen was a career woman, putting her work first. She was still only in her early twenties and to achieve the level of success the band desired required absolute focus. "I never had a boyfriend on the road, I didn't agree with it . . . I never met anybody I wanted to have on the road—it's the same thing as guys carrying wives or women . . . when you go out you go to work," she said.[3]

The double standards of gender conditioning were reflected in Karen's experience—male musicians frequently toured and left wives and girlfriends at home, but once they were married and pregnant female artists were expected to retire. Country singer Patsy Cline's husband Gerald, for instance, could never get used to her touring schedule, and in the rock world Patti Smith semi-retired from music once she married Fred "Sonic" Smith and had children. Knowing that her ultimate goals of love and marriage were incompatible with life on tour, Karen ended up in a state of perpetual singleness, forming quick, intensive bonds that were temporary as long as her primary commitment was to the band. She resented anything that might threaten or compromise the Carpenters' upward trajectory—and that included girlfriends who took up too much of Richard's time.

*

As the Carpenters' profile rose Karen decided it was time to cultivate a sleeker, more sophisticated image. In 1972, a hairdresser named Maria Luisa Galeazzi, who ran a beauty salon in Downey, was encouraged by a friend of Agnes to get in touch with the duo. Galeazzi called Karen and ended up joining the tour as her hairdresser and stylist. That was fine until Richard started dating Galeazzi and the two became very attached. Karen was furious, feeling she had to fight for his attention or sensing abandonment when he traveled separately with his new girlfriend. Any resentment was fueled by Agnes, who was unsure about Galeazzi's intentions. "Richard and I spend a lot of time together, every minute. We have a disagreement every now and then but never a time we don't talk. Or we call a truce and discuss what we have to," Karen said.[4] Galeazzi was a threat to that working intimacy, and Agnes played on Karen's fears about this, urging her to fire the hairdresser.

It's a common trope in touring bands that partners are viewed with suspicion and threaten the unity of the group. Musicians' partners are expected to keep a low profile. The situation with Richard and Galeazzi could only be resolved by her quitting as Karen's hairdresser. Her replacement was Sandy Holland, another pretty blonde woman from a beauty salon, but when Richard started going out with *her*, Karen made it clear that this wouldn't be tolerated. Keen to keep her job, Holland stopped dating Richard and remained Karen's stylist for the next seven years. "If I'm with a girl Karen doesn't like, she gets in her three cents" worth and then doesn't leave it at that," Richard said later. "I wish [she] wouldn't . . . interfere in my personal affairs."[5] The power battles would continue for a number of years. There was a sense of double standards in the way Karen's lovers were closely vetted by family and management, but Richard felt entitled to date freely. It was also expected that she would give up the drums, but no question that Richard would be restricted in his arrangements or production or the choice of material the band would cover. "Richard was the boss," says their drummer Cubby O'Brien. "Whatever he told her to sing or play she always deferred to him. He [had] the last word."[6] Maybe Karen objected to Richard's women and guarded her role in the band so jealously because as time went on their working relationship was one of the few areas in her life where she could be sure of the family's attention and where she felt that she mattered.

Maria Galeazzi later complained that although she loved Richard, she felt she had been bounced out of "the system," the close-knit Carpenter family network, where outsiders were treated with wariness and perceived as a threat. Musicians and colleagues remember the Carpenters as courteous people, but not always easy to get close to. "Richard and Karen were very cautious about hanging out. They'd rather stay in their hotel room and watch videos and movies," recalls O'Brien. "When we were in Japan they didn't like to sightsee with the rest of us, they kept themselves to themselves." While Karen could be possessive over Richard, he too (after the dismissal of their road manager Paul White) was uneasy about her dating from within the entourage. "We had a rule in the band that nobody is going to get involved with Karen. It was a case of 'don't touch,' something we discussed and agreed between us. Richard would have had a fit, he wouldn't like that," says O'Brien.

A former drummer with the Mickey Mouse Club and the bandleader Spike Jones, O'Brien was professional from the start. He replaced Jim Squeglia, who had a more defiant attitude, wanting to improvise on stage even though the Carpenters insisted the musicians had to play like the records. Squeglia also had a few hugs with Karen and joined her for the odd dinner date—which alarmed their manager, Sherwin Bash. After Bash warned Squeglia away from Karen, the drummer went back to New Haven, failed to turn up for a rehearsal, and was fired. O'Brien knew that the best way to keep his job was to make sure he never had a romance with Karen.

What they did have, though, was a friendship and a rapport that built steadily through the years they played together. O'Brien was Karen's drumming partner and her connection with the instrument she loved. They met early in 1973 when the Carpenters were on *The Carol Burnett Show* and O'Brien was part of the house band. He was approached by Bash, who said the Carpenters were going to be doing a summer tour and would he be interested going on the road with them. "Oh, man, I'd love to!" O'Brien enthused. This was the transitional period, when Richard and the management were coaxing Karen away from the drums so that she would stand upfront and sing. It needed someone with sensitivity to help her with that transition.

"I walked around with a headset on for a couple of weeks and learned all the songs. Karen and Richard wanted the drums to sound exactly like the record, so if Hal Blaine did '*dagadoom, dagadoom, crash*' that's what they wanted to hear. So for the first six months Karen and I played everything in tandem. Then she finally started getting away from the drums and Bob Mackie made gowns for her and she started to like being out front," says O'Brien. He also remembers her missing the drums terribly. "There was always a big number in the show for her to play. We'd do 'Strike Up the Band' with a long ten-minute solo for her with the band. She loved playing, she was one of the first female drummers who got recognition as a good player."

Karen and O'Brien had drumming conversations and talked about different players they liked. O'Brien had grown up in Los Angeles and had drum lessons with Karen's idol, the jazz drummer and bandleader Louie Bellson. Karen was delighted one night when he introduced her to Bellson and her other childhood hero, Buddy Rich, after the two went head to head in a Battle of the Drums set on *The Tonight Show*. "Louie Bellson was very gracious and sweet to her," says O'Brien. "Then I took her over to Buddy. He had a caustic sense of humor. I said to Buddy, 'This is Karen Carpenter,' and he said sarcastically, 'Karen Carpenter, you're my favourite drummer!' I'm sure she wasn't . . . but he was very nice to her anyway. Buddy was a mentor for her, as he was for everybody of our age. Probably the best soloist of all time."

O'Brien remembers Karen as fitting in well with the band. "She was always right there with the jokes. She was like the down-to-earth girl who became a star, she was very level-headed." Once on tour O'Brien got his finger caught in a window spring and he had to go to the Emergency Room. "I had this big bandage on the middle finger of my left hand, so when I was playing the drums it looked like I was giving everyone the finger. Karen joked, 'What're you *doing*, you're flipping everybody off in the audience!'"

She enjoyed the camaraderie of the road and was quick to point out anything ludicrous or surreal, like when they played outdoor arenas and she opened her mouth to sing and insects would fly in.

"What are you going to do? Have you ever tried to choke with class?" she said. One humid night in Detroit as she sang "Superstar," Karen could feel a moth fluttering in her blouse. "It was going berserk down there, it couldn't get out." By the time she reached "Goodbye to Love," she was thoroughly distracted. "I was cracking up, singing 'I'll say goodbye . . .' and I didn't know what the hell to do. I was thinking, *[Richard's] going to break my neck because I'm ruining this song.* The tears were rolling down my face from laughing. Finally I just shook my blouse and let him out."[7]

Joking or playing with the gang was when Karen seemed most content, like when she pitched in the band's softball team. Tony Peluso shot a few home movies while on tour and there is footage of a healthy Karen, looking happy and curvy in denim shorts and a baseball cap, running and throwing a ball. The video footage is a poignant reminder that, in the early days of the Carpenters' career, Karen's weight was a stable 120 pounds and she was more carefree.[8] They would play charity games against the promotion guys from different radio stations around the country. "There would be a coupla thousand people in the stands. I was more nervous playing short stop than when I was playing drums," O'Brien recalls. "The whole band formed a team with Richard pitching and Karen playing centerfield. It was always fun to play a local station."

*

As their show trundled through state after state Karen gradually became more confident in her lead singer role. "She became accustomed to it and I think she really liked the adoration she got from audiences," says O'Brien. Richard, however, was more awkward and reserved. "He didn't like touring as much as Karen did. He liked to be in the studio, he's a studio guy." In 1973, the Carpenters had one of their busiest years of touring the hits and building an audience and Sherwin Bash kept them fairly constantly on the road. Fretting that the exhaustive itinerary left him with little downtime to write, Richard prepared for their next album by revisiting songs from their childhood for sources of inspiration, from the rock 'n' roll that he and Karen grew up listening to in that New Haven basement, to the '60s surf pop of their teenage years in Downey. "People are going back to the '60s and '50s because those were times when they were happier, before the energy crisis and before things got so tough," Richard said, referring to the global scene of oil shortages and economic tension following Arab–Israeli conflict in the Middle East.[9] It was important to him that the Carpenters offered escape from those tensions.

Now & Then has an authentic power, capturing a period and a scene steeped in 1960s nostalgia, when the car was king. Richard and Karen both loved vintage cars and once they started earning serious money that was one of their indulgences. Karen was a fast driver who would zip up the freeway in her Mercedes. "I love fast cars. Love 'em," she said, proud of the fact she kept her cars in impeccable shape. "It's beautiful and it runs like a champ. When I wanna get in a fast car I just walk down to . . . the garage and go tearing off into the distance."[10] Richard, meanwhile, liked drag racing at the Ontario Speedway, a new motorsport park that opened in 1970 with a state-of-the-art track. The super speedway featured celebrity races, where Hollywood stars like Paul Newman were paired with professional race-winning drivers and in 1971 it hosted a stunt by Evel Knievel, when the motorcycle daredevil did his record jump over nineteen cars.

During their live set the Carpenters celebrated hot rod racing in their rendition of the Jan & Dean hit "Dead Man's Curve." This was part of a quickfire 1960s medley that became side two of *Now & Then*, with Tony Peluso voicing comic links between songs as a radio DJ. Opening with John Bettis and Richard's nostalgic composition "Yesterday Once More," the medley moves from the Beach Boys' "Fun Fun Fun" to a couple of girl-group hits, "One Fine Day" and "Da Doo Ron Ron" and includes a screeching "Dead Man's Curve" and a deeply moving rendition of "The End of the World." Concluding with a reprise of 'Yesterday Once More," Karen's voice dazzles and shimmers until it gradually fades out, like a faraway radio signal.

Now & Then evokes Karen and Richard's teenage years in Downey, a culture of drag racing and souped-up cars that is immortalized in Tom Wolfe's book *The Pump House Gang*. Wolfe writes about the Hair Boys—car kids with smooth, impeccable haircuts who would cruise with their girlfriends to Harvey's Drive-in on Firestone Boulevard and drag-race through the streets. "The Hair Boys . . . keep moving into *high style*. It may be because they have always been dedicated to such an ornate, glistening, high-style sculptural object, the American automobile, in the first place."[11]

That veneration of the automobile is portrayed on the three-panel fold-out cover of *Now & Then*, which features Karen and

Richard outside their Downey home in his bright red Ferrari Daytona. A&M's chief photographer Jim McCrary took the photograph, and afterward the picture was turned into an air-brushed illustration. Even though Richard complained about what he saw as a low-budget approach, the sleeve has become iconic in its hyperreal depiction of 1970s suburban California. The fact that Karen and Richard are shadowy figures inside the car emphasizes the picture's mysterious allure. Art director Roland Young said he wanted to represent the power in the Carpenters' songs. "The *Now & Then* cover captured them with an elusive cinematic image. They are cruising in their car, driving by their mom and dad's home in Downey . . . I wanted an illustration, not a photograph. Notice the missing shadow on the garage door, no street lamps. It's not real, but so real."[12]

While side two of *Now & Then* streamlines the past, side one is rooted in the Carpenters' present, leading off with "Sing," a fetching tune written by Joe Raposo for the children's TV series *Sesame Street*. This open-hearted appreciation of music was heard by some at A&M as mind-numbingly simplistic, but Richard's instinct that it would be a hit paid off, because in the spring of 1973 it went gold and earned the Carpenters two Grammy nominations, one for Richard's arrangement and the other for Best Pop Vocal. Overdubbed with the Jimmy Joyce Children's Chorus, Karen's voice emphasized the track's wide-eyed idealism. In stark contrast, the Leon Russell song "This Masquerade" has a dramatic, pensive quality. Bob Messenger's flute and the cocktail piano add to the dreamy sense of someone in lonely reflection, alienated and disconnected from a lover they have lost. Dark and resonant, it is considered to be one of Karen's best performances.

Another stand-out track is the Hank Williams song "Jambalaya," which celebrates a riotous Cajun wedding party on the south Louisiana bayou. Following on from the success of "Top of the World," this song was aimed at the country market, but Karen sings it with a straightforward pop vocal. It seems the recording session for this track was far from smooth.

JayDee Maness is a pedal steel guitarist with a strong country style—he played with Gram Parsons and the Byrds and has received the Academy of Country Music's Steel Guitarist of the Year award eighteen times. Maness was one of the guitarists on the "Jambalaya" sessions and remembers Karen making her feelings known to Richard. "They had a tiff and argued quite a bit. I have a theory as to why—she might have wanted more control and Richard had all the control. Every note had to be exactly in place," he says. "While Richard and I were working out the part she was sitting in the little booth waiting to sing, knitting or crocheting, either not interested or bored. It was a battle, maybe she didn't want a steel guitar in place. When I heard the record back the steel guitar was barely audible. I thought, *What's the point here?*"[13]

Now & Then is an homage to 1960s pop, so maybe Karen felt that too obvious a country texture would be confusing. "The Carpenters were in the pop genre, they could never be labeled country," says Maness. Although many recording sessions were harmonious, musicians sometimes picked up on tension between Karen and Richard, particularly if they had creative disagreements. Richard is frequently represented as the architect of their entire sound, but Karen was credited on this album as coproducer. It's clear that she had aesthetic input too and was a constant presence in the studio. Maness found Karen's diffidence curious. "Maybe she was a little shy. I remember Joe Osborn was there too, playing bass. Those two had history as friends but she didn't talk to Joe either. I wondered why there was not more conversation with her, I don't know if that was Richard's doing." When the moment came for Karen to sing, however, her delivery was exquisite. "That girl could really sing—a beautiful voice, without any effort. I've seen vocal sessions where you spend laborious hours trying to get a vocalist in tune, but she was ready and she pretty much had her part done. I remember hearing her sing and thinking, *Wow.*"

Even though it was recorded with frayed tempers during a hectic schedule, *Now & Then* was a masterful follow-up to 1972's *A Song for You*. It was the first Carpenters record made without Jack Daugherty and the siblings' first joint credit as coproducers—Richard had long complained that he did all the real production work while Daugherty took the credit. Karen's coproduction role shows how central she was to the process, too. She also drummed on most of the tracks (apart from "Jambalaya"), in a way that was tight, fiery, and inspired.

Released in May 1973, the album was critically acclaimed and became their best-selling international record, going to number one in Japan and number two in the US, Canada, UK, and Netherlands. Its success coincided with the film *American Graffiti*, George Lucas's coming-of-age comedy drama about the drag-racing escapades of California high-school kids in 1962. This record delves into the power of nostalgia and music as a creative force, embodying a glowing version of America's past.

On May 1, just before the album release, the Carpenters returned to the White House to perform at a state dinner for President Nixon and the West German chancellor, Willy Brandt. By this point there were already questions about Nixon's administration and rumors of "dirty tricks." The following year evidence emerged of his team bugging the offices of Democrat opponents, phone-tapping activist groups and using the FBI and CIA as political weapons in his paranoid investigations. Although the Carpenters garnered huge publicity with their White House performance, not everyone at the record label was happy. "To me the Carpenters sounded like where they were from, which was Orange County," recalls Clare Baren, A&M's head of video and TV production. "At A&M everyone was Democrat, but Orange County didn't vote the way we voted. It was a traditional Republican stronghold. The Carpenters were keen on doing the White House performance—well, he *is* the president—but we just hated it."[14] Bruce Ravid, who was A&R for Capitol Records and who had close friends at A&M, agrees that this complicated the picture for the Carpenters. "My attitude was, *Oh, typical. The Carpenters are playing for Nixon.* Anybody that I talked to was embarrassed about it," he says.[15]

For Karen and Richard, however, the show was less about politics and more a recognition of their achievement—as Richard admitted later, "I was never into the youth rebellion."

Dressed in angelic white, exuding radiance and grace, his sister looked almost regal. At that point the Carpenters were at the summit of their career. They may have been young America at its best, but like the David Lynch neo-noir mystery film *Blue Velvet*, a dark psychology lurked beneath the lustrous image.

BOOK 4
Horizon

CHAPTER 9

1974

I love living at home—our parents are the greatest . . . Do you want some iced tea? Mom makes the best iced tea in Downey.[1]

In the summer of 1973, UK music writer Chris Charlesworth arrived in Los Angeles to be *Melody Maker*'s man in America. He moved into the Chateau Marmont and spent most of his time interviewing rock 'n' rollers like the Rolling Stones, Deep Purple, and Blood, Sweat & Tears. But one of his less typical assignments was going to the Carpenters' house in Downey to interview Karen and Richard. A&M publicist Dorene Lauer drove him there and played Carpenters cassettes all the way down the Santa Ana Freeway. "They were not my kind of act," he recalls. "Very MOR. And they lived in Orange County, an island of Republicanism when most of California was Democrat."[2]

When he arrived, however, Charlesworth was pleasantly surprised to be met by the whole family. "They were really sweet people, they struck me as the sort of family who got dressed in Sunday best and went to church. They were kind and welcoming and their mum made me a cup of tea. I was probably an exotic creature." The house was large, with a recording studio extension at the back, a swimming pool, a miniature Japanese garden, a bar with a wall rack of 300 wines and a living room that looked like a show house, with wood-paneled walls and a glass table inlaid with swords. "It was full of brass cabinets with photos and trophies. It was immaculate, not a speck of dust anywhere," says Charlesworth. "The whole neighborhood was immaculate like that—not posh like Beverly Hills or Bel Air, more upmarket suburban. Extremely tidy homes with nice cars parked everywhere." In the music room there was a deep-pile carpet, banks of speakers, a vinyl collection of several thousand albums and two director's chairs emblazoned with **KAREN CARPENTER** and **RICHARD CARPENTER** respectively.

Charlesworth chatted to Karen and Richard for an hour and the latter did most of the talking, telling him about starting out in New Haven and the early days in Los Angeles with Spectrum. "He looked a bit sallow and thin. He was quite charming but didn't seem to belong to the rock 'n' roll world. And Karen looked like a bank teller, not Hollywood flash at all, no glamor, no tight pants and plunging neckline," says Charlesworth. "At that point I was immersed in the Los Angeles rock scene—men with denim shirts unbuttoned to the navel and girls flaunting themselves in the Troubadour and the Whisky. Richard was the opposite, he looked like an estate agent. They seemed like a suburban couple, even though they were brother and sister."

Charlesworth was struck by the fact that even though Richard was twenty-six years old and Karen twenty-three, their parents were very much in evidence. "It did seem odd that at their age and at that point in their careers they were still living with Mum and Dad." Agnes and Harold did not seem controlling, just "very mumsy and dadsy and delighted with their son and daughter." There was some attempt to monitor public relations, however, because someone taped the interview. "Much bigger stars didn't do that . . . Lennon didn't and Led Zep didn't give a hoot about that." Underlying this meeting was a collision between two worlds, two music cultures. Charlesworth recounts how when Karen had won the 1971 Playboy award for Best Drummer in the World, Led Zeppelin's drummer, John Bonham, was "absolutely furious, fucking livid. Bonzo didn't think it was funny."

*

The Carpenters may not have appealed to hard-rock fans but they were firmly ensconced in the pop world and part of the attraction to fans was the sense of a united family. They were featured in the teen pop press alongside idols like David Cassidy and the Bay City Rollers. Much was made of the Carpenters as musical siblings—with Karen represented as the cool younger sister who could sing and play drums.

In the Carpenters' Downey house, there were signed photos of the band with other showbusiness family groups of the 1970s such as the Osmonds, the Boones, and the Jackson 5. These families knew each other—they had industry contacts in common and would meet backstage at the same shows and that is how Karen met and dated the oldest Osmond brother, Alan. "I knew Karen and Richard as we both worked in different theaters in Las Vegas," Alan Osmond recalls with enthusiasm. "I went out with her and found her to be as great a person as she was an entertainer!"[3] Starting out as a barbershop quartet in Ogden, Utah, the Osmonds came to the attention of crooner Andy Williams after they performed at Disneyland and appeared on his TV show throughout the 1960s before making it big as teen idols (with the addition of Donny and youngest brother Jimmy) in the early 1970s. Parents George and Olive accompanied the brothers everywhere and were an important part of the story.

In a decade of rising divorce rates, there was an appetite in popular culture for idealized representations of family, and the big pop families slotted in with that trend alongside fictitious TV hyper-families like the Waltons, the Brady Bunch, and the Partridge Family. A combination of greater economic freedom for women and more liberal divorce laws meant that the annual rate for divorce jumped from 3.5 to 5.2 per thousand by the end of the decade. The Carpenters' family values were reassuring to their fans and as a result Agnes and Harold were often mentioned in articles about the band. "They always got everything we needed, [we] couldn't afford any of it," Karen once said, referring to the sacrifices their parents had made in the beginning. "That's one of the reasons we're so close."[4] In 1971, the A&M PR department even sent out a press release about the Carpenters' home, detailing the interior decoration—right down to the black, red, and ocelot colors of the Spanish-style den, the dining room with the glass-topped table that was "ideal for California meals" and a kitchen with all the modern conveniences, including a waste-disposal unit and a refrigerator that shot out ice cubes. "For an ace cook like Karen, the kitchen of the new house is a dream come true."[5]

However, as Karen was to discover, those traditional family values could be stifling when it came to forging a separate identity. The more exposure the Carpenters got, the stranger it seemed that Richard and Karen still lived with their parents in the home on Newville Avenue. With their newfound wealth the siblings bought a four-bedroom property for their parents five minutes' drive away at 8341 Lubec Street, but Agnes and Harold didn't want to leave. As their manager Sherwin Bash said, "Agnes couldn't understand why they would want to separate and be living in two different houses."[6] Her dominant influence could be embarrassing—one evening, for instance, when Richard was kissing and cuddling a woman in his bedroom, Agnes opened the door to see how he was. In a bid for independence, Richard and Karen decided to move into the Lubec Street house instead. Agnes was seen as needy and overprotective, but she was a matriarch not unlike Katherine Jackson, who made all her sons' suits and costumes and who was on the management team, or Olive Osmond, a formidable figure known by all as "Mother Osmond."

The Carpenters forged links with the Osmonds partly because the two groups shared management with Ed Leffler and there were parallels in the way the two bands were promoted as a wholesome family unit. Olive Osmond actively boosted the showbiz family juggernaut during interviews, asserting that "if kids are talented, you should push them." Her husband, George, was a disciplinarian, turning the boys' bedroom into a dormitory filled with army bunk beds and waking them with a bugle each morning. They practiced songs and choreography with military precision, and he even held inspections to check whether their beds and clothes were tidy. In 2003, the Osmonds spoke openly about the pressures they experienced in the 1960s and '70s. "It was abusive to a certain extent," recalled Donny. "We had to be this perfect family. We weren't allowed to be normal, to have fights or express our feelings . . . in our family you just get the show done. Do your job and don't complain."[7] Merrill, one of the most talented brothers in terms of his singing and musicianship, was suicidal as a teenager and suffered from bulimia into his early twenties. "We were like a machine," he said. "We all [had] that nervous feeling of having to measure up to something that can't be measured up to."

Both Olive and George held the family together with a strong sense of discipline—Olive described discipline as "a form of love" and praised the job she saw her boys doing of promoting the Mormon faith. "I think they're very good missionaries for Christianity," she declared. Despite her declaration of protecting the family unit, Jimmy Osmond has spoken about being left at home alone at the age of fifteen while his parents went away on a trip. He walked to the local drugstore, was beaten up by a gang and didn't leave home for two weeks. Nobody contacted him during that time, certainly not his parents. "I realized then that nobody was gonna fix Jimmy but Jimmy," he said.[8] George Osmond also made some ill-advised investments and in the 1980s the family lost much of their $80 million fortune.

Richard and Karen also met the Boone family singing group at various functions and events. They had mutual friends in the Osmonds and the producer Mike Curb. The oldest Boone sister, Cherry, would later become Karen's friend and confidante, partly because, like Karen, she developed an eating disorder that she felt the pressure to hide. The Boones' father was Pat Boone, one of the best-selling singers of the 1950s and during the 1970s and '80s a prominent conservative Christian preacher. "Being a celebrity's kid and a preacher's kid at the same time was a very strange juxtaposition of pressures," recalls Cherry Boone. Her father wanted the Boones to be "a shining light" for other families, but that meant hiding personal problems and failures. "That's not what you put up on the stage or when you're doing a TV special. That can be a little schizophrenic—feeling you have to present a certain image when you're in public and yet there are things that you're struggling with that would suggest that everything's not squeaky clean and perfect."[9]

There was pressure on showbusiness pop families to maintain a shiny wholesome image because so much money was riding on it. The families were so successful partly because of their ability to sing brilliantly accurate and vibrant harmonies. The story of close-harmony groups in pop is dominated by sibling acts, from the Bobbettes and the Delfonics to the Everly Brothers, the Beach Boys, the Shangri-Las, and the Ronettes. Brother-sister duos are more rare but memorable, like US gospel duo BeBe & CeCe Winans, British stars Tom and Dusty Springfield in the

Springfields and, most recently, Billie Eilish and her brother Finneas O'Connell. Having grown up together, the closeness of the family unit on the road creates its own private ecosystem, making it hard for outsiders to penetrate the inner circle.

Many in the family's orbit noticed how much Agnes Carpenter was a dominant presence, and it could be argued that she took on a "stage mother" role, heavily invested in her children's success. According to Lisa Gee, author of *Stage Mum*, "The term is derogatory and misogynist—you have stage dads, too. But in common parlance a 'stage mother' is a female parent who both pushes her children to perform and tries to push everyone else out the way so her children can hog the spotlight and she can bask in the reflected glory."[10] To be fair to Agnes, she and Harold were responding to their children's talent and following them round the country was a rapturous experience. "It's unbelievable, it feels amazing when your child is doing something stunning," says Gee, whose daughter Dora started her acting career as Gretl in the stage version of *The Sound of Music*. "The silence that comes in your head when you know your child is doing what they are supposed to be doing. It's transcendent. It's your job as a parent to enable your offspring."

Problems arise, however, when one child is focused on more than the other. In the Carpenters' case, Agnes was particularly devoted to Richard, pushing his interests to the fore. Her sister Bernice said that "Agnes always thought Richard was the greatest," phoning her often to talk about his musical achievements and tending to focus on him at Karen's expense. After all, he was the reason they had moved nearly 3,000 miles from New Haven to Los Angeles when he was a teenager and he was the one who had displayed musical talent from the beginning. Karen would feel obliged to echo this view, effacing her own work by foregrounding his. "He's so talented it just makes me weep that everybody just walks right by him," she once said. "He's the brains behind it."[11] That favoritism was to gradually erode her self-esteem.

Agnes was also wary about letting other parties take control of her children's career, afraid that the family would be exploited. From the early Spectrum gigs at the Troubadour she had been accustomed to taking their earnings and giving them an allowance, and even after the band signed to A&M Agnes assumed control of the finances. Karen, however, had a savvy business sense and by 1972 was worried that the money coming in was too much for her mother to manage. As the band became successful, Karen wanted more financial independence and more professional advice. She and Richard were no longer children being given the equivalent of pocket money—they were superstar performers who needed a sturdy accountant. Agnes had opened accounts in numerous banks and lost track of what income was individual, what was corporate, and what they needed to pay tax on. At the request of Jerry Moss, A&M lawyer Werner Wolfen took over their affairs, which he said were in a "big, big mess."[12] Agnes resisted his take-over at first, before gradually letting Wolfen steer the finances, but she still had a marked emotional hold over her children.

In comparison, Harold was described as sweet and pleasant to everyone and particularly close to Karen. He was as quiet as Agnes was garrulous, but his passivity left a gap, an absence. Evelyn Wallace, a family friend who worked in the Carpenters' office at their home in Downey, remembers Agnes frequently yelling at him. One day he came into the office looking worried. "Agnes kind of has a mean streak in her sometimes," he said to Wallace. Maybe this was a quiet cry for help. Harold found safety in retreat. He liked his private time, read the paper in the den—a room at Newville with a bar, color TV, pool table, and leopardskin couch. He preferred comfort to confrontation, but deferring to Agnes meant that he wasn't always a solid presence in the household. "Karen's mother was a very strong person, an A-type person, and her dad was not. He was 'I'll go along with anything, whatever you want to do,' one of those guys," says Cubby O'Brien.[13]

Friends and potential suitors were heavily vetted by Agnes. Soon after they moved into Lubec Street, Richard began a relationship with Sherwin Bash's sparky, charming 21-year-old daughter Randy. Within three weeks Agnes declared that she didn't like her, and this influenced Karen, who decided that Randy was an unwelcome distraction. In the same way that she had frozen out Maria Galeazzi when they were on tour, Karen refused to speak to Randy, treating her like an annoyance. "Richard can have his girl travel with him—she has no career," she said dismissively.[14] Later when Richard moved Randy into Lubec Street, Karen objected. Although his girlfriend packed her bags she still came back every night to sleep there, so Karen ended up returning home to Newville Avenue and Mum and Dad.

The move for Karen was temporary. Feeling suffocated by her mother and the awkward situation with Randy and Richard, she longed for her own apartment, her own space to furnish in the way she liked and the freedom to make her own decisions. Even though there were four bedrooms at Lubec Street, it was a modest 3,000 square feet and every time Randy walked around with not much on, the house felt too small. At the two-storey family home in Newville Avenue her parents had the master bedroom downstairs, while upstairs Richard had claimed two rooms for himself by knocking through the adjoining wall to create his own master bedroom. By contrast, Karen had a smaller girly chamber, dominated by a king-size bed and her collection of stuffed animals. She knew she needed to move to a place where she was no longer a child, where she could envisage her own future. She also needed more privacy. Camera security had been installed in the front porch to monitor unwanted fans who would come and ring on the bell and the house was vulnerable to stalkers. By now everyone knew the whereabouts of Newville Avenue, especially since it had been immortalized on the cover of *Now & Then*.

Karen asked Werner Wolfen to start looking for a condominium located away from Downey, further into Los Angeles. She was, however, a little scared of Agnes and one day took the extraordinary step of asking Evelyn Wallace to tell her mother of the plans. Wallace felt uncomfortable doing this, but she loved Karen and would do anything for her. Soon after Karen left the house Wallace broached the subject with Agnes and was dismayed by the hysterical reaction. Agnes grabbed the phone and rang her daughter in a fury. "She was screaming at her and calling her a traitor," recalled Wallace.[15] It would be two years before Karen finally got her wish, while in the meantime feeling stuck in the role of dutiful daughter and sister.

Rolling Stone writer Tom Nolan picked up on the frustration of these family dynamics when he spent a few days on tour with the Carpenters in 1974. Describing Karen as a "sheltered and pampered" princess, he noted with distaste how she giggled, made faces, or balled up her chewing gum like a gauche teenager and stuck it in the ashtray. He detailed the siblings' bickering (probably aggravated by Randy's constant presence at Richard's side). But he also spotted the occasions where Karen supported Richard and the moments when she sought reassurance from him, but none was forthcoming. Outwardly at least, it appeared to be an unequal relationship. Nolan was bewildered by how diffident Karen could be in interviews, but he also detected that beneath lay a sense of powerlessness. Like a bird in a gilded cage, Karen had been pushed into the traditional role of band singer, the "amiable thrush," and her creativity and contribution were sometimes overlooked. "So long has she deferred to her brother, it seems, she cannot express a distinct personality of her own," he observed.[16]

It's striking to see footage of Richard playing the piano live on stage, gazing at Karen in a way that was sometimes unnerving, almost single-minded. There is the sense that the Carpenters was ultimately his project, that he felt he was the person to best understand and frame her voice, building his production around it. Many people, therefore, assumed it was his vision rather than a mutual one between the siblings.

As the Carpenters' fame increased, so Karen's role as the star singer became more protected and circumscribed, and it was the hermetically sealed nature of this world that later contributed to her sense of loneliness and isolation. At this time Karen met someone who helped her explore feelings about her family situation. "She was led to believe that Richard was better than her and was loaded with self-doubt," says songwriter Nicky Chinn, who met Karen via Ed Leffler in 1973.[17] The pair of them shared an off-the-wall humor and love of pop music and quickly connected.

Along with his production partner Mike Chapman, Chinn was one of the architects of glam rock in the UK, writing huge number-one hits for acts like Sweet, Mud, and Suzi Quatro. Drawing on styles as varied as cabaret, science fiction, and art pop, glam rock was an extreme collision of platform boots, florid costumes, glitter, bubblegum pop and loud rock stomp. "I remember first hearing Marc Bolan's 'Ride a White Swan' and it was so good we just got swept along. 1970s glam rock was unique—it was a style of music and image that had never been done before. When we came along we were able to buy into it in a big way, we understood it. We had a knack for that kind of music, we knew what we were doing," recalls Chinn. He also remembers that, like the Carpenters, Chinn and Chapman had their detractors in the music press. "We were having too much success and people get pissed off about that. We were often referred to as the sausage factory because we had a lot of hits. The same thing happens in the Carpenters. They were seen as a bland brother-sister thing and meanwhile they were turning out amazing music."

Chinn and Karen dated and for a while were romantically involved, going to restaurants and spending long hours together in the Beverly Hills Hotel Polo Lounge—a favorite hang-out of musicians and artists in the 1970s. They also went to Las Vegas together to see Karen's friend Petula Clark. "We just drove around and had a good time. We were both young and successful, so there was no disparity. And I admired her talent tremendously," Chinn recalls. They became very fond of each other. "Karen gave me a present, a gold chain with a 'Number One' on it. That was lovely, I wore it around my neck," he says. Later, during the 1976 American bicentenary celebrations, she gave him a sweater emblazoned with a "200 years" logo. "Two hundred years over here in the UK is nothing. But we celebrated the Declaration of Independence and had a great time together." Chinn remembers Karen as being funny and irreverent. "We laughed a lot. Richard was much more serious. I always remember us in the back of a limousine talking about a hit act around called Mott the Hoople and she called them 'Hoop the Mottle.' Richard said, 'You can't talk like that!' He was very serious. He and Karen were opposites."

However, something alerted him early on to the fact that she was struggling with seriously low self-esteem. One night they passed John Lennon as they were leaving Le Restaurant on Melrose Place in Los Angeles. The former Beatle stopped and said, "I just gotta tell you, love, I think you've got the most fabulous voice." And he walked on.

Karen turned to Chinn with disbelief. "He couldn't have meant that!"

"You know what, Karen? If there's one thing I know about John Lennon—he doesn't say things he doesn't mean."

Chinn was saddened that she couldn't accept such a momentous compliment. "That's when I realized her opinion of herself was so low, even though she is clearly one of the great voices of all time."

Chinn was diagnosed with bipolar disorder at the age of sixteen and has struggled with it his whole life, so he recognized something in Karen. "I've listened closely and you can hear the pain. Karen didn't just sing a song, she understood every word and she put her emotions into it. And you can hear the pain in her voice very, very often, because she was a girl in pain." He interpreted her humor as a "wonderful exterior. If you didn't know her, you would think nothing was wrong."

Chinn spent time in Downey and got to know the family. He describes her parents as "very strange" and maybe part of the uneasiness he felt was because of the attention that Agnes in particular lavished on Richard. Karen could be very guarded with her emotions, but she did confide in Chinn about the effect this had on her. "The only thing she ever opened up about was saying that Richard was the favorite and that had always been difficult for her. I could tell how much pain that caused her," he says. "Richard was the center of attention. He was the talent. He was the arranger. If you grow up with your brother as the favorite and basically being told you're not as good, then if you have a tendency to get ill, you will. And clearly she had that tendency, that was the root of it."

By the end of 1974, people started to notice a change in Karen. Although she had been dieting and eating salads for some time, her weight from the age of seventeen (when Agnes took her to the doctor and put her on a diet) to twenty-three years old had remained relatively stable at around 120 pounds.

But as Carpentermania grew and the band were increasingly in the spotlight, so Karen's anxiety about her weight intensified. She became very self-conscious when she saw photographs of herself, and even though people tried to reassure her that she looked just fine, she was convinced she needed to diet some more. "Karen always felt that she was too heavy," says her friend Gayle Levant. "I have a friend who took off a huge amount of weight and looks so beautiful. I'm so proud of her. But she says that when she walks by a window where she sees a reflection, she still thinks of herself as a heavy person. And that was like Karen, she went by what was in her head."[18]

There is footage of Karen in February 1974 singing "Jambalaya" with the band live on stage at the Grand Gala du Disque awards show in Amsterdam. She looks healthy and happy in a halter-neck trouser suit that displays her curves—but this was one of the pieces of footage that alarmed her and fueled a growing obsession with dieting. "She was really pretty, gorgeous eyelashes," recalls the Carpenters' video director Clare Baren. "I never thought of her as fat, but she had that complex. Now you can have a big ass and be a huge star, like Lizzo. But it was different for women in the 1970s. All the managers, agents, and supervisors handling Karen's career were men. I'm sure she got told 'You have a big ass' by the wrong people, many times."[19]

Even though people were starting to get concerned, Karen batted off any enquiries about her well-being, keeping her focus on the band. Her weight yo-yoed, but for a while she managed to keep relatively healthy, maybe partly helped by the intervention of her new boyfriend Mike Curb, MGM vice president and music industry whizz kid, who insisted that when they went out to restaurants she should eat and enjoy food with him. The romance with Nicky Chinn had by then fizzled out. "I was still young enough and successful enough that I wanted to be out there partying. But at the same time there was a super amount of love and respect for each other," he says. Karen dated Curb for a year, but because they both had busy schedules the romance had little time to develop. The Carpenters' music career was uppermost in her mind.

It's notable that Karen flitted from boyfriend to boyfriend with little break. Men found her expressive eyes and good humor magnetic, but she was insecure about her looks and her attractiveness as a woman and found it hard to open up and relate on an intimate level. She could not hold down a relationship for long, but equally she could not live without one. Her parents provided a model of marriage, dedication, and fidelity that she aspired to, but as long as she was dominated by her family, that kind of commitment also felt smothering. As a result Karen would sometimes yearn for men who were safely out of reach, like her suave, elegant boss Herb Alpert, who was married and unavailable.

Love and romance felt like difficult terrain, so Karen focused instead on areas where she was more in control, like her work. Perfectionism and the need for control are key aspects of eating disorders like anorexia and bulimia, and Karen exhibited this obsessive behavior from the beginning of the Carpenters' career. It was vital to her that each gig was perfect. Although many accounts emphasize Richard's role as bandleader, Karen had a very proactive role in the stage shows and was confident about organizing and driving the band forward with a single-minded vision. "On top of being at the front and doing all the lead singing, she's listening to every note . . . and she hears every mistake," Richard said. Karen would pull aside a musician after a show if he played a bum note, even Richard.[20]

Jeff Dexter, a British mod DJ and club promoter, noticed this about Karen during the Carpenters' tour of the UK in 1974. He remembers wangling his way to the stage door at the Talk of the Town in London's West End the afternoon of their first performance, where the band were soundchecking and running through rehearsals. A charmer and a gentleman, Dexter was captivated by Karen, but she refused to be distracted. "I tried my hardest to get off with her, every trick in the book. She was absolutely gorgeous, but she was having none of it. She was focused on the show and all the timings and finessing of it," he laughs. "She was the boss. Richard knew his music, but she was the boss. During rehearsal time they'd be halfway through a song and she'd stop everything and make them do it again, saying, 'No, it has to be right.' She was the one in control of all the fineries— the stagecraft, directing the musicians, etc. She was an amazing performer, both with her singing and her drumming—real precision work."[21]

The Talk of the Town concert was a triumph, performed with the expertise Dexter saw in rehearsals. Opening with a complicated '60s medley, they segued swiftly from one song to the next. One moment Karen was singing the Crystals' hit "Da Doo Ron Ron," hitting the drums at the front of the stage and conducting with her drumstick, then without missing a beat she jumped to "Leader of the Pack," a death ballad immortalized by the Shangri-Las. After a set that featured all the Carpenters' hits she bowed and ran off stage, scarcely taking a moment to linger.

In 1974, another year marked by constant traveling, a new young tour manager called Rebecca Segal joined the team. This was a bonus for Karen, usually the only female in the entourage. "There were not a lot of women out on the road, you've got guys around you all the time. I felt that in every tour I did, it came with the territory," Segal says.[22] Her father, Ben Segal, was a top promoter who founded Oakdale Theatre near New Haven, a concert venue "in the round" with a spinning stage that featured everyone from Broadway stars to rock bands like the Who, the Doors, and Led Zeppelin. Through the venue Rebecca got to know Sherwin Bash and joined his management team in the early 1970s. "I had done a four-month tour with Alice Cooper and wanted to be a tour manager. There were very few girls doing what I was doing. I had applied to a number of managers that I'd met and nobody would give me a gig," she recalls. Bash, however, had noticed her talent and hired her, to work first with Herb Alpert and then with the Carpenters, as his representative on tour dates.

"Karen and I are both Connecticut girls, born just a few months apart. We were similar in age and [had] both grown up in showbiz, so there was a connection, an unspoken thing that was understood," says Segal. "Karen was friendly, she was lovely with me and we got along fine, but there was a sense you weren't going to get any closer. There was always a part of her that was a bit reserved. She and Richard were not aloof, but they were not the most communicative. But they were both very competitive. It was important for them, for instance, where the band were on the charts."

Throughout 1974, Segal worked with the Carpenters on their European dates and a full tour of Japan as well as US shows until December. Adulation for the band was reaching fever pitch. Their drummer Cubby O'Brien remembers the Japanese shows in particular. "They were the number-one group there and we worked big boxing stadiums with 15,000–20,000 people. The crowd would throw stuffed animals at Karen so by the end of each show there would be piles of cuddly toys on stage. When they performed 'Sing' a little Japanese children's choir would come up and sing it with her. Japan was a great experience, always a lot of fun."

Karen loved being in Japan. She got on well with the country's top promoter, Tatsuji "Tats" Nagashima—"He owns Japan," she said. "You'd recognize him even if you didn't know him."[23] His father worked at Mitsubishi Bank, so he spent part of his childhood living in London and New York and learned to speak impeccable English. The family moved back to Japan during the Second World War and, after the war, Nagashima, a big jazz enthusiast, organised performances in Japan by foreign artists such as Louis Armstrong and Benny Goodman. He brought the Beatles to Japan, and by the 1970s his company Kyodo Kikaku promoted artists as varied as the Supremes and Led Zeppelin. "The great thing about Tats was he straddled both worlds. He'd been brought up in the West, he was a great bridge for us," recalled Paul McCartney. "He was loved by a lot of people. He had a twinkle in his eye, a good sense of humour. He was a very special man."[24]

Miki Berenyi, lead singer and guitarist with British dream pop band Lush, remembered seeing the Carpenters frequently on TV in the 1970s when she went to visit family in Tokyo. 'The Carpenters were incredibly clean-cut, so American-looking, and in Japan there was a real fascination with a western image that was quite fetishized. Pop television there was absolute family entertainment. Grandparents, little children—everybody was watching it," recalls Berenyi. "In the 1970s and early '80s, Japanese pop was totally manufactured and girl idols like Seiko Matsuda seemed very childish, very pure."[25]

Berenyi's cousin, rock musician Keigo Oyamada (aka Cornelius), remembers as a small boy in 1973 performing "Sing" with his family on a mainstream Fuji TV program called *Love Love Show*. "The Carpenters were used in commercials and as theme songs for TV dramas and I heard them often in my daily life," he says.[26] The band's smooth image and melodies chimed with that sense of innocence in Japanese pop. Not surprisingly "Sing" became one of their biggest hits in the country and Karen learned to sing the song phonetically in Japanese—there is a YouTube video of Karen on stage with the Kyoto children's choir, a cuddly toy pinned to her waist, bending down and singing call and response with the group of engagingly cute six-year-olds.

Rebecca Segal was tasked with finding and rehearsing the children's choir for each city they visited on the 1974 tour and didn't quite share Karen's enthusiasm for the song. "It was one of my least favorite songs ever. But somebody said, 'Oh, Rebecca, you line the children up and teach them the song and make sure they remember when to walk on stage.' Excuse me, how did this thing wind up on my lap? So I had to go, 'Hi, kids, how are you? Excited to be singing? Let's try it out.' I can't sing, but I'm singing along with them. And every time I just wanted to finish up and have a shot of tequila and smoke a cigarette. I think maybe after the tenth time, I finally took care of my game. I said, 'Can you please come down and do this with me? I'm gonna ruin this song.'" After that Karen would come over and say hello to the children and help Segal with rehearsals.

Touring that year was high pressure, but the Carpenters wanted to stay on top of the charts, so it was necessary to keep up the momentum. "You get into a rhythm and you're also in a bubble, like you're in suspended animation for three or four months at a time, seeing the same people," recalls Segal. "You were not grounded in any way, but everybody had to tour a lot those days to get on the radio and stay on the radio. That's how the whole business worked. There was no Spotify—you needed to be out there."

Sandwiched between tour dates from the summer of 1974 to early 1975 were recording sessions for *Horizon*, their sixth studio album. Now into their fifth year of touring, the expertise gained from performing live night after night can be heard in the assured quality of this album, perceived by many fans to be their best. Karen had developed a mature, skillful approach to recording. Nicky Chinn, for instance, believes that she focused on getting into the right mindset before she delivered a song.

"We talked about the recording sessions. She found them very easy because she understood a song so well. She did preparation beforehand, she wanted to be in touch with the lyrics. For Karen to prepare, it wasn't about the notes, she knew she could sing those. It was the lyric she wanted to understand. If she could, that was what she worked on before she went into the studio. She was a brilliant artist."

Karen obviously prepared as much as she could, but sometimes Richard could be controlling before a session, not revealing the title or the nature of the song they would be working on. Maybe he thought this would keep the process spontaneous, but this deeply irritated her and compounded any feelings of frustration or powerlessness. "I keep saying, for days before, 'What's the song' and he keeps saying 'Oh, you'll be okay. It's easy for you.' He doesn't let me know what my work is! And I hate that about him," she said in a *Melody Maker* interview.[27] Even though Richard may have stalled with the material, Karen was a quick study, able to digest the meaning, flow, and melody in an instant. Chinn also observed at close hand her flawless pitching. "I've been in studios with acts of my own, when we're on take twenty-seven. But Karen would walk in, do one or two takes and walk out. That was how good she was. She was note perfect always."

Bookended by "Aurora" and the short closing song "Eventide," *Horizon* was a concept album, but unlike the broad sweep of *Now & Then* it had a more subtle, intimate feel. It was recorded in A&M's Studio D with state-of-the-art 24-track Dolby technology, so each instrument could be heard with pristine clarity. As a result, on John Bettis and Richard's composition "Only Yesterday," the strongest track on the album, Jim Gordon's kick drum, Tony Peluso's guitar riffs, and Karen's yearning vocal are combined to create a sparkling wall of sound. The track has been called power pop, but it has a transformational force that goes beyond that generic description. "It's not muzak. We have fairly strong backbeats . . . maybe next to Led Zep it seems quiet, but next to muzak it sure as hell isn't quiet. There is a hell of a lot going on with the arrangements and the color," Richard said in a reflection on the song.[28]

Throughout this album, the lyrics seem aptly and acutely personal to Karen—particularly "Desperado," originally recorded by the Eagles in 1973. In this song the protagonist sings to a hard-bitten rancher who refuses to be tied down, chasing after romance only when it is out of reach. He mistakes being a loner for freedom, all the while closing his heart to love. With her bare, intimate delivery, Karen could be singing the song's message about love to herself. Tommy Morgan, the harmonica player from "Rainy Days and Mondays," played on this song as well. "When you have vocals like hers, it is easy to play harmonica around them," he says. "Listening to the track it was a really exposed vocal, you can hear inside her thoughts as a singer."

Karen sang the song with a slight country rock feel and this time she was positive about the slide guitar, played here by Thad Maxwell, the former Tarantula guitarist who back in 1969 had hidden behind the curtain to watch the Carpenters audition for A&M executives. By the mid-1970s he was playing with Linda Ronstadt and innovative country guitarist Thumbs Carllile and the Carpenters booked him on to the session. Maxwell remembers Richard standing right next to him in the studio. "He said, 'Okay now, play that chord but give it a sharp five and a flat seven.' Pedal steel guitar has about thirteen pedals on it . . . so there I was contorting myself with knees and feet and fingers to make some of the chords he heard in his head. They were not ordinary pedal steel chords, so it was challenging."[29]

He was struck by the fact that Karen sat quietly in the recording booth with the engineer Roger Young, watching Maxwell through the glass. "She was eating fruit—bananas and apples—and when I came in to listen to the playback she was very appreciative and very easy to talk with. She'd had a significant amount of success by then and she didn't have to be that way. It was nice to see that she could be a normal, decent person," he recalls. He could see that even though Richard had final say as producer, for this album Karen was credited as associate producer and had a strong vision as well. "Her being the lead singer gave her a lot of clout in those discussions, pretty much equal with the producer."

When they took a break during recording Richard went outside into the quad with Young and fired up his Ferrari. "They raised the hood and stood there listening to his Ferrari idle," he says, while Karen munched on her fruit. "She didn't seem to be struggling with her health at that point. I've thought long and hard since then as to whether I saw any signs or evidence of her eating disorder, and I did not. She seemed healthy and engaged."

Another dynamic track on the album is "Please Mr. Postman," an R&B pop song previously recorded in the 1960s by the Marvelettes and the Beatles, here speeded up and given a twist with Karen's deft, sure-fire performance on the drums. Recorded in July 1974, the song was released four months later and became one of their biggest worldwide hits, reaching number one in the US, Australia, Canada, and South Africa.

*

Even though the *Horizon* sessions went well, Karen and Richard were preoccupied with private challenges. He was strung out from touring and had got into the habit of taking Quaaludes as a sedative to help him sleep. By 1975, he was becoming dependent on them, taking them earlier and earlier in the day. This disconnection is apparent on "Solitaire," a song by Neil Sedaka about a lonely card shark who has lost in love. The duo perform as if in a dream, distant and separate from each other—like he is in one room playing piano and she is in another, her voice walled off in musical cladding.

Horizon is a snapshot of where Richard and Karen were as artists—adrift in their personal lives but developing depth and range as musicians. Its crisp, clear sound also shows their mastery of studio technology. This is where Bernie Grundman, the mastering engineer who gave every Carpenter album a silvery polish, really came into his own. "I was fortunate in that I got into the business right in that period when mastering became a creative part of recording," he says. "Sometimes mastering can completely transform the whole recording and make it more effective for the listener, a better emotional connection. That's our goal, to try to find that place."[30]

A fan of high-end audio, Grundman began his career in the 1950s running an after-hours jazz club in his home town of

Phoenix before moving to Los Angeles to the groundbreaking jazz label Contemporary Records, working with inspirational figures like the label's founder, Lester Koenig and recording engineer Roy DuNann. Grundman grew his reputation as an audiophile's engineer, so Herb Alpert poached him for A&M and while at the label he was very much part of finessing the Carpenters' sound. They had special amplifiers similar to ones in the Contemporary jazz studio. "So we were able to get a really good high-quality sound, especially with Karen. She had such a pure, natural voice; to capture that we really needed a good system and mastering was done with the least amount of processing, with the purest signal we could get," Grundman recalls. "The vocals were so good that you didn't need to cover up anything with reverb, or do pitch correction, none of that. Even though the records weren't really cut loud her voice was present on the radio, just like the announcer." Noting that each album was like a journey, a moving, fluid experience, it was very satisfying to Grundman that with *Horizon* the band were able to take a step up in terms of the technology. He remembers Karen coming to his mastering sessions. "We would talk a little bit . . . both her and Richard were very sensitive, always thinking about how to make things better. We had a pretty good rapport, it was pretty easy to tell what they were looking for."

He thinks their sound reflected their roots in Orange Country. "It's a very conservative, very quiet area in California. I don't think they [had] been out in the world much, so they had this innocence about them. That was kind of refreshing, they were very naive about a lot of things," he says. "But they certainly really had worked on their music together. They had a vision, you know, because their first album had that sound right away—they had been on that for a long time and it just got better."

The Carpenters' musical vision matured on this album, partly because they were finding ways to express through the music feelings that may have been repressed for far too long.

CHAPTER 10

1975

Some people center their whole lives around us. That's getting awfully heavy . . . It's an eerie feeling. I don't dig being *responsible* that way. I mean . . . we only wanted to make a little music.[1]

The Carpenters had legions of devoted fans, some of whom became obsessive, stalking them or attempting to gain access to their family home in Downey. "One time I got this beautiful bouquet of flowers in a box. I wondered what it could be, it wasn't anyone's birthday. I opened it up and there was a cake, right in the middle of the beautiful flowers," said Karen. "Some kids pull the funniest things that you just can't get upset, they think of wild ways."[2] From time to time she would be sent rings and marriage proposals and that would put her in a quandary, because to send them back would seem rude. "It's very touching. Some of them spend quite a bit of money," she said.

Some of the attention lavished on Karen was scary, like the man in Houston who came in during a soundcheck and sat down at her drums. When he was approached by the police he screeched, "Don't touch me! I'm engaged to Karen Carpenter!" After his arrest they found he had a wedding ring and plane tickets for a honeymoon. There was also the man who pulled up outside their Downey home in a Pontiac GTO muscle car with "JESUS SAVES" stickers claiming that all the songs Karen had been singing over the past four years were for him. The stalker came back day after day, sitting in his GTO and staring, sometimes screaming up at her bedroom. All the police could do was escort him to the city limits and hope he didn't return.

Karen thought deeply about the fans and the intensity of their needs sometimes troubled her. "A lot of kids write and ask me for advice," she said. Some would write saying they had been addicted to drugs but the Carpenters' music had helped them quit. Others would say that they were lonely, that their parents didn't love them, that they just lived for the music. One girl had lost her boyfriend in Vietnam and was suicidal, another told Karen that her stepfather was hateful and her brother interfered with her. A Vietnam veteran wrote to Karen, saying that a letter from her helped him cope after being injured and discharged. A twelve-year-old girl was dying and wanted a drum set, so the Carpenters gave her one. She stayed alive for their show in Utica, New York, and then passed away a few weeks later. "That's a hell of a responsibility . . . strange to think you could have that much power," mused Karen.[3]

Those years of relentless touring were exhausting, but what the Carpenters offered could transform communities, appealing to young and old. "They're really special. Lotta groups been through here, but . . . they are the only ones really worth seein'," said a fan in Wheeling, West Virginia.[4] The Carpenters' entourage would drive past disused rail yards and wrecked mobile homes to play to grateful audiences in small cities like Richmond, Virginia, or Hershey, Pennsylvania. They would play old theaters where the sound system was compromised, or ice-hockey rinks where backstage smelled of damp socks, but before each event they would soundcheck religiously and make sure the show sounded perfect. With each meticulously planned tour, staying at Holiday Inn after Holiday Inn, the Carpenters were bringing their music to the people. At one special concert they played to 15,000 children. "I was flabbergasted because I stood there and sang 'Rainy Days and Mondays' and I saw a baby sitting there singing every word with me," Karen said.[5]

They also made it a point of honor to sign autographs—in fact, Agnes scolded Richard and Karen one night when they rushed to their car in the rain without stopping for a signing and fans complained. Occasionally the pressure would get to them. One morning, for instance, during a hotel breakfast a burly man presented Karen with five napkins to be signed. "Oh fuck!" she exclaimed. Although Karen could be overwhelmed by the attention, she cared about the audiences and they responded—the emotion in her voice either soothing or resonating with the crowd. She enjoyed being recognized when she was out in the street or signing checks in a shop and was thrilled at the validation of her as an artist. She even thought it was fun when they chased her car down the freeway. Her ability to connect with fans was profound, but this wasn't always appreciated or understood by the Carpenters' record company.

In 1975, the group were still having global hits but there was an ongoing discussion at A&M about making the band more relevant to a new generation of hip, rock-savvy music fans. Clare Baren remembers the Carpenters had an office on the second floor of the A&M compound but they were seen as separate from the label's other artists. With their low-rise buildings set around a quad with a small car park and room for tables and chairs, the old Charlie Chaplin studios had an easygoing collegiate atmosphere and were a focal point for musicians and producers. 'Across the lot I saw the producer Lou Adler every day with Carole King and Henry Lewy, the engineer for Joni Mitchell. It was the most creative place. I used to sit in the middle of the lot holding hands with Cat Stevens, chatting. It was the friendliest place," says Baren.[6]

The Carpenters were different from the rest of the bunch, and there was some uncertainty about how to market them. Baren remembers her friend Paul Williams, an A&M songwriter, asking for suggestions on how to promote the band. "I didn't listen to the Carpenters at home, I was into rock 'n' roll. My first reaction was, *These two young people shouldn't be singing love songs looking at each other*. I said, 'This is creepy, they're brother and sister!' It was really *tough*, because you couldn't give her a boyfriend or him a girlfriend. You didn't even know if they wanted boyfriends or girlfriends, no one asked. We didn't really wanna know what was going on privately. Even though we know she had her issues and we know he did, they never ever fought in front of anyone. They never dissed each other, were never rude. They were so well brought up it was almost scary."

When it came to promoting the *Horizon* album Baren decided to make it less about them as a duo and more about creating short, evocative films. The first video she made with them was for "Please Mr. Postman," which was shot at Disneyland. "We had the whole park for a day, before the public was let in, so we went on rides and filmed them having fun but not looking at each other lovingly. Our shoot in Disneyland was the most fun we ever had. You'd make the performance as good as it could be with a tasty background. It was always a challenge, but the songs were amazing and her voice was superb, so you didn't have to do that much."

Baren's choice of the Disneyland location was an inspired move, because she tapped into Karen's deep idealization of Mickey Mouse. Although the Disney character was a small mouse with a falsetto voice, he had huge presence and in the 1950s and '60s became an emotive master symbol of amicability and fair play. He is the intrepid friend who in every film solves a problem or out-smarts a villain and wins his girl Minnie, overcoming any obstacle in his way. Not only can he reshape reality, but he is a judicious leader and overall nice guy. Karen associated Mickey Mouse with her 1950s childhood in Connecticut, a place of familiarity and safety, where she and friends Joe and Debbie Vaiuso would sit together at home watching *The Mickey Mouse Club*. Rigorous work schedules and her own secret, self-imposed dieting regime left her feeling lonely and cut off, longing for close friendship. The cartoon character surrounding her in the talismans of soft toys, T-shirts and key rings was a form of comfort, symbolizing the love and attachment she craved. Shooting in Disneyland allowed Karen to express a playful, breezy side to her personality. An artist stepping out in a video with Mickey Mouse could be seen as the epitome of high camp, but for Karen the attachment was less about irony and more a statement of true devotion.

In contrast to the childlike joy of the Disneyland shoot, the next video Baren produced was more reflective. "Only Yesterday" was shot at Huntington Gardens, a special place in Pasadena with 120 themed acres, including a Japanese garden, a rose garden, a cactus desert and a huge botanical park. Because it was the Carpenters the management gave the film crew the whole place for the day, letting them roam and ramble through the acres. Unlike the cheery, nostalgic power of "Please Mr. Postman" there is a more poignant tone to "Only Yesterday," a song about finding a love that alleviates old pain and sadness and enables one to face the future. As she walked in the sunshine through the trees and shrubbery Karen seemed to connect deeply with the lyrics. "It's not natural if you're lip-synching quietly, so she sang out loud. Even though she didn't sing at full volume her voice was so spectacular," recalls Baren.

For most of the video shoot, Richard and Karen were very cooperative and polite, but as the day wore on Baren noticed Richard getting tense. "Setting up shots takes a while and what I didn't realize then was Richard was taking pills to stay calm or sane. He would keep saying, 'Are we ready yet?' If you took an hour to set up I could see Richard getting impatient and I'd say to the director, 'You've got to pick it up, you've got to move, Richard's getting antsy.' That was the only tension. If we were with a heavy-metal band they'd break the equipment or stick a foot through the drum kit if we took too long. But the Carpenters never had a tantrum, never insulted anyone. But on the other hand it wasn't slap your hand, hug hello, or be warm and friendly."

Horizon was a turning point for both Richard and Karen. Although the album was one of their biggest global sellers, it was the first to miss the top five in the US, peaking at number thirteen. Their career was beginning to plateau, and that worried them. That sense of unease is reflected on the album cover, a photograph which is actually one of the strongest images of the duo, with Karen half-frowning and averting her gaze while Richard stands pensive behind her. No bright smiles, no shiny perfection—this time there was a sense of emotional realism.

The picture was taken by Ed Caraeff, a rock 'n' roll photographer who snapped the iconic shot of Jimi Hendrix burning his guitar at the Monterey Festival in 1967 and who worked with everyone from the Doors and Frank Zappa to Carly Simon and Linda Ronstadt. Right from when he was a shy fourteen-year-old student escaping from high-school bullies by creating his own magic world in the darkroom, Caraeff liked to express a mood or feeling in his photos. "The night I shot Jimi Hendrix, 99 percent of people there hadn't seen him or heard his music. A German photographer in the pit casually mentioned to me, 'Save some film for Jimi Hendrix.' I didn't know what to expect when two skinny white Brits and a short, thin black guy came on stage. But then he started to play. To this day I have never seen or heard anything like that. Jimi was so cool, so casual about the whole thing and so confident."[7]

Caraeff was surprised when someone from A&M contacted him about photographing the Carpenters. "I don't know why I got the phone call. I had no business card, no portfolio, an unlisted phone number. It was all word of mouth," he says. After listening to *Horizon* Caraeff decided to try something different for the album cover shot. He had two key approaches—either very art-directed, like the cover for Elton John's 1973 album *Don't Shoot Me I'm Only the Piano Player*, where he created a classic cinema on the back of a Universal studio lot, or natural reportage style, like 1972's *Honky Château*. "I took that candid photo in Elton's hotel room just before his Troubadour show. It was natural light and I sepia-toned it," he says. With the Carpenters he opted for the latter approach, aiming to capture their essence as musicians. "The goal was to make them look great, not like the other very posed, lit studio shots. I knew they were from Downey, ten minutes from where I grew up and I knew she played drums."

They came to his rambling 1920s house in Coldwater Canyon, which was at the end of a long driveway shaded by trees. "Right off the bat there was a different vibe," he recalls. Karen was quiet and thoughtful. "She said no more than hello and her brother did all the talking. He was the point man—she seemed to defer everything to him." Caraeff made sure Richard and Karen were comfortable and then took them outside at 5:30 p.m. just as the sun was beginning to go down. "The light goes over the canyon at a certain time, what I call magic time. It's a very flattering light.

I know when I've got the photo, I can feel it. I just captured the moment."

Caraeff was aware that the Carpenters had been branded square and uncool. "Their visual style was indicative of who they were, you can't wave a magic wand and get style. Jimi Hendrix, for instance, was naturally like a *Vogue* man." The Carpenters would have benefited from an imaginative stylist and Caraeff says he brought his own relaxed style to the shoot. "I was able to photograph people in a way that made them look good. I spent a lot of time thinking about the lighting, camera angle, clothes and the darkroom work."

He was also known to have the best marijuana in town. "Along with David Crosby I was a connoisseur of weed. I was very discreet about it." The Carpenters once said they were in favor of legalizing marijuana so maybe they would have been tempted to partake. "I have no memory of that, but I would have had it available!" One thing Richard did ask about later was the cover of *Don't Shoot Me I'm Only the Piano Player*. "I got a phone call from him, he wanted to buy the vintage car used on the album cover. It was from a prop house at Universal Studios . . . so he got in touch with them and bought it."

Horizon repositioned the Carpenters as a band and was described by *Rolling Stone* writer Stephen Holden as their "most musically sophisticated album to date." They had hit a creative peak, but one that was difficult for them to sustain as their lives became more and more affected by personal demons. When their career took off in 1971, Richard battled feelings of anxiety, brooding constantly about the need to record hits in the middle of a busy tour itinerary, and this affected his ability to sleep. His mother Agnes had similar problems with restlessness and she recommended Quaaludes, which had helped with her insomnia. Richard took one Quaalude every night for the next four years. However, he began to notice that if he took one or two and stayed awake he felt high and enjoyed the sensation. By the time the Carpenters were shooting videos for the *Horizon* album he had built up a tolerance and was beginning to take more and more. He also ate less, because they worked so well on an empty stomach. He was managing the habit, but only just.

Karen, too, was finding the touring a strain and the novelty of being on the road had definitely worn off. "You get to a point where you can't remember where you are. That's not good. In the past we'd talk to people and they couldn't remember places they'd played and we'd think, *How does that happen?* Well, I've got news for ya. After a while you have no idea," she told a radio interviewer. "For a while we were doing things that no human can take. It can finally get to you."[8] Chuck Findley, the flugelhorn player on "Close to You," noticed that when he saw Karen on the A&M lot she had a distracted air and looked tired. "I'd say, 'Karen, are you gonna be taking a little holiday, be in town for a little while?' 'Well, no, we leave tomorrow morning, you know.' [They were] forever playing, constantly in and out recording and on the road. It was just too much . . . too busy."[9] Driven by perfectionism and a sense of duty to the band, Karen found it impossible to take time off. During the recording of *Horizon*, for example, she had sores on her vocal cords and the doctor advised her to stop singing for a month. "I was home for two days and then I was back in the studio. *Horizon* just drained everything, every drop of blood out of us," she said later. She kept a torch by her bed, so even after she went to sleep she would wake herself up to write down a "to do" list. On top of that she was becoming more and more obsessed with counting calories, keeping to a stringent diet of thin salad and iced tea, which lowered her energy level.

There was an intimation of Karen's impending crisis during a conversation with some A&M staff members, an informal chat at Hollywood's Au Petit Café for the label's newsletter *Compendium*. She and Richard were talking about their most memorable "goose bump" musical moments. He mentioned the raunchy feel of Led Zeppelin's "Whole Lotta Love" and the aching beauty of "Bridge over Troubled Water." She picked out the bridge in Simon & Garfunkel's "Old Friends." What's notable about this song is how it begins as a melodious reflection by two elderly men, sitting on a park bench thinking about their friendship. But in the bridge section the music is disturbed by dissonant, clashing strings and the sense of suppressed agony and old rivalries beneath the surface.

As well as battling exhaustion, Karen was feeling as lonely as the love songs she sang. She took out her frustration on Richard by monitoring his relationships, chafing when he spent too much time with girlfriend Randy Bash. As well as criticizing his choice of partner, she had exacting standards for herself—the man Karen intended to marry had to be strong, wealthy, confident, and loving too, because she was tactile and loved to be hugged. "My man should have a good sense of humour, dress well in modern gear . . . and be a musician," she said in 1970, and those requirements remained pretty constant throughout her life. On the one hand she wanted a successful career, but she also felt a sense of failure about the fact that she was still unmarried and without children. Cubby O'Brien noticed that it was difficult for her to trust men. "I felt sorry for Karen in a way," he says. "She always felt when she had a boyfriend that they liked her because she was Karen Carpenter."

Early in 1975, however, Karen met a man who fulfilled every category on her mental checklist. Terry Ellis, producer and co-founder of Chrysalis Records, had just moved to Los Angeles to develop his label in America. He and his Chrysalis partner Chris Wright had already achieved huge success with Jethro Tull, Ten Years After, and Procol Harum and within a year he was to sign a New York punk band called Blondie. As well as being savvy about the business, 32-year-old Ellis was bright and engaging. He and Karen met through Frenda and Ed Leffler and began dating almost straight away. They had an easy compatibility and in many ways would have been an ideal match. He gave her valuable advice on stagecraft and how to project herself as a confident performer, encouraging her to make it more of a show and reminding her of the golden rule to never turn her back on the audience. He also struck up a rapport with Richard—the two shared a love of fine wines and the latter respected his knowledge and experience of the music industry. His special relationship with Karen, however, was affected by outside forces that neither of them could control.

*

The Carpenters' 1975 *Horizon* tour started well but ended badly. They were scheduled to tour America for six weeks, playing Lake Tahoe and Las Vegas before flying to Japan and Europe. Sherwin Bash had booked Neil Sedaka as support and this proved to be a lethal combination. "To tell you the truth, the managers should never have put them together, it was not a good pairing. Neil Sedaka would start introducing people who were in the audience, so if he introduced a star who'd come to see us then Richard didn't like it at all," remarks Cubby O'Brien. "It didn't work out too well, it was a clash."

Neil Sedaka was a Brooklyn-born teen idol and Brill Building songwriter who rose to fame in the late 1950s and early '60s with hits like "Oh! Carol" (a tribute to his high-school girlfriend Carole King), "Happy Birthday Sweet Sixteen" and "Breaking Up Is Hard to Do." In the mid-'60s, however, his career suffered because of the Beatles and the British Invasion and he spent some time out of the limelight during what he called "the Hungry Years," until Elton John revived his career in 1973 by signing Sedaka to his Rocket label. The album *Sedaka's Back* was released in late 1974 and yielded three hit singles, so by the time he secured the support slot with the Carpenters, Sedaka's comeback was in full swing. "I think they were thrilled because they love the music and he was affable but also someone else was getting their applause. It's not like it was jealousy, but more, *We got to stay on our game*," recalls their tour manager Rebecca Segal. "When you have a massive, massive audience you've got to just keep feeding that machine. You've got to have hits to make people keep wanting to come back."

Sedaka's success threatened the Carpenters' pop supremacy. A vivacious performer with a forceful personality, Sedaka would sing, smile, clap, and dance while playing the piano. As the tour went on, it became obvious that he was beginning to upstage the duo. Matters came to a head one night in Las Vegas, when Sedaka introduced Tom Jones and Dick Clark to the crowd, two celebrities who had come to see the Carpenters. Showbusiness protocol is that the headline act makes such introductions. Already strung out on pills and operating on a short fuse, this transgression sent Richard apoplectic. Afterward during an irate phone call with Bash, the latter said, "Do you want me to fire him?" Richard agreed and Sedaka was bumped off the tour. "'Breaking Up Is Hard to Do' indeed," chuckles O'Brien. This rebounded on the Carpenters when Sedaka accused them of sacking him because he was too good. "I'm in a state of shock," he said. "They felt I was too strong. I guess I was going over better than they had expected."[10]

Even though Richard issued statements to the contrary, the damage had been done and the Carpenters were ridiculed in the press. Reviewers were already taking swipes at the band— the *Columbia Flier*, for instance, criticized their "whiteness and milksop stage presence," saying that in her pink and orange gown Karen looked "a little too sweet . . . like the most expensive candy in the dime store." The Sedaka debacle did nothing for their image and strained their working relationship with Sherwin Bash, because Richard blamed the latter for planting in him the idea to fire Sedaka.

The band were not in a good way. By now Karen's constant dieting had developed into the eating disorder anorexia. "She was rapidly losing weight. I remember walking into the dressing room one day and she was sitting with her back toward me. She just had a towel on and I remember having to not gasp," says Segal. Malnourishment led to exhaustion, and even though Karen performed well on stage, she had to sleep in the dressing room during breaks to conserve energy. "I had to find designers who would make her clothes. I said to one designer we worked with, please make sure the clothes are kind of flowing. Then Karen took a jacket off on stage and you could see the audience recoil." Critics began to make references to Karen's gaunt frame. "She is terribly thin almost a wraith and should be gowned more becomingly," wrote the reviewer for *Variety*. "She was totally in denial, but that body dysmorphia is common. I was a chubby girl too," says Segal, who remembers the social stigma around girls with a fuller figure. "Because she'd been a chubby girl, in her mind she was thinner and more attractive."

As the tour went on, Segal became more concerned. "You are clearly seeing someone who's suffering but I don't think that Karen and Richard were raised in a way where communicating their emotions was a natural thing for them to do, or even encouraged," she says. "There were a few times on the road that I would look at her and think, *Somebody's got to do something here*. I did say to one person, 'Somebody should be aware that she's not eating.' But not much was known about anorexia then, so I don't think people understood the kind of slippery slope she was on. How do you raise that? I can't imagine that Karen or anybody wanted to go down that rabbit hole." Segal was also aware of her role as a young person on the team, seeing the power dynamic around Sherwin Bash, the Carpenters, and their mother, Agnes, and knowing her place was not to question that. "As a young woman I wasn't afraid to speak my mind. But I was mindful that I was one of the few women in that position and it could all go away. I mean, you're in a business that's somewhat fickle."

Before their homecoming show in New Haven in July, Harold Carpenter voiced concern about his daughter. "Have you seen Karen lately?" he asked their old friend Theresa Vaiuso, when she came to collect him and Agnes from the hotel.

"Only on TV. She looked pretty good to me."

"Well she's not fooling me. That girl's got anorexia nervosa."

Harold saw the warning signs, but found it hard to persuade his wife that Karen's condition was more than dieting gone too far. By late August, however, the reality of her disorder hit home when she collapsed, too ill and undernourished to perform the Carpenters' tour dates in Europe and Japan. In summer 1975 her weight had gone down to 91 pounds, so she checked into Cedars-Sinai Medical Center for five days with a severely weakened immune system and was ordered by doctors to rest, eat, and recuperate. This was the first of several hospitalizations and the moment that her family and friends realized Karen was seriously ill.

Sherwin Bash told her to get professional help, but claimed that Agnes was of the view that "we can take care of ourselves . . . it's a family matter." At the time very few people understood the urgency for treatment so it was assumed that rest and good food was all Karen needed. Meanwhile the Carpenters' upcoming world tour had to be rescheduled. She felt personally responsible for the loss to the Carpenters of up to $250,000 in refunded tickets. In a statement to the press Dr Robert Koblin explained, "She is suffering a severe case of physical and nervous exhaustion." Karen's distress was exacerbated by the fact that Richard fired Bash over the fall-out with Sedaka, which for a short while left the Carpenters without management. Richard asked Terry Ellis if he would do the job, but Ellis said that because he was dating Karen there would be a conflict of interest and he agreed just to manage them until they found a permanent replacement.

Richard, John Bettis, and Terry Ellis went to Tokyo and London for emergency press conferences, apologizing to the fans. "She's just kept up too tough a schedule and really run herself down," explained Richard. "She wanted to show that she could do just as good as the guys and really pushed herself . . . Now she's got nerves thinking about having made the decision to cancel the British tour. It's troubled her all week."[11] In an interview with *Melody Maker*, Richard did refer to the fact that Karen "went on this huge diet and lost a lot of weight." He even admitted that "diet for Karen really became an obsession." But he did not mention the severity of her condition and was reluctant to use the word "anorexia," framing the problem instead as flu and exhaustion brought on by weight loss and overwork. In 1975, eating disorders were seen as frightening and taboo and making Karen's anorexia public would have damaged the band's image and the "brand."

The Carpenters were still very popular in the UK, and there had been feverish anticipation about their upcoming concerts, so there was genuine concern and speculation about Karen's health. In the pop press and tabloids there were rumors that she had cancer, so to counteract this Evelyn Wallace issued a statement from the Carpenters' fan club saying that Karen had developed colitis, because of "overwork, dieting and lack of rest . . . her collapse was inevitable after the rigorous schedule of the past summer months." This didn't stop the speculation, however, or the sense of mystery surrounding Karen's illness. The Carpenters had always been a picture-perfect example of beaming California health and talent and this abrupt postponement of their tour dates showed them to be fallible people with real-life problems.

After the hospitalization, Karen went back home to Downey and took time off to recover, building her weight back up to 104 pounds by the end of October. Though troubled by the postponement of their UK tour, Karen could see how much she had been punishing herself. "All my strength is not back yet and that alone gets me upset," she said. "I'm not used to being slower than [normal]. Being idle is annoying."[12] Ellis advised her that slowing down wasn't a crime, that it was necessary for her and for the band's survival. "Your health is more important and you'll be more creative if you have some rest," he said. It is striking that, despite her hospitalization, Karen was in denial about the seriousness of her anorexia, convincing herself that it was just a question of readjusting her diet and regaining her strength. Acknowledgment of the disease would have meant a complete change in her lifestyle, a total break from work and a commitment to long-term therapy, but jeopardizing her career seemed too high a price.

THE STORY OF KAREN CARPENTER

Once Karen was feeling a little better Ellis took her on holiday to his house on Tortola, in the Virgin Islands, and when they came back she moved into his Beverly Hills home. It looked like she was finally breaking free from her family and Agnes in particular. Ellis remarked that away from her mother's influence Karen would "come alive." However, it was soon clear that there were signs of incompatibility—she loved to get home from the studio and put her feet up with a TV tray watching reruns of 1950s sitcom *I Love Lucy*, whereas Ellis preferred to socialize and dine in fine restaurants. Though it might have seemed a trivial activity, for Karen watching TV comedy was a valuable form of relief and mental distraction. In *I Love Lucy*, Lucille Ball plays Lucy Ricardo, a young housewife in New York City who with her best friend Ethel (a former vaudeville star) is constantly trying to get into showbusiness and appear beside her bandleader husband Ricky, played by Desi Arnaz. Even though she sings off-key and many of her performances end in disaster, Lucy's spirit is irrepressible. Likewise, in 1960s spin-off *The Lucy Show*, Ball plays a zany woman following her own whimsical path, trying to raid her late husband's trust fund to hatch madcap projects with her divorcee friend, Viv.

Karen loved these shows, watching them over and over again. Lucille Ball's clowning was her escape and her release. The Lucy characters had a subversive appeal, daring to be the Fool—naughty, carefree, and playful in a way that Karen, often consumed by worry and self-doubt, found it hard to be in everyday life. At the same time, when she was relaxed Karen was a natural comedian. Ball's goofiness chimed with an anarchic humor that, as the Carpenters became more successful, with more and more people depending on them along with the attendant studio deadlines and responsibilities, she didn't always get a chance to express. That lightness of spirit is what Ellis hinted at when he said that away from the Carpenters juggernaut Karen would come alive.

In any normal relationship, small incompatibilities could be worked through, but Karen's anorexia meant that going to restaurants involved stressful and elaborate strategies to avoid eating. Her mother's indomitable personality also proved to be a significant obstacle. When Ellis suggested that Karen see a psychiatrist, Agnes was completely against the idea, saying that the family didn't need to see "people like that." To Agnes, someone from a Second World War generation used to overcoming hardship and the rigors of rationing by sublimating their fears, therapy was an unnecessary indulgence. She was also worried about Ellis's influence as the band's temporary manager. What if he persuaded Karen to move to the UK with him? And what if he got her to leave Richard and sign to Chrysalis as a solo artist?

Even though Karen was in love with Ellis and he offered her a way out, she wasn't quite ready to leave home and this was compounded by pressure from Agnes to end the relationship. Panicking at the thought of a serious commitment and not ready to change her life, Karen packed a suitcase one night when Ellis was away and fled back to Downey. At first Karen dismissed the affair, telling a journalist that "we had a thing going . . . but we weren't exactly matched," but very soon came to regret leaving Ellis and the opportunity of genuine truc love.

CHAPTER 11

1976

I don't think I'll ever lose my love to sing. With each day that passes you learn more. I'm able to express myself better now. I was afraid to do what I wanted. After you become "established," you tend to go ahead and do what you feel like.[1]

"I've moved!" In the autumn of 1976 Karen sent a vibrant yellow card to her friends, with her change of address emblazoned in bold red: "CENTURY TOWERS, 2222 Avenue of the Stars, Los Angeles 90067." Finally she was independent and moving into her own apartment on the twenty-second floor, with a doorbell that played the first few bars of "We've Only Just Begun." Her excitement was palpable. Here she was, a 26-year-old woman at the top of her game living in Century Towers, a gleaming high-rise designed by I. M. Pei, architect of the glass Pyramide du Louvre in Paris and home to film stars and celebrities including Burt Lancaster, Lana Turner, Diana Ross, and

Ruth Handler, the woman who invented the Barbie doll. The development boasted valet parking, 24-hour security, a swimming pool, a putting green, and tennis courts, and just across the road were the studios of 20th Century Fox. With the help of their lawyer Werner Wolfen, Karen had purchased two condominiums in the block and turned them into a duplex. From her floor-to-ceiling windows she had magnificent views of the city and the Hollywood Hills. She could drive with the top down just twenty minutes along La Cienega Boulevard to reach the A&M recording studios—a completely different experience to negotiating the heavy traffic from Orange County. She was a long way from Downey; she had arrived.

Karen had the duplex decorated by renowned interior designer John Cottrell with a mix of "funky and top-class" comfort—so the living room sported sleek lines, a large audiovisual system and 7-foot TV screen, while the kitchen was homey in a French country style. "I like big fluffy couches. I want it to be top-notch, top class, yet I want people to feel they can put their feet up," she told Cottrell.[2] This apartment symbolized the new Karen, someone aspirational and refined, someone transformed from tomboy to poised celebrity. Good friends like Frenda Leffler and Carole Curb, sister of Mike Curb, met her for lunch in nearby Beverly Hills and took her shopping in designer boutiques. Since they first met in 1970, Frenda had coached Karen on how to walk and talk "uptown," to leave behind the tough-guy defensiveness, the girl in the on-the-road gang who strode like a "truck driver."

Karen had fun experimenting with hair and make-up and doing her nails and buying clothes, but after a while fashion became another thing to obsess about and "get right." Carole noted her walk-in wardrobe where clothes were hung exactly a quarter of an inch apart and rigidly grouped according to type, with trousers in one section, blouses in another and shoes all color-matched. Olivia Newton-John also noticed how the place was always immaculate. "She was very clean, very tidy. Obviously she had issues and probably could have had obsessive-compulsive disorder," she said.[3] The compulsive tidying was reminiscent of Agnes Carpenter's obsessive cleaning during Karen's childhood. There is the sense that Karen's hard-won independence also triggered anxiety—in trying to attain that elusive sophisticated status, Karen lost touch with something that kept her anchored. The wisecracking tomboy was part of Karen's identity and strength as a musician, it wasn't something she needed to hide. There was a sense of Karen as a woman out of time. Ten years later in a more diverse industry where female artists were coming through as instrumentalists and singers, she would have found it easier. Or if she had been born ten years earlier Karen could have carved out a career as a massive torch singer like Patti Page or Peggy Lee. The 1970s was a cusp era, when women were redefining themselves, caught between the old models of passive, decorative femininity and a more liberated self-assertion.

Karen's uncertainty about her looks comes through in her choice of clothes. During the Carpenters' formative years she sometimes wore clumpy midi-dresses, or flouncy gowns that but-toned up at the chin, unflattering outfits that covered her body and made movement awkward. She wore the more formal dresses in her role as lead singer, but seemed much more comfortable in jeans or, as the decade went on, wearing tailored trouser suits and a more androgynous style.

There was also a side to Karen that was unremittingly hokey and childlike. Her bedroom was chock-full of Mickey Mouse paraphernalia and stuffed animals, including a large purple elephant and an 8-foot rabbit sitting on a love seat. A fan of needlepoint, she was constantly embroidering small tapestries and cushion covers, an activity that she found calming and which satisfied her eye for detail. This repetitive, circumscribed work became her method of laying down thought patterns, often when she had idle time on the plane or waiting backstage, or in the hotel room at night after a show or when she was at home alone. It was somewhere to weave the worry and obsessive feelings and it was also an outlet for her visual flair. In the teenage autobiography Karen wrote for a school project in New Haven, she mentioned a love of drawing and that she had won a prize for creating a poster. She had inherited her dad's talent for design, sewing graphic communication into those cushions. The needlepoint was also a vehicle for her humor—one of the canvases she stitched for her parents featured a yellow-brick road leading to a dollar sign and the words "YOU PUT US ON THE ROAD." As time went on and the touring schedule took its toll, that slogan could be read as an accusation.

Even though Karen enjoyed the freedom of her new condo, she returned to Downey two or three times a week and resisted her parents' efforts to get her to ingest more than salads, iced tea, and, on a good day, a piece of fish with no sauce. Family friend

Evelyn Wallace would visit once a week with a gardener to help tend Karen's indoor potted plants and she noticed that the large double-door fridge was permanently empty. Most poignantly, the full range of spotless pots and pans in the kitchen were rarely used. Karen may have moved uptown, but that hadn't cured the anorexia that was beginning to govern her life.

*

The year 1976 marked a new phase for Karen, not just on the home front, but also professionally. In January Jerry Weintraub had taken over as the Carpenters' new manager. "He was a big player, a wheeler-dealer maverick who didn't want to be in the rock cartel," says Chris Charlesworth, *Melody Maker*'s editor in Los Angeles. Weintraub started out in the 1960s as a talent manager agent and then made showbusiness history by being the first to organize large arena tours for artists as varied as the Four Seasons, Neil Diamond, and Led Zeppelin. He worked with Colonel Tom Parker on Elvis Presley's 1970 comeback tour and coaxed Frank Sinatra out of retirement in 1974, transforming him from "a saloon singer into a stadium singer."[4] The year before he began managing the Carpenters, Weintraub had branched out into film production as producer of Robert Altman's multi-award-winning movie *Nashville*. "Jerry got us the TV deals. He's thinking more long-range. Before, we'd just record and tour . . . now TV is looking up," said Karen.

More than most pop managers at the time, Weintraub understood how to develop an artist's longevity. For John Denver, for instance, he secured TV and film roles, as well as making sure his live concerts were dynamic and engaging. He adopted a similar approach with the Carpenters, thinking about long-term strategies and cutting down live dates to allow more time for the recording studio. After 1975's *Horizon* tour, the band were depleted, so Weintraub made sure that the first few months of 1976 were devoted to recording *A Kind of Hush*, what was to be their seventh album.

The title track, a version of the 1967 Herman's Hermits hit, is vintage Carpenters, with Karen's velvety voice highlighted by stabs of lazy trumpet and accented arrangements. Elsewhere, John Bettis's lyrics show his instinctive understanding of her emotional reality. Karen sings about seeking perfection in the imperfect world of "I Need to Be in Love" and in the tour de force "I Have You" she sings about how safe music and the power of song make her feel.

Even though the Carpenters were now international stars with new top-flight management, Karen didn't change the way she related to her friends. Harpist Gayle Levant, for instance, always found Karen optimistic and easy to work with: "She never, for all the time that I knew her, became infatuated with herself. I never saw that 'It's all about me' or 'I'm one step above you' kind of ego that some artists had. She wanted to make the best record she could with Richard, and I'm just grateful that she didn't change."[5]

She also seemed to have recovered some energy after her collapse. Drummer Cubby O'Brien played on these sessions and noted that Karen was actively involved in the process. "Richard liked playing with all the knobs and mixing, and the two of them would do their own background singing and overdub and overdub," he recalls. Since 1973's *Now & Then* album she had been credited as associate producer or coproducer with Richard and for this project clearly took part in decision-making in terms of production. "They listened and listened and listened. Richard was a fanatic about sound. They'd go back and change maybe one bar of music or change one note of her vocal. He knew what he wanted to hear and how to get it and of course Karen wanted to be a part of that, they were definitely a team."

Even though there are some memorable songs on the album, *A Kind of Hush* was less successful than previous records, peaking at number thirty-three in the US. It sold better in the UK and Japan, but it had an uneven quality, a sense of marking time. Quirky or more experimental tracks like "Goofus" and "Boat to Sail" sounded at odds with the sparkling ballads and their closing rendition of Neil Sedaka's "Breaking Up Is Hard to Do," complete with the musicians whistling, shouting, and laughing, had a comic insouciance that was in a league of its own. Maybe this was a way of saying sorry to Sedaka for their unseemly bust-up in Las Vegas the previous summer.

With the slight downturn in sales, Jerry Weintraub looked at how the band could revamp their career and decided it was time to revolutionize their stage show. Their previous tours had a straightforward, no-frills focus on Karen and Richard and the band playing the songs—which worked fine when they started, but by the mid-'70s big-name tours were becoming more like theatrical productions. Encouraging the Carpenters to create something arena-scale, Weintraub enlisted Broadway producer Joe Layton to work with Richard and Karen.

A gifted director and choreographer, Layton had already had success with stage shows for Bette Midler and Diana Ross and won an Emmy award for a Barbra Streisand TV special. The fact that Karen admired all these singers augured well for the production. Also, a groundbreaking new designer called Bill Whitten worked on their costumes. Starting with a small shop in West Hollywood in 1974 making custom shirts, within two years he employed fifty people and was doing stagewear for acts like the Jacksons. He went on to make Michael Jackson's famous rhinestone glove and crystal-encrusted socks, as a way of emphasizing the star's quick movements with his hands and feet. Whitten encouraged Karen to change her bulky, layered clothing to wear more fitted gowns. This caused a stir with her family, particularly Richard, who objected to her wearing outfits that emphasized her weight loss. "We had enormous problems about clothes, what seemed to be the bone of contention," said Layton, who sensed Karen's nervousness every time it came to a fitting.[6]

Though she felt self-conscious about her image, Karen entered into the spirit of the new show, a theatrical extravaganza that included five costume changes and a spoof 1950s segment where Richard roared on stage on a motorcycle and Karen dressed up with fake chest, bouffant wig and lipstick. "We're hams. We enjoy dressing up," Karen said, while Richard remarked, "Guess we're now trying to graft charisma onto our act." There was a comic Spike Jones–style reworking of

"Close to You," complete with kazoos and hooters and a rather unsettling moment during "We've Only Just Begun" where Karen and Richard held hands and looked lovingly into each other's eyes. Richard said that they "didn't love each other like that," but had responded to comments from people who'd seen previous shows. "Friends and managers said that it was ridiculous that we didn't touch each other throughout, so we put that in." It's quite a jump for a sibling act to go from no touching to holding hands, a gesture that, though meant to be humorous, came across as a little forced and odd.

The Carpenters were trying, however, and attracted large crowds and generally positive reviews for their tour, which started with postponed dates in Japan before snaking across the US through the summer and ending with the rescheduled European tour in November, visiting Germany, the Netherlands, and the UK. During preparations for the show one of the first things Layton said, like many before him, was that Karen "hid behind the drums." Once again her talent as an instrumentalist was being trivialized, as though the drums were a decorative prop rather than one of her primary means of expression.

As if in reaction to this, Karen found a striking way to assert herself. There was a section in the show when she changed into jeans and a T-shirt and really came alive, leaping around the stage, thwacking an array of drums and congas. Her T-shirt was emblazoned with the words "LEAD SISTER," a term that had popped up the previous year when a translation error in a Japanese magazine described Karen as "lead sister" rather than "lead singer." She loved the phrase, using it to communicate her musicianship. "Now we have incorporated into the show an entire seven- or eight-minute drum spectacular. It is just drums. I don't sing a note," she enthused. "We end up with twenty-three drums on stage . . . I love to play—I really do—and I love to sing, but I wouldn't want to give either one of them up."[7] With this section Karen displayed a mischievous fighting spirit, taking eight minutes to demonstrate to the world her drumming and *not singing a note*. She stepped into her role as the cool, capable sister that all the Carpenters' girl fans wanted her to be—equally as talented as her brother and equally as important. Their tour manager, Rebecca Segal, noticed here the complexity of Karen's musical statement. "Being a drummer is big, aggressive and hard-hitting. It's an emotive instrument," she says. "You are getting emotions out with those drums and you contrast that with Karen's silky voice. I always thought there was a kind of the duality in her that said 'Hear me, hear me!'"[8]

Critical reaction to the show was favorable, if a little bemused. "There's an air of desperation about the show—but at least it's a positive effort to blitz the audience with something beyond Carpenters music," wrote Ray Coleman in *Melody Maker*. *Variety*, meanwhile, praised the "slick staging" and said, "Karen Carpenter displays boundless energy and flair with her lengthy drum solo."

Karen's star turn was a breakout moment, part of her gradual bid for independence and an identity separate from the family. This became more apparent on the European leg of the tour, where the Carpenters were accompanied by their parents and also Richard and Karen's first-cousin, eighteen-year-old Mary Rudolph, who had joined as wardrobe assistant. Although she was the adopted daughter of Agnes's sister Bernice, she and Richard embarked on a relationship (and she was later to become his wife). No one in the family entourage remarked on Richard's new relationship—no one, that is, apart from Karen, who was furious at him dating her kid cousin. Their tour roadie Michael Lansing, for instance, observed that "no one said a word."[9]

In order to distract herself from the claustrophobic backstage atmosphere, Karen began to flirt with A&M's UK promotions officer, John "Softly" Adrian, and he responded. A former actor and model, Adrian was called "Softly" because he once appeared in British TV detective series *Softly Softly*. He also had a subtly seductive manner that appealed to Karen, and before long the pair of them were involved in a secretive affair. Karen was happy to break away from the entourage in snatched moments, like going on a limousine ride around the Scottish moors before the Glasgow date, or wandering around Portobello Road market in London.

As the romance grew, someone from the Carpenters' inner circle rang Derek Green, head of A&M UK, to say that Karen was becoming infatuated with his promotions guy and was thinking of inviting him back to Los Angeles. The conversation with Green turned into a kind of background check into Softly's motivations. Although he assured them that his colleague wasn't a gigolo, after he hung up the phone Green felt duty-bound to "buy off" Softly with a two-week holiday in the Caribbean, implying that if he continued his affair with Karen he wouldn't have a job when he got back.

Thinking this was an elaborate plan of Karen's to end the affair, Softly acquiesced and phoned her, saying that he didn't think their relationship would work, partly because he was a simple promotions guy and she was, well, Karen Carpenter. Both were engineered into finishing a blossoming romance—one that might have naturally fizzled out, given the geographical distance between them. The poignant thing about this episode is the lack of control that Karen had in the situation and the underlying assumption that she didn't have the strength or sophistication to know her own mind.

CHAPTER 12

1977

We didn't see *Star Wars* until we were mixing ["Calling Occupants of Interplanetary Craft"]. The [track] was an enormous undertaking, but from the time we started we couldn't wait to get back at it. We let other things slide "cos we were working on "Occupants." We kept thinking, *When will this thing be done?*[1]

On March 10, 1977, the Sex Pistols stood outside Buckingham Palace and publicly signed to A&M Records. During the after-party Johnny Rotten insulted executives, Steve Jones hooked up with a fan in the toilets, and Sid Vicious smashed a toilet bowl and trailed blood round the building. The band then recorded "God Save the Queen," an antimonarchist song that in the year of the royal Silver Jubilee went straight to the epicenter of the punk movement and became an alternative national anthem.

Twenty-five thousand copies of the single were pressed by A&M, but in the ensuing media outrage most of the Sex Pistols' tour with the Damned and the Clash was canceled and most copies were destroyed (only for the song to be released by their next label, Virgin, and go to number two in the UK charts). The Sex Pistols' relationship with A&M was short-lived and they were dumped after a week. A&M's John Deacon said, "Unfortunately the group's behavior since signing with the company compelled reconsideration of the situation."[2] Although the Sex Pistols departed, that signing set the tone and along with other punk and new wave signings like the Dickies and the Police, there was a new mood at the record label.

A&M video director Clare Baren shot videos with the Police for "Roxanne" and "Can't Stand Losing You" in a rough hand-held style before their set at the Whisky A Go Go in Los Angeles. She wanted to do something a little more experimental with the Carpenters, but felt that the band had already been type-cast. "The Carpenters weren't the biggest thing any more and things were passing them by. The industry was changing, too. Their songs were solid MOR love songs and their image was quaint. Thinking back, I wish I broke out of the mold more. I was always trying to make them feel comfortable and please them, but I think Karen really wanted to break out. I believe the label were not willing or interested in trying to make the Carpenters edgy, for fear they would look ridiculous. They had a place, a very successful place and to pretend that they were the Sex Pistols would've been a big mistake."

Chris Briggs, who was head of A&R at the label in the 1980s, says that A&M had a distinctive philosophy that allowed for both the Sex Pistols and the Carpenters to coexist. "Herb Alpert is a properly out-there member of the alternative society. He and Jerry Moss were entrepreneurial leaders and owners who cared what the artists thought and they wanted us to sign stuff that worked internationally. It was a lovely place to work—we socialized together and worked all hours and didn't mind." He says the Carpenters needn't have worried about the Sex Pistols. "I think that Malcolm McLaren set the whole thing up to get dropped. It was like a performance art stunt, I didn't feel there was a career there." According to Briggs, the fact that A&M had acts at two musical extremes shows their versatility. "It was a very eclectic roster. There was no intergenre snobbery and artists were given time to develop, not bullied to have hit singles."[3] With their next album, *Passage*, Richard and Karen were given space (and the budget) to reinvent themselves and 1977 proved to be one of their most experimental years.

At first Jerry Moss was keen for the Carpenters to try a new producer. *Horizon* and *A Kind of Hush* had stalled outside the top ten and he was concerned about the downturn in sales. "I was perfectly willing to let someone else take over my role; it would be a lot less work for me and I was not 100 percent myself," Richard said later.[4] In 1977, he was still struggling with sleeping pills and found it difficult to stay focused. A call went out, but the Carpenters had already established such a distinctive sound no one wanted to take on the role of producer. As a result, Richard carried on as producer but looked to other songwriters for a change of direction, and Karen helped by playing a key role as associate producer.

193

By this time, the Carpenters were a notable musicians' band, attracting dazzling players and arrangers, so that allowed room for exploration of different genres. A stand-out track on this album is "B'wana She No Home," a Latin funk song that shows how Karen, now aged twenty-seven, was maturing. It was no longer just about singing ballads piled high with harmonies; Karen could also perform sophisticated pop with a wry emphasis and a light touch. On this track the vocal arrangement was scored by Gene Puerling, founder of vocal groups the Hi-Lo's and the Singers Unlimited. He had also worked with jazz swing group the Manhattan Transfer and 1950s crooner Rosemary Clooney and he brought out a different side to Karen. In the song she plays the part of a wealthy recluse in Ecuador who has a servant instructed to say, whenever anyone comes to the door, "B'wana" (Sir or Madam), the mistress is not at home. In return the trusted servant is free to drive her car and spend her money. Playful and savvy, the song shows Karen branching out with ease into jazz soul and this laid the template for the sound she was to explore two years later as a solo artist.

Also featured on the album were characteristic Carpenters love ballads, such as the pared-down country-style song "Two Sides," where Karen sings with aching ambivalence from the point of view of a woman putting her lover on hold, too afraid to show her shadow self, the dark side. For Karen, who was still putting a lot of effort into denying or disguising her anorexia, the sentiment was apt. "She was a tiny little thing, but her looks didn't affect her pipes," recalls Jay Graydon, who played guitar on the track. "When she sang in the isolation booth it was like ear candy, she had the gift. She sounded like she came from the 1950s, she would have been a massive star back then, singing jazz standards. She had incredible pitch and control, as smooth as silk."[5]

He remembers the session as being friendly and "like a family." This is a hugely ambitious record—the Carpenters' version of "Don't Cry for Me, Argentina," for instance, involved the large Los Angeles Philharmonic Orchestra and a host of choral singers. Peter Knight was flown over from London, the British orchestrator and musical director who had worked on Scott Walker sessions in the 1960s and was famous for his elaborate, sensual orchestration on the Moody Blues album *Days of Future Passed*. Michael Boyle, a bassoon player with the London Philharmonic Orchestra, remembers Knight as a gifted, intuitive arranger. "He was the best of those BBC arrangers, very good at balancing the voicing and instruments and bringing out the best in artists," he says. "He was also very funny. I remember after one long recording session he said, 'Well done, everybody. Next time I'll get you in for some paid work!'"[6]

By 1977, Richard and Karen were at the center of the Los Angeles musicians' scene and managed to make their large-scale production work. According to Jay Graydon, what made many 1970s records special was the fact that they were made by a community of studio musicians used to listening and playing together on countless sessions. "In retrospect it was the most fun we ever had—sometimes twenty dates a week, it was like a drunkard's dream. We all had jazz backgrounds, we took it seriously and it was tight." An example of this is how he locked in with the drummer on sessions for *Passage*. "I know when Ed Greene plays sixteenth notes on a high hat he'll swing it just a little bit. I know from the downbeat of the song where we'll be in the groove and where his high hat's gonna be. By the third take you know you've got it." Gayle Levant agrees. "I don't think all of us realized what we were experiencing and the impact it would have for future generations. I hope it still does. Because we would run from one session to the next, all day long, all week long. And we just had such a good time."

With her intuitive phrasing, Karen was locked in with the musicians. She could also be an enigmatic presence and this was most evident on the album's epic song "Calling Occupants of Interplanetary Craft." Subtitled "The Recognized Anthem of World Contact Day," this piece of sci-fi pop was originally written by Canadian progressive space rockers Klaatu. Peter Knight turned the song into a symphony, conducting 160 orchestral musicians for the Carpenters' recording.

World Contact Day was a fictional event, a futurist leap into an imagined universe where humans were able to contact alien life forms. This topical theme was fueled by the blockbuster success of the film *Star Wars*, which opened while Karen and Richard were working on the track. "We didn't see *Star Wars* until we were mixing. In fact, we left it one night to go watch [the film], then right back to the studio," she said. Recording "Calling Occupants" fired up her imagination, and she spoke about looking for scripts and wanting to act. "Our all-time love is to do a college musical. It would be set in the 1970s. It would have modern technology plus a classic serial sci-fi approach."[7]

That futurist approach was apparent in the cover design for *Passage*, where the traditional Carpenters' logo was replaced with their name painted in swirling italics against abstract musical notes floating away from a stave. "It's like a horrible 1977 child's version of *Doctor Who*," says design historian Jon Wozencroft.[8]

The band's new direction worked well in Europe's pop market. Released as the lead single, "Calling Occupants" did well internationally, going to number one in Ireland and number nine in the UK, but it didn't make the top ten in the US, stalling at number thirty-two. Harold Childs, head of A&M promotion, observes: "There comes a time with every artist when radio gets tired of them. During that period it was difficult to get them on the radio, so they did more TV—that was a little easier."[9] Karen, who had worked closely with Childs, taking a deep interest in their marketing, was disappointed at their US sales. "We wanted to spread a little, but a lot of the time the public won't let you. It's strange, because as an artist you wanna grow, but you always have to keep upmost in your mind what your public wants from you," she said.[10]

Aware that the Carpenters had felt overworked by touring, during 1977 their manager Jerry Weintraub booked them onto a more leisurely circuit of suburban music fairs like Painters Hill in Maryland and Westbury Music Fair in Long Island, with extra dates in Lake Tahoe and Las Vegas. This only underlined their status as a lounge act for the older generation. That schedule may have been fine for Perry Como, but at twenty-seven and thirty-one respectively Karen and Richard were hardly ready to be pensioned off. That summer Karen's hero Elvis Presley died at his home of Graceland, in Memphis. "The King" was only forty-two, but in the seven years since he flirted with her backstage at Las Vegas he had changed beyond recognition, bloated by overeating and prescription drugs. His death symbolized the end of an entertainment era and if the Carpenters weren't careful they would be written off along with his generation of pop artists.

Despite their global popularity, critics had lambasted or laughed at the Carpenters for a few years, seeing them as hopelessly out of step with the trends at the time. "What are we gonna do with these two? Look, ain't saying I don't love 'em—they've always been one of my favorite swoontracks, especially with them so perverted looking and all," confrontational Detroit critic Lester Bangs wrote in 1973. "It's not even art, much less rock 'n' roll—it's more like a public service . . . they're wholesome as Wonder Bread in their tummies."[11] Throughout the decade the Carpenters created a musical space that was separate from the propulsive energy of genres and scenes springing up around them—from the progressive sounds of Yes, ELP, and Genesis to heavy-metal acts like Led Zeppelin, Black Sabbath, and Alice Cooper, to the brutal, grungy protopunk of the Stooges and the New York Dolls, or art pop glam like David Bowie and Roxy Music. They were accused of embodying polite white cultural values—the *NME*'s Nick Kent, for instance, dismissed the Carpenters as having a "thoroughly innocuous WASP-ish neutroid charm . . . the epitome of sterilized middle-America youth"— with limited reference points to black music and artists of color like Stevie Wonder or Marvin Gaye.[12]

In the cultural context of the time, pop music critique was undeveloped. Pop was seen as the province of teenage girls and gay men and therefore not taken seriously as an art form. Bruce Ravid, working in 1970s Los Angeles as an A&R and radio plugger, says that promotion was "extremely genre-specific." He was developing the newly emerging format of alternative rock, which was less about slavishly following mainstream top-forty sounds and more about letting DJs choose their own music. "I don't think there was a lot of love for the Carpenters. Nobody could argue about their integrity or her vocal power; they were incredible. But I wouldn't say there was any love left for them, not in this world. They were considered top forty and the whole top forty versus progressive alternative was very polarized back then."[13] Writer and music anthropologist Wendy Fonarow grew up in Los Angeles and remembers this period in a different way. "Every year, there was a countdown on the main radio station on Fourth of July weekend and every year Led Zeppelin's 'Stairway to Heaven' would win. I was appalled. Where were the Carpenters? Where was all this beautiful pop music? Masculinist music was always getting represented as cool. I remember thinking it was antiwomen," she says.[14]

In many ways, the Carpenters were out of step with their time, inventing a new pop language. As Clare Baren says, "I didn't know any other brother-sister act like them. It was a weird precedent and there was no playbook." Critics tended to read the band at face value, apart from odd, instinctive moments, like when Bangs hit on a nerve with his review of *Now & Then*, suggesting that there might be "grey clouds passing over Carpenterland because [Karen] manages to sound almost used in Leon Russell's 'This Masquerade.'"

Richard in particular was stung by the music press ridicule, but there was an appreciative audience that did get them and which was expanding. Younger fans who had read about the Carpenters in the pop press were now growing up. They were aware that there had been a gap when the band temporarily faded from the scene, but now they were doing something experimental and singing weird songs about space. It was no longer just the harmonic overlayered love songs—now they were singing about extraterrestrials. To many fans this seven-minute intergalactic opus was an inspired move. From Karen's echoing vocals to fairground rhythms, military brass, rock guitar, sweeping strings, and a celestial chorus, "Calling Occupants" was not so much a song as an event. And maybe the reason the song was so powerful was the cryptic clue that lay at its heart. Karen had disappeared for a while because of a mystery illness and now she was back. But was she back? As her voice drifted, disembodied, out into "the vast unknown," there was the sense that, on a personal level as well as to the wider world, Karen was floating further out of reach.

BOOK 5
Help

CHAPTER 13

1978

I just got tired out and was exhausted and lost too much weight. I ended up in bed for two months. I just needed some sleep. Every now and then people need to sleep! That's basically what it took, I just needed to relax.[1]

By 1978, Karen was living in the grip of anorexia but also in denial about its effect on herself and those around her. "Things started to change on tour. Karen wasn't healthy. When you travel with somebody you know a lot about them and we could tell she wasn't happy," says the Carpenters' drummer Cubby O'Brien. "She would complain about her fat stomach and yet she was getting thinner and thinner. She'd wear heavy clothes and cover up everything, so you couldn't see as much of her body."

Many musicians have struggled with alcohol and drug addiction and research shows a connection between anorexia and addiction. As Chris Briggs, a scout at Chrysalis in the 1970s before he joined A&M as A&R director, says, "I've worked with a lot of artists who've had dysfunctional upbringings and music is one way of healing that. The eating disorders are viewed in the same way as substance addictions. In the '70s when people didn't know much about this they thought AA was a religious cult and hadn't made the connections. Imagine if your drug of choice is available in Sainsbury's. You're not waiting for the dealer to turn up, it's on the shelf. It's easier for someone to cut themselves off from drugs and then recover, whereas if the source of your problems is in the fridge you can't get away from it."[2]

All the signs were there with Karen. According to psychiatrists Lauren Godier and Rebecca Park, the behavior of anorexia parallels the development of substance abuse, in a number of distinct phases.[3] Compulsive, ritualized behavior is central to anorexia—first there is the pleasurable, reward-seeking phase. For Karen, that was in the early days when she lost 20 pounds and people complimented her on a trim figure. There was a feeling of achievement, that she was fitting into a Twiggy-style model of success—or at least, on her way to achieving that look. Then, in the same way that a substance is taken in larger amounts and over a longer period than intended, she kept dieting and counting calories. She bought a hip-exerciser cycle, used it each morning and made sure it was packed in with the tour gear. She went out of her way to exercise regularly and restrict her food, because not to do so meant she and her body were out of control.

The next phase is when compulsive behaviors and craving and controlling the "high" increase over time. For Karen, this was the phase of shifting food around her plate, picking at salads and drinking iced tea while other band members heartily ate their burgers, never resting, waking herself in the middle of the night to write down by torchlight everything she needed to do the next day. Even though she was hungry, she could still perform; in fact she was driven by a burning energy and an empty stomach—what is described by some anorexics as an intoxicating "hunger high."

Once the behavior becomes all-consuming, however, there is "functional impairment" and a failure to fulfill responsibilities at work.[4] This point was reached in 1975, when Karen collapsed, was hospitalized, and had to postpone the European and Japanese tours. As the body becomes more malnourished the brain's cognitive abilities are affected, so the anorexic's self-concept becomes distorted. "I still have to lose weight," Karen said to her friend Elizabeth Van Ness after she came out of hospital.[5] The two of them were looking at her figure in the mirror. By then Karen had also developed body dysmorphia, seeing her arms and hips as hopelessly plump, while her appalled friend saw just skin and bones. Like a sufferer of substance abuse, Karen felt scared and unsafe when she wasn't denying herself food.

The last phase of addiction is when the disorder becomes a barrier to recovery and despite the need to intervene the behaviors become ingrained. Though everyone around her advised her to eat, Karen found ever more elaborate ways to avoid food. As her friend Nicky Chinn says, "A lot of people with mental illness, but in particular eating disorders, are very manipulative. And they really do it very, very well. Her business manager said, 'Karen was the most honest person I've ever met. Except when it came to her illness.' She manipulated everybody. Now that I look back, I can remember her shoving food to the side of her plate. Or saying, 'Would you like a taste?' All of these things to avoid eating, basically. And she just got thinner and thinner and thinner."

Carpenters tour manager Rebecca Segal remembers one evening after soundcheck when the band were in the food tent, having a meal before the show. "I'm watching her and everyone is talking and no one's really noticing. I'm thinking to myself, *She's not eating, she's just very talkative and animated and pushing food around on the plate making it look like she's eating.* I don't think I saw her take a bite of anything. At that point she had a doctor but he may not have known what clues to pick up on and what questions to ask."

Karen's appearance was disturbing, not just to her family and close friends but also to people she came into contact with during promotion or touring. In February 1978 "Sweet Sweet Smile," a cut from their album *Passage*, was a top-ten hit in the *Billboard* Hot Country chart, so the Carpenters did an interview with Nancy Naglin from *Country Music* magazine. Reflecting on that encounter twenty-two years later, Naglin wrote that Karen seemed enigmatic and detached. "I was struck by Karen's fragility . . . the translucent quality of her skin." In an effort to get the star to open up, Naglin asked Karen about her charm bracelet. Each charm meant something, a personal marker— like the little gold record that was a Christmas thank-you gift from A&M. "Dutifully enumerating them, she sounded like an emissary from a private world . . . Her unnerving ethereal presence haunted me," recalled Naglin.[6] Around this time Harold Childs saw Karen on the studio lot. "I thought, *Is she all right, is she sick?* She had lost a lot of weight and I didn't know why."

In the 1970s, there was a lack of discourse around mental health and eating disorders, which led to a culture of silence. Internalizing their disease as shameful, sufferers felt compelled to hide it, and that in turn made it harder to seek treatment or counseling. People around Karen could see that something was wrong, but did not know how to reach out to her and felt afraid to intervene. Karen's friend Cherry Boone O'Neill suffered anorexia at the same time and recalls feeling very isolated. "I remember I was struggling with it for probably a good five years before I read an article that described what I was going through and gave it a name. Even when my mom got me to a doctor he didn't say, 'You have an eating disorder called anorexia.' He just said, 'I've seen this kind of thing before. And if you don't start eating and putting weight on, we're going to have to put you in hospital and force-feed you.' The words 'anorexia' and 'bulimia,' even the term 'eating disorder,' were not a common part of people's vocabulary. It was not a part of public discourse at all," she says.[7]

As her anorexia took hold, Karen seemed to withdraw to a remote space where she was untouchable. Medical anthropologist Karen Ali writes about the concept of liminality, an in-between state of "indefinite temporality and undefined spatiality." It's a term usually applied in anthropology to delineate a rite of passage, where the initiand (usually a young person) is separated from society in preparation for rejoining it as an adult. The term also applies to people with chronic illness, cast in ambivalent suspension between the "healthy" and the acutely sick. Those suffering from eating disorders can live in that liminal space, creating an altered reality "through extremes of dietary restriction, bingeing and purging."[8] One former anorexic woman told me that just being focused on food and eating quietened her brain. "It subdues your feelings and you're drained and tired. It's a very pleasing form of power. People expect less of you, tiptoe around you. It keeps people away from your body, keeps the world at bay."[9]

After her breakdown in 1975, Karen would move in and out of this liminal world—there were periods when she was actively engaged with life, particularly when she was performing and recording, but then she would slip into patterns of anorexic behavior, particularly if she was under stress. As well as restricting food, one of her methods was the overuse of laxatives, a daily practice that she kept secret for as long as she could. Every so often her friends tried to help, but in relation to her anorexia Karen could be tricky to deal with, assuring them that there was no problem. Cubby O'Brien remembers how her female friends would rally round. "Dionne Warwick was a friend of hers. Olivia Newton-John, Petula Clark. They all stepped in and tried to convince her to see a doctor. She was very well liked among her peers, they cared for her and recognized how talented she was," he says.

But despite the concern of those close to her, Karen's need to create and maintain a private space became ever more demanding, and it also affected her romantic relationships. She had a pattern of dating people for six months to a year before finishing it and drifting on to the next suitor. After John "Softly" Adrian, however, Karen got together with someone with whom she had a realistic chance of a future and lasting happiness.

One day she was in a line of traffic near the A&M studios when she saw a man in a sleek chocolate brown Porsche convertible who looked like her friend Tom Bahler, the composer and arranger she had known since the Ford Maverick campaign in 1969. Suddenly he did an impatient U-turn and roared away from the traffic. This caught her attention, and later that day Bahler got a call from her secretary.

"Hi, I'm a secretary for Karen Carpenter."

"Oh, great," he said, thinking it was a prank call. "What's up?"

"Were you driving on La Brea this afternoon?"

"Yeah, at about 4:30."

"Did you hang a U in the middle of La Brea, in all that traffic?"

"That would be me."

"Well, Karen wants you to call her. Here's her private number."

An amused Bahler called Karen and the two of them met for coffee. Before long they were dating, spending a lot of time together in Beverly Hills drinking endless pots of coffee or whiling away hours at her condo in Century City just talking. "I had so many good times in that apartment because we would listen to music and we'd sing things together and tease each other. I'd say, 'You know, your pitch isn't as bad as Richie says.' We had a very loving, fun relationship," says Bahler.[10] One night when they were listening to the radio in his car, he learned the versatility of her vocal powers. The song "Lovin' You" came on, a record sung by soul legend Minnie Riperton in a four-octave range. Suddenly

Karen was singing right up there with Riperton's impossibly high whistle register.

"Holy moly!" exclaimed Bahler. "What is with you?"

"I've got a real large range."

"But you sing low on your records."

"Well, here's the deal. I studied up on every really popular woman singer and they all sang in the basement. So that's where I concentrated."

Bahler at that point was working as coproducer on the soundtrack of *The Wiz*, the 1978 film that was a reimagining of *The Wizard of Oz* with an African American cast starring Michael Jackson and Diana Ross. This work amplified for him how serious Karen was about her craft. "This was one of the things I loved about her. She was so smart, she was a researcher. So was Michael Jackson, by the way. Every great artist I know is a researcher of their genre. She wanted to know everything."

As they spent time together Karen and Bahler's relationship grew stronger. "The more we hung out the more we liked each other. I know she was comfortable with me because I was successful at what I did," recalls Bahler. "I didn't have Carpenter money but I was fine, I had my own money. Her family was very diligent and worried about somebody trying to take advantage of them, so I kind of passed that test." Their relationship was progressing so well that Bahler took a week off from recording *The Wiz* and they went on holiday to Hawaii with Richard and his on-off girlfriend Mary, staying in a luxurious suite in the Kahala resort in Honolulu. This was when he first became aware of her eating disorder. "When I first met Karen in 1969 she wasn't a thin girl but she was very attractive, with a beautiful personality. In Hawaii she came to the hotel pool in a bikini and she looked like she was from Biafra. It didn't turn me off, but it turned my concern off the charts." Bahler was shocked. By then he and Karen shared a lot and she had been honest with him about Richard's challenges with prescription drugs. He had supported Karen in talking about her brother's problems, but sensing she was in denial about her eating, he felt unable to discuss her own issues. "I was thinking, *Oh my God, but this isn't your business to talk to her about this.* So I just played like I didn't notice and said, 'You look great in that.'"

Bahler was falling for Karen, yet his instinct was to let the relationship develop slowly and to be supportive without confronting her head-on about the anorexia. Richard, however, was becoming more and more worried about his sister. Back in Los Angeles he pulled Bahler aside and asked him a favor. "Hey, man, I'm so glad that you and Karen are together, she listens to you."

"Well, thank you. We got a good thing going."

"You know she's got an eating problem."

"Yes, yes, I'm aware."

"Would you try something for me? Because I don't think she's gonna get mad at you. Take her out to dinner. And would you try saying, 'We're not leaving this table "til you eat'?"

"Really?"

Bahler found the idea very unappealing, but trusted that Richard knew Karen better than him and decided to try and help. The next time they went out to dinner, toward the end of the meal, Bahler asked Karen to finish her food. "We're not leaving until you're finished."

"Really?"

"I'm not the only one that's concerned about your eating. So will you do this for me, please? I don't care how long we stay. I'm with you, as long as I'm with you, I'm okay."

Karen ate and didn't make a fuss. But although she finished the food on her plate in the restaurant, she felt cornered about her anorexia and later on that made her aggressive.

"We got back to her apartment," recalls Bahler. "And she went into the bathroom, left the door open and threw up. She came out on the verge of defiance and said, 'See, you can't make me.'"

Bahler then realized the depth of her problem. "The next day I called Richie and I said, 'Man, okay, I tried it. This is what happened. I would hope not to be put in that position again. I care for her and I'll do anything. But that didn't work.' That was a tough point."

Despite that incident, Bahler and Karen's relationship continued to grow until it was clear to both of them that marriage might be a possibility. She said to him, "You know where this is leading, don't you? And are you okay with that?" Feeling that Karen was the woman for him, Bahler said that he was on board, that he wanted to be with her. "Finally she said, 'I need to know if you have any secrets. And I'll tell you right now that I don't have any.' She implied in so many words, *If you're dealing with me, you're dealing with my family*," says Bahler.

The only problem was Bahler had a daughter from a previous relationship. When he started dating Karen, that affair had been over for ten years and he and the mother were just friends. After he told Karen this, she went very quiet, said she needed time to think and asked him not to call. Three weeks later she contacted him and they went for a drive before pulling into the car park at A&M to talk. Karen was almost shaking as she said, "I haven't really had a night's sleep in three weeks. I don't know what to do with this. My mom is worried that your daughter's going to come along and want to get her hands in our pockets."

"I'm very sorry, I could take that as an insult. I appreciate her protecting you, but those are strong words. I know my daughter and her mother would never do that."

"Well, I just can't go forward with this."

"You know what? I appreciate the way you're handling this," said Bahler. "You and I have been friends for ten years and we're still friends."

Bahler remembers the break-up as amicable ('I loved her ever since she was a teenager, I understood'), because he knew deep down that it would be fruitless for him to take a stand against Karen's family. But in capitulating to her mother, Karen once again cut off a potential avenue for happiness and fulfillment. Agnes sowed seeds of doubt, which fueled Karen's tendency to flee when people's flawed reality didn't match the idealized, perfect relationship she had in mind. This meant shutting down possibilities to have the family she desperately wanted. As Sylvia Plath wrote with devastating clarity in her poem "The Munich Mannequins," "Perfection is terrible, it cannot have children."[11] Cherry Boone O'Neill is frank about that anorexic desire for perfection. "Anytime you have a bar of perfection that you're shooting for, you're always going to be disappointed. The thing about being a perfectionist is, you are always measuring yourself (and other people) by the impossible. So you're constantly seeing failure, how you're falling short."

In contrast to her fluctuating romantic relationships, the working rapport Karen had with Richard was constant, the one thing that seemed secure. In an interview she said that each of them would like to find a marriage partner but busy schedules made it difficult to date people. "We have so much to give and we've accomplished a lot on our own. It would be nice to share it with somebody [but] at this point, we're just sharing it with each other."[12]

In 1978, her brother was entering his own liminal, spaced-out world. Richard's addiction to sleeping pills had worsened and, despite a short stint in a detox unit in late 1977, he found it almost impossible to stop taking Quaaludes. His whole day was dominated by fighting the withdrawal symptoms of slurred speech, panic attacks, and shaking hands, counting down the hours to when he could go home or back to the hotel room to take more pills and sleep. He was taking up to twenty-four pills a night, in doses of six at a time. The addiction affected Richard's playing, so he began to lose confidence and drop from the Carpenters' set songs that involved more complicated piano sections. Though the band's live dates during 1978 were restricted to just a few residencies in Lake Tahoe and Las Vegas, by September he was even overwhelmed by that. On September 4, 1978, just five days into a two-week engagement, Richard announced to the band and the crew that he was quitting.

Walt Harrah, a session singer who had joined the tour, noted that both Richard and Karen seemed aloof, alone, and depressed. When he made the decision to quit, Richard thought that the Carpenters would tour again when he had recovered, but that was to be their last major concert. The band were dismayed. As Tony Peluso remarked, "This whole giant career ended like that—boom, in the middle of a season."[13] Peluso, Gary Sims, and Bob Messenger received severance pay and money for a pension plan, as acknowledgment of their past eight years of work, companionship, and loyalty.

Karen was subdued and quiet after that final Las Vegas date—she had already tried to help Richard. In 1976, she had approached Norman Weiss, the president of Jerry Weintraub's company, to say that she was worried about her brother's reliance on sleeping pills. At that point it wasn't affecting his performance, but now it was. The band were due to play one more show, a benefit on December 3, 1978, for the Carpenters Choral Scholarship Fund at their old alma mater, California State University. They were on the bill with Frank Pooler's choir and the university orchestra, so it was an emotionally charged event. According to the student paper, the *49er*, the show built momentum with the performance of Pooler's choir but the Carpenters' appearance at the end came across as anti-climactic, as predictable as a "Las Vegas lounge act." Because of his symptoms of anxiety and his shaking hands, Richard had cut most of the material from their show, just about managing an odd, lackluster medley of themes from *Close Encounters of the Third Kind* and *Star Wars*, while Karen had to rescue it with

215

her rendition of "Ave Maria" from their forthcoming album, *Christmas Portrait*.

The following week the Carpenters were due to fly to London to appear on the prime-time TV show *Bruce Forsyth's Big Night*, to promote *Christmas Portrait* and their new compilation, *The Singles 1974–1978*. Richard, however, could hardly get out of bed and refused to make the trip, telling Karen that the promotion could wait. Adamant that they had to honor their commitment, Karen decided to go on her own with the live band. In a manner both single-minded and singularly in denial about her own health issues, Karen planned to keep going and keep up appearances for as long as she could. As soon as the plane landed in the UK she was doing interviews, apologizing for Richard and saying he had the flu and batting off enquiries about her health, saying, "I've got my energy back and I'm raring to go!"

The trip to London was pivotal for Karen, the moment she began to see the possibilities for herself as a solo artist. It seemed to galvanize her out of her detached state. She was a witty, gracious presence on *Bruce Forsyth's Big Night*, ripping through "Please Mr. Postman" and singing a very personally expressive version of "I Need to Be in Love." Dressed in white silk trousers and a red shirt shot through with gold thread, she looked perilously thin but animated at the same time. When Karen finished, the audience response was so rapturous she was visibly moved, tears welling in her eyes.

She had a quickfire exchange with Forsyth. A vaudevillian comedian of the old school, Forsyth was a cheeky gentleman who liked to banter with his guests, keeping it just the right side of risqué. Karen rose to the challenge, enjoying the chat and engaging him with charm. The pair of them duetted on a Christmas medley that included renditions of "Winter Wonderland" and "White Christmas." Karen's performance went down so well that immediately after the show there were rumors of a Carpenters split. She worked quickly to dispel the speculation, telling the *Sun* newspaper that she had no plans to go solo. However, it was clear that though Richard was incapacitated back in Los Angeles, she still had the energy to work. *Christmas Portrait* was a very important record for her; it was one that mattered to her personally and one that Richard now describes as "her first solo album."

Christmas Portrait is an extraordinary release, with a long, winding history. It emerged in August 1977 when Karen and Richard were filming *The Carpenters at Christmas*, their second TV special for ABC. The siblings had always loved Christmas—the feeling of being cosy with the family went right back to their New Haven days when as children they would listen to Spike Jones's *Xmas Spectacular* LP, a riotous mixture of exuberant parody, souped-up Christmas carols and gentle reflection.

The Carpenters wanted to record something with a similar spirit and as the TV special took shape, they decided to put those songs on an album, due to be released at the same time as the December '77 broadcast. "Spike was a massive actor. People don't know that it takes more talent and perfection to pull off crackpot things than it does to do serious things. Spike was the best. His album was a combination of nutty and serious. We grew up with that album and loved it to death. And got around to doing this album, which we've wanted to do for nine years," Karen explained.[14]

The sessions for *Christmas Portrait* took longer than expected and grew in size and ambition. Richard was battling his addiction at the time, so he enlisted Peter Knight for the orchestral arrangements, along with Billy May, the composer-arranger who had worked on classic albums with Nat King Cole, Frank Sinatra, and Peggy Lee. Karen was delighted to be singing with an eighty-piece orchestra and seventy-voice choir—this fed into a sense of Christmas wonder that was childlike in its intensity. In the same way that she collected fluffy toys for her bedroom, Karen loved collecting Christmas songs and carols and couldn't get enough of them. "I enjoy doing this type of music all year round," she said, enthusiastically recording between breaks in touring over a period of fourteen months. "People were . . . saying, 'Why in heaven's name are you doing Christmas stuff in the middle of August?' It never occurred to me [that it was strange] because I could do it any time of the day or night, any time of the year."

There is naiveté in the way that Karen, at the age of twenty-eight, was still attached to Christmas and cuddly toys, and friends remarked on her guileless innocence. On one level it's clear that a possessive mother made it difficult for her to grow up, but a key part of anorexia is arrested development. Sufferers experience delayed emotional maturity and can get psychologically stuck at the age they developed their eating disorder. Harvard psychiatrist David Herzog notes that many sufferers try to avoid teenage experimentation or uncontrolled behavior like dabbling in drugs or casual sex or being lazy and not achieving the right grades. "They believe there's no room for wrong. For some reason, wrong is unbearable," he says.[15] Karen did not want to disobey or defy her mother and therefore didn't allow herself to experiment. Her friend Paul Williams said that she needed to escape from her family and her own self-imposed strictures. "Part of her needed to run out of there . . . kick the locks off a lot of doors . . . Part of me wanted to snatch her out of it and say, 'Let's go raise hell, Karen; let's go do something that we'll be horribly embarrassed about in the morning.'"[16]

Her delayed maturity could be dated back to when she was seventeen, when she began performing and was being scrutinized by audiences and record companies and the family doctor put her on the Stillman diet. Or it could go back further to when she was thirteen and the family moved 3,000 miles to an apartment on the wrong side of the tracks in Downey, a small, suburban California town where she knew nobody and had to make a whole new set of friends. Memories of snug Christmases in Connecticut, of sledding and snowballing with schoolfriends Debbie and Joe Vaiuso, were idealized pictures that could give her comfort. No wonder it felt safer to retreat to the rituals of childhood when the world became stressful. Karen said that if ever she was in a bad mood or upset, she would put on their Christmas album. "That'll bring me to tears. Songs like that can shake you up, "cos they're so gorgeous."

Eventually released in October 1978, *Christmas Portrait* was packed with seventeen tracks (unusual for an LP at the time, when ten songs was the average). The mood spanned traditional carols sung with 1940s-style Hollywood schmaltz, to brisk, jaunty versions of "Sleigh Ride" and "Winter Wonderland," performed with the same verve as the Ronettes and Darlene Love did on the 1963 Phil Spector production *A Christmas Gift for You*. Most effective, though, was Karen's bluesy, almost gospel interpretation of "Little Altar Boy" and the J. S. Bach–Charles Gounod version of "Ave Maria." The latter sounds almost chilling, the toy piano introduction contrasting with Karen's grand, bravura delivery. Here she sings like an operatic diva, as if tapping into something deep and troubled within. There is also "Merry Christmas, Darling," the song that connects Karen to Frank Pooler, her old voice teacher and mentor. He wrote the lyrics as a lovestruck eighteen-year-old and asked Richard to add the music in 1966 when he and Karen sang in his Cal State choir. Ever since the song was released in 1970 it has been a hit in America each Christmas.

In December 1977, they had tested out their Christmas set with a spectacular show in Las Vegas's MGM Grand. "The casino is the size of a football field. Somehow it worked—everyone was in terrific Christmas spirit . . . it was a pleasure," recalled Karen.[17] But by the following year that spirit had evaporated. When she came back from London, Richard was in a dire mood and she still had to face the eating disorder that was drastically affecting her health. Their usual cozy family Christmas was blighted by tension and bickering; they had become a family torn by crisis. Karen kept telling Richard that he needed to go into rehab, while he retorted that she needed to eat. "She had every right to be mad at me," Richard said. "Trouble is she was no example of how to deal with a problem." By the new year, it was clear that the siblings both needed treatment if they, and the band, were to survive.

CHAPTER 14

1979

I think the record industry can handle anything that is put in front of them. They don't fall short of anything. This business is confronted with new things every hour.[1]

A concerned Karen arranged a meeting with Richard, A&M lawyer Werner Wolfen and Jerry Weintraub and, while they were all sitting in the latter's office, Richard fell asleep in the chair. "Either sit there and kill yourself or deal with it," Weintraub said sternly. Their manager's brusque treatment of Richard is in stark contrast to how powerless the Carpenters' team felt about Karen's disease in the face of her airy denial that she had a problem. "I couldn't do anything about it . . . nothing seemed to work for Karen," said Weintraub.[2] He did not know how to tackle her eating disorder, but at least there was a tried and tested treatment model for Richard's addiction.

Jolted into action by Weintraub's tough words, he agreed to go into rehab, so on January 10, 1979 Karen and Wolfen took him by rented Learjet to Menninger's chemical dependency unit in Topeka, Kansas. Karen and Wolfen stayed one night in a nearby Holiday Inn, leaving Richard at the center in a spartan room with no TV. Far away from sunny Los Angeles, Richard found himself isolated in a wintry Kansas that was dark and desperately cold at 20 degrees below zero. He said later that it was one of the most difficult periods of his life. In the ensuing days, however, the therapy sessions and companionship he found with other residents helped him explore his addiction issues and rebuild his confidence.

Like Karen, he suffered from anxiety, only they dealt with it in different ways. Her way of coping with stress was to keep busy to the point of hypermania, while he had self-medicated into sluggish mental oblivion. Karen was unsure how long he would need to stay in rehab and that sent her into a panic. "It was okay for a little bit, but then I was anxious to go back to work," she said.[3] Her comment shows an impatience and only a passing regard for Richard's welfare—maybe because it felt too threatening to stop and reflect on her own difficulties. To acknowledge the depth of his distress meant that she would have to recognize they were both in crisis.

Karen's UK trip had empowered her with a sense of independence, so after Richard went to Kansas she took a more active role in Carpenters affairs, frequently going into their office at A&M. Alan Oken had just joined the label in the department of Artist Development and he remembers Karen as being very much at home and in charge. He spent a day with her recording promotional messages for the National Association of Recording Merchandisers (NARM), a high-profile industry organization that held a conference every year. "At that point she was in the upper echelons of stardom. She didn't need that much direction, she handled it and was rockin' on her own. She was a smart cookie," he says.[4] Entranced by the atmosphere at the label, Oken says that with the movie lot, A&M's soundstage and the recording studios, "there was an overall sense that something cool was going on. I'd come to work in the morning and hear Herb Alpert playing his horn, hear it wafting over the lot. I saw Dylan one day, Bruce Springsteen the next. Once I was sitting in my office, looking over the edge of the balcony and there was Springsteen in his car, listening to music he had just made." Karen was clearly comfortable in this environment and when she worked with Oken she kept him and the engineer engaged, telling jokes and posing riddles. "She was light and bouncy and fun," he said. "But, boy, she was thin!"

Despite her emaciated state Karen kept on driving herself forward. The previous year when radio presenter Bill Moran asked about the Carpenters' career in the US, she had said, "It's a very touchy question to us . . . if somebody would just let us know what the problem is. We don't know what top-forty radio is looking for."[5] Dismayed at their downturn in sales, she began to explore other options, intrigued with the possibility of a new audience—after all, she said, "this business is confronted with new things every hour."

With Richard in rehab, Karen decided to record her own solo album, an idea she had been considering for a while. She figured that didn't mean the end of the Carpenters as a band, because her solo work left room for Richard to score a film or produce other artists. As well as offering something new to the fans, Karen wanted recognition among her peers as a solo performer. She noted the transformation in her good friend Olivia Newton-John, who the previous year had astronomical success with a starring role in the musical *Grease*. Playing Sandy Olsson, an Australian high-school transfer student who has a summer romance with John Travolta's greaser Danny Zuko, Newton-John made a dramatic transformation from goody two-shoes to a vision in leather and skin-tight Spandex. That image is immortalized in the video for "You're the One That I Want," a duet with Travolta that became a global number one. Until that point, Newton-John had been languishing in the country and adult contemporary charts; *Grease* catapulted her to global stardom. Inspired by the film's phenomenal success, Newton-John reinvented herself for her tenth studio album, *Totally Hot*, dressed in leather for the album cover and singing songs with a funky rock edge. This sparked Karen's innate sense of competition—maybe *she* could explore a new direction?

Karen also noted the number of women singers—from Dory Previn, Barbra Streisand, and Diana Ross to Anne Murray and Linda Ronstadt—who were getting Grammy awards, while she had not yet received one, at least not as a female vocalist. It was time for her to try. Two weeks into his rehab, Karen paid Richard a visit and broached the subject, telling him she wanted to make a solo album. He reacted with fury. Worried about her working without him and also concerned about her health, Richard suggested that instead she needed to go to a specialist center like him and get treatment for her anorexia. "I don't have anorexia, I have colitis," she responded, feeling browbeaten by him, trying to avoid thinking about her eating disorder and the implications that had for her future.

Although outwardly Karen put on a brave front, privately she knew she had to get help in conquering her illness. She asked Frenda Leffler about treatment and the latter contacted a few psychiatrists in Beverly Hills who specialized in eating disorders. Karen went to a number of appointments, but each time her nerve failed and she insisted that Leffler go in the room with her. Unsurprisingly, these consultations led nowhere.

Then one day Cherry Boone O'Neill's mother Shirley saw Karen at an event and knew by looking at her that she was struggling with an eating disorder. "My mom told Karen that I had moved away and gotten help and that I had just had a baby, all of this great stuff. So she gave Karen my phone number," says O'Neill, who was writing a book about her recovery from anorexia. Immediately Karen contacted O'Neill for advice and O'Neill became an ally and confidante. "[Karen] knew that she had a kindred spirit, that I wasn't going to judge her," she recalls. Both women were prone to perfectionism, both had overprotective families, and both relied on excessive dieting and exercise.

Karen knew she had to deal with her anorexia and her addiction to laxatives, but was finding it hard to stop the obsessive behaviors and her ritual purging of food. O'Neill's book *Starving for Attention* gives a glimpse into the private hell of an eating disorder and a sense of what Karen must have been going through. At thirteen years old, O'Neill discovered Eskatrol in the family medicine cupboard, her mother's amphetamine-based diet pills. At first they suppressed her appetite and gave her euphoria and the energy to keep to an obsessive exercise regime. After her family confiscated the diet pills she relied on laxatives, building up the dosage until she was taking sixty at a time, because ingesting a whole box meant she could discard the evidence. O'Neill suffered anorexia over ten years, going through periods of recovery and relapse, bingeing and purging between concert tours, traveling, and recording. She pulls no punches in her book, detailing the effects of laxative use—the soiled bed linen and soggy mattresses, the diarrhea, low-grade fever, nausea, dehydration, sunken eyes, and hollowed cheeks. But it all seemed worth it when she could look in the mirror and see what she wanted to see. "My body image determined my self-esteem. No fat, no flab equalled no fear, no failure," she wrote.[6]

In 1979, O'Neill was happily married and in recovery, but Karen was still caught in the "no flab, no failure" mindset. She was convinced that social acceptance and success was tied to controlling her weight. As the feminist author Susie Orbach wrote in *Hunger Strike*, "Anorexia is an attempted solution to being in a world from which one feels excluded . . . the craved-for self-esteem is elusive. It is almost impossible to consolidate."[7] O'Neill had given up showbusiness and moved away from Los Angeles to Oregon to seek therapy and recover, but Karen had no intention of leaving her singing career behind. Her focus was now on recording her ambitious solo album and she was brimming with ideas. Initially there was a lot of support for the project—both Herb Alpert and Jerry Moss thought it was a good proposal, as did Weintraub. While Carpenters record sales slowly declined, there was a feeling at the label that something else could be done with Karen's magical voice. As Derek Green, head of A&M UK, put it, "Wouldn't we do better with her alone?"[8]

Alpert suggested Phil Ramone as producer, who in 1977 had produced Billy Joel's *The Stranger*, a punchy, charged satirical album that, along with the Grammy-winning *52nd Street*, had catapulted Joel to huge chart success. Ramone had also produced Paul Simon's *Still Crazy After All These Years*, which in 1976 won Grammys for Album of the Year and Best Male Vocal Pop Performance. Ramone was a skilled producer renowned for his ability to coax dynamic performances from artists as varied as Aretha Franklin and Bob Dylan. His working methods were very different to Richard's, with emphasis on raw energy and live spontaneity in the studio. Karen was happy to work with Ramone and met the producer at his duplex in Beverly Hills. He also visited her apartment in Century City and was very amused to hear the first few notes of "We've Only Just Begun" chiming as her doorbell.

Karen flew to New York on February 16 for further meetings, where they listened to songs and demos and discussed the musical direction of the album. She was as keen as him to try something fresh and different, exploring funkier textures and more mature lyrics. "We pride ourselves in being trendsetters for the easier listening sound [but] we were knocked for being dressed cleanly, for taking a bath," Karen said, aware that what the Carpenters had once pioneered now restricted them. She assumed that Ramone would come to Los Angeles and record at A&M Studios with their usual band of top-flight session musicians, but he persuaded her to travel to New York instead and change her approach. Determined to make this happen, Karen sank $400,000 of her own money into the project. She was very nervous about working separately from Richard, but knew this was her bid for musical freedom. All her close friends agreed. "Doing something out of the family was important, a show of strength, of independence," said Olivia Newton-John.

*

After six weeks at Menninger's, Richard had recovered enough to come back to Los Angeles. However, he was not ready to work and knew he needed extended time off and to get away from stressful situations that had made him ill in the first place. He traveled, visited friends, and lived for a while in Long Beach with Gary Sims and Dennis Strawn, brother of Doug. While on his break Richard felt that, despite her protestations, Karen wasn't strong enough to record an album on her own and he also saw her solo project as a kind of treachery. Werner Wolfen told him firmly that it wasn't treachery but an opportunity. "Why should her career wait on you?" he said. "When you're ready to do a great album, she'll be there."[9]

Jerry Weintraub approved the solo project, but he was worried about Karen's health issues. Watching a talk show one night he was impressed by a guest called Steven Levenkron, a 38-year-old therapist in New York City who specialized in eating disorders and who was promoting *The Best Little Girl in the World*, a novel about anorexia. Levenkron had been doing clinical work since 1970 and had developed an expertise in helping young people overcome their mental health issues to lead healthy, productive lives. Thinking that he might be the ideal person to treat Karen, Weintraub got in touch with Levenkron. After the TV appearance, the therapist had received an avalanche of calls from parents anxious about their daughters—little was known about anorexia and eating disorders then, much less methods of treatment or indeed that it could affect boys as well—so it was a few days before Levenkron returned his call. Weintraub explained that his client was Karen Carpenter and they were afraid for her health. Levenkron had a full schedule, handled all his patients equally and did not give celebrity clients special treatment. In fact, he preferred not to work with celebrities because they were often resistant to making the necessary lifestyle changes to get better. He told Weintraub that Karen needed to speak to him directly if she wanted treatment.

Karen knew she had to convince people that she was strong enough to work on a solo project, so when Weintraub suggested she get in touch with Levenkron, she agreed. During a meeting on March 27 with Richard and Weintraub at the management office, she rang Levenkron. She was wily, however, moving out of earshot to make the call, telling the therapist that her problem was colitis, not anorexia. "Everything I eat just flows right out of me and that's why I'm skinny," she asserted. Knowing that he could not force Karen to pursue treatment and reluctant to take on someone so resistant, Levenkron said briskly, "Well, go and see a GI [gastrointestinal] specialist."[10]

After the call Karen lied to Weintraub and Richard, claiming that Levenkron told her she was not anorexic. Like many anorexia sufferers, subterfuge was automatic for Karen, a way of controlling her world and an eating disorder that, while it made her ill, paradoxically also helped her feel safe. Although skeptical, Richard and Weintraub were pleased she had made the call—that in itself was a step forward. They were also reassured when she checked herself into Cedars-Sinai hospital for a few days of tests and rest. That gave them the impression she was no longer in denial and that she was committed to eating and getting healthy again. In reality, it was a tactical way of ensuring that the recording sessions would go ahead and that no one would block her trip to New York.

Once out of hospital, Karen started packing all her suitcases with color-matched satin shoes and jackets, ready to take with her to New York and the sessions with Phil Ramone. Although she desperately wanted to record her solo album, she felt unanchored without her brother's blessing. After all their years of working together she was scared to venture out on her own and needed to feel that the project was sanctioned by him. On April 30, she telephoned him in Long Beach and started to cry. "I can't do this without your support," she mumbled through tears. Reluctantly, Richard told her to go ahead. "Just promise me one thing," he said before she put the phone down. "Don't do disco."

On May 1, Karen flew to New York, took up residence in a suite at the Plaza Hotel on 5th Avenue, and began having production meetings with Ramone, whittling down the songs and planning a recording schedule. Although they had a good working rapport, her fancy midtown location wasn't the most conducive for thinking about or creating music. The suite was luxurious, with views of the Manhattan skyline, but it was a little impersonal and hugely expensive. After two weeks Ramone and his girlfriend Karen Ichiuji suggested Karen would be more at home staying in their large house in the quaint upstate town of Pound Ridge. The two Karens bonded immediately and Karen Carpenter came up with a nickname for her new friend, shortening her surname to "Itchie." Though tonally less than racially sensitive in the twenty-first century, the name reflected Karen's enthusiastic wish to forge a friendship that made her feel secure.

Karen moved all her suitcases into Ramone's home in Pound Ridge, excited to begin a new period of experimentation with her sound and style. "Our house became this big musical commune," said Itchie.[11] When listening to demos with Ramone, Karen would enthuse about disco, gravitating toward tracks that were explicit and sensual. Once, on the daily 43-mile commute into Ramone's studio in Manhattan, she expressed interest in a song that was overtly sexual. Ramone rejected it, saying that it would come across as inauthentic. "Well, that's what I would really like to sing," Karen replied. At twenty-nine years old, she was discovering her sense of autonomy and desires as a woman and wanted to make a record reflecting that new reality. She was tired of being marketed as asexual and square—as the *Chicago Sun-Times* reviewer wrote, "the girl next door you'd never peek over the fence at." Inspired by the driving pulse of disco, she was also determined to change her musical style.

Disco as a genre emerged from the dancefloors of the black and gay club scenes and became a music of liberation, signaling an era of creative freedom for LGBTQ artists, female performers, and people of color.[12] Songs of self-declaration and sexual empowerment, like Diana Ross's "I'm Coming Out," Cher's "Take Me Home" and "Why" by Carly Simon, revolutionized the sound of many female stars. "The 1970s disco era was an incredible time for me. Everyone wanted to dance and be happy and feel release. It was that moment of realization of our power and letting people know 'I'm here to stay and my voice needs to be heard,'" recalls Stephanie Spruill, who was to sing backing vocals on the Carpenters' 1981 album *Made in America* and whose powerful soprano graces classic records like Donna Summer's "Hot Stuff" and Gloria Gaynor's "I Will Survive." "In the past, whether it was surviving abuse or just being a woman—they didn't want our voices to be heard. That was changing by the 1970s, with women like Gloria Steinem and Maya Angelou speaking out. We were standing on the shoulders of all the great women who spoke truth to power."[13]

The burgeoning women's liberation movement of the 1970s was an exciting, revolutionary force, prompting a change in consciousness. More and more women were delaying marriage and motherhood to further their education or pursue careers. But the fight for equality threatened the status quo, leading to feminists being branded in the media as strident, men-hating "women's libbers." Like many women who were new to the concept of feminism, Karen couldn't see past the ball-breaker stereotype and was wary of declaring political support for the women's movement. At the same time she was strong-willed and forth-right and had never let the fact she was a woman hold her back in her music, either as a vocalist or as a drummer. She loved the unfettered energy of singers like Donna Summer and the mes-sage of self-determination in their music. Her decision to cut free from the safe haven of A&M studios in Los Angeles to record an album in New York, the home of disco, showed a yearning to stretch herself as an artist, even though it was very challenging for her. "I was scared to death . . . I basically knew one producer, one arranger, one studio, one record company and that was it," she said.[14]

In 1979, New York was smelly, dirty, and crime-ridden, with side streets piled high with rubbish and subway cars covered in graffiti. The live sex shows, X-rated videos, and porn cinemas of 42nd Street spilled out onto surrounding blocks in Manhat-tan. The city was precarious, paranoid, and on the edge of bank-ruptcy, but artists and musicians flocked there because of cheap rents to create a vibrant, restless arts scene.

At that point, New York had a very distinct musical identity. DJ Larry Levan span an explosive dance mix every weekend at Paradise Garage, the Danceteria had just opened, playing new wave videos and British post-punk alongside funky freestyle sounds, while drag performers stalked through the Pyramid Club in the East Village and the Mudd Club in Tribeca featured underground cabaret and an art gallery curated by Keith Haring. And a young Madonna had arrived in the city, practicing ska pop with her first band, the Breakfast Club, by day and dancing in the clubs all night. To be in New York at that time was like getting a shot of adrenaline, akin to sticking one's fingers into an electric socket.

Rob Mounsey, one of the key arrangers on Karen's solo album, describes the New York sound as "more high energy and less manicured than LA . . . more chaotic, rougher and more anarchic."[15] A graduate of Boston's Berklee College of Music, Mounsey arrived in the city in 1976 and quickly built up experience as a session musician and arranger, working with artists such as Diana Ross, Cissy Houston, Roberta Flack, and jazz trumpeter Tom Browne. "1979 felt like a very vibrant time in the business. I was really lucky to be in New York, there was a lot of work for musicians, performers, writers and producers," he recalls. "Everyone was making a record and people were making money making records. There was a very busy studio scene— you'd see a crowd of about 200 people working every day in different studios and there were a lot of clubs. I was a hired musician who helped make a lot of those records."

The year 1979 was a key one for irrepressible records including Anita Ward's "Ring My Bell," McFadden & Whitehead's "Ain't No Stoppin' Us Now," Sister Sledge's "He's the Greatest Dancer" and, of course, jazz funk classics like "Rise," the number-one hit by Karen's A&M boss Herb Alpert. Blondie were also riding high, mixing new wave and disco with "Heart of Glass." Karen was listening to these hits and also admired the way the Bee Gees had reinvented themselves. "As an artist you wanna grow. Look at the Bee Gees. They were cookin', but then had a cold spell, cube city. Until they went disco and now they're hot as a pistol," she enthused. "That's a gift that the Bee

Gees have, they can go in any direction you point "em."[16] Karen wanted to explore a funk and soul sound, one she had already captured so accurately on the Carpenters' 1977 track "B'wana She No Home." New York was the place to do that.

Situated on 7th Avenue and 52nd Street, Phil Ramone's A&R Studios was at the heart of the New York scene. Ramone had produced Billy Joel's (appropriately named) *52nd Street* album there and, just before Karen arrived, he had been working on the follow-up, the new wave–inspired *Glass Houses*. Ramone chose Joel's backing band for Karen's solo sessions, because he liked their full-tilt exuberance. Fired up with a brash, combative energy, drummer Liberty Devitto, guitarist Russell Javors, and bassist Doug Stegmeyer were Long Island natives who had been playing with Joel since the mid-1970s. They attended most of the sessions for Karen's solo album, which were packed into three weeks, recording basic tracks from 12 noon until 8 p.m. every day.

Karen had come from a sheltered background, but she was willing to experiment and enjoyed the camaraderie of the studio. "We liked Karen a lot. She was extremely smart and a very good musician in her own right and appreciative of what everyone did," recalls Mounsey. At first, though, she found the rock 'n' roll swearing a little challenging. "She came from a very conservative, square southern California family and had trouble getting away from that good-girl attitude. The musicians could be a salty bunch of guys, using unprintable language, especially the F-bomb. Every time the F-word went by Karen was sorta bothered. She talked about it, 'Oh, that word, I don't like that word!'

We respected her, so the guys tried to clean it up, but everyone thought that was funny."

Devitto distinctly remembers "not being able to say what we'd normally say with Billy and the guys. She didn't want us swearing, but her sense of humor was so great. That's what surprised me. I thought we were going to get this stiff, conservative person and all of a sudden it was like, *Oh my God, she's fantastic!*"[17] On Joel's albums during that period Devitto played the drums with a crisp, pummeling attack and he took a similar approach in the sessions with Karen. "New York-style drumming is very aggressive—we play a little bit ahead of the beat. There was a lot of adrenaline and energy in the studio," he says. "It was pretty insane because we were recording *Glass Houses* at the same time. So when Billy was writing songs we were recording with Karen. She was so great, she just wanted to fit right in with us. She wanted to change her image—go from that squeaky-clean American apple pie persona to a grown-up woman."

Devitto evolved a style that was inspired first by the Beatles and then Dino Danelli, a frenetic drummer who played with New Jersey garage band the Rascals. "I was an Italian from Long Island, but unlike Ringo I didn't have straight hair or a British accent. So when the Rascals came on the scene and three out of the four of them were Italian with wavy hair, I could relate to them. Dino blew me away. He showed me that a drummer could be as much of a focus as the lead singer."

Karen enjoyed Devitto's spiky humor. When they were about to start recording the song "Make Believe It's Your First Time," Devitto said over the microphone, "Y'know, Karen, it should be 'Make Believe It's Your First Time and I'll Guarantee You It's Mine'!" There was so much laughter in the studio the session had to stop. Another time it was Devitto's birthday and Ramone brought in a cake from an erotic baker with a large icing penis.

Devitto held the cake up to Karen. "You wanna piece?"

Karen gave a wry smile. "I don't think I've ever been that close to one of those before!"

Devitto remembers that day with fondness. "That's the kind of humor she had, she just fit right in with us," he says.

Gradually Karen became more comfortable with the musicians, singing songs like "Making Love in the Afternoon" with cheerful brio. Russell Javors remembers the band as being "kinda rowdy. We weren't the studio presence Karen grew up with! Phil said, 'Let her be one of the guys, she's never really done this.' My understanding was she'd never been on a plane by herself, which I found pretty amazing. We treated her with our own brand of respect. I think she enjoyed being in that environment. Don't get me wrong, we were consummate professionals, but we had our own style," he says. Ramone was amiable but protective of Karen, always in control, keeping an eye on proceedings and aware of his producer role. According to Javors, "he was like the Godfather. You had to earn your way into the room with him, so you didn't mess around—but he gave you the freedom to express yourself."[18]

Mounsey intuited that there were two sides to Karen, that an ingrained sense of propriety was keeping in check her more earthy persona. "I think that it was hard for her to shake off that very square upbringing. But she wanted to have a broader point of view," says Mounsey, who enthused with her about R&B and funk artists like Bootsy Collins, James Brown, Parliament, and Funkadelic. "I think she wanted to connect with that a little. She was a real musician who had antennae reaching in all directions."

One of the biggest "what if" questions around Karen's solo work arises from the fact that Rod Temperton, a key arranger and songwriter on the album, offered her the songs "Off the Wall" and "Rock with You." Much to Ramone's dismay she decided to pass and they ended up becoming colossal hits for Michael Jackson. Many now believe these tracks could have been the hits to spectacularly launch Karen's solo career. Instead, she went for the subtler soul sound of Temperton's tracks "Lovelines" and "If We Try." An eccentric British songwriter from Cleethorpes, Lincolnshire, Temperton had already had global success with Heatwave's "Boogie Nights" and "The Groove Line" and later went on to write "Thriller" for Jackson. He worked with a feverish attention to detail, chain-smoking and drinking coffee throughout the writing and recording sessions.

Ramone pushed Karen to sing in different ways. On Javors' song "All Because of You," for instance, she had to sing such long, sustained, soulful notes in a higher register that at one point she hyperventilated and had to breathe into a paper bag. Maybe the lyrics were a little edgy as well. "I don't think she would have sung a song like that with the Carpenters, with the line 'I can't sleep at night, all because of you,' but that was a challenge she was willing to take," recalls Javors.

What's striking about Karen's solo album is how many songs contain direct reference to sex, from the snappy disco rhythms of "My Body Keeps Changing My Mind" to the lush club pop of "Remember When Lovin" Took All Night." Rob Mounsey could see that Karen was willing to explore ways of expressing herself that were at odds with the Carpenters' audience and with songs that would go down well on the gay nightclub dancefloor. "The Carpenters' image was America's favorite, very Disney-esque, Nixon's favorite band, but on this record she sounds mature, less guarded. She's not a little girl any more; she's a woman. And she was trying to project that with real feelings, real emotion, not Hallmark emotions."

The risqué lyrics sent out a few shockwaves when halfway through the sessions Karen went to Los Angeles for a visit and came back two weeks later saying that her mother Agnes was horrified by the early demos, particularly sexually suggestive lines in the song "Still in Love with You." Javors saw this as a sign that the sessions were working. "I was so proud her mother hated my lyrics!" Even though Karen was ready to joke with the guys, she did have a limit. Devitto remembers one day in November she gave each of the musicians a copy of *Christmas Portrait* as a gift and he proceeded to draw beards, berets, and moustaches on the picture of Karen and Richard. When she saw it she was furious. "We worked really hard on that! I can't believe you defaced the cover!" she shouted.

"Whoa, okay. I reached your limit. Now I know where to stop," said Devitto.

Karen was dedicated to perfecting her work and insisted on getting the songs right in a way that felt authentic. Mounsey, for instance, remembers how she changed the words to his song "Guess I Just Lost My Head." Originally written from the viewpoint of a man singing about his crush on a woman, Karen rewrote a line to make the song more gender-neutral. Even though it presents an intriguing image, Karen felt the notion of a man wearing a flower in his hair prompted a rewrite. "We wouldn't worry about that now, but at the time it was seen as bizarre, a little too gender-bending," says Mounsey. "So she rewrote the line in a way that was clever."

Mounsey noticed that Karen was demanding of herself, particularly when it came to vocal arrangements. "She and her brother had this patented process of building those pretty choir parts. Usually it would just be the two of them, but on this session it was just her. They're very striking because they're so unique to her sound. You hear other Karens come in, very tight and correct, like pretty shiny steel bars. She built those very carefully; it was all mapped out in her head. I worked with Brian Wilson of the Beach Boys and he did very much the same thing."

Javors, likewise, was fascinated by the precision with which Karen tackled the new wave rock feel of his song "Still in Love with You." "It was kind of raucous, so I thought, *Wow, how the hell is she going to do that?*" Karen liked Javors's phrasing and tried to copy his vocal style, but became frustrated when she couldn't master it. Eventually, she asked him to join her in the vocal booth so they were standing nose to nose. "I lip-synched so that she could watch my mouth and copy my phrasing. We did that a bunch of times until she was happy. What amazed me was, I thought she'd have a big voice, but it was like a whisper. When we sang together she wasn't belting it out, what came out was a pure rich tone. Karen sang with her soul, but had such control."

Karen trusted the musicians partly because Ramone cultivated a family atmosphere in the studio. He had a jovial, engaging personality and was comfortable working with superstar artists. As the arranger Bob James says, "He was always able to hang in there with whatever an artist's idiosyncrasies were and keep his eyes on the prize."[19] Karen also felt safe and nurtured on an emotional level because Ramone's wife, Itchie, was a constant companion, often sitting in studio sessions. She also gets a credit on the album as production associate. Itchie's brother Doug remembers Ramone and his sister being very supportive. "They always looked out for you and you always knew they had your back. When my sister first met Karen she rang me to say that they really hit it off. They were close to the same age. Those two Karens got on so well."[20]

Maybe Itchie got on with Karen because both of them were strong individuals with an upbeat energy and, to a degree, both outsiders, Karen because of her tomboy roots and her love of the drums and Itchie because of her Japanese heritage. "We're sansei, third-generation Japanese. Our grandparents migrated from Japan and both our parents were born in the US. Because his family lived on the West Coast, during the Second World War, our dad and his entire family were incarcerated in a concentration camp," recalls Doug Ichiuji. While in the camp the Ichiujis' father volunteered for the US Army and became part of one of the most decorated teams in history. His troop fought in Europe and liberated Dachau. "All while his family were incarcerated—that's the irony of the whole thing."

As a result of this, Itchie and her brother grew up in Maryland with parents who were forceful about conforming and assimilating into American society. "She was four-and-a-half years older than me and took the brunt of that transition, made to fit in with the Caucasian crowds," Doug says. Though she was a cheerleader in high school and a popular student, when the Beatles came to the US, spearheading the British invasion, Itchie rebelled. "She was part of that frenzy. I remember arguments—my mother did not want her to listen to the Beatles, she figured it would do something to her mind." Itchie sang and played guitar in high school and for a short while dated Peter Yarrow from the folk group Peter, Paul & Mary. She was politically active and went on anti–Vietnam War demos and benefits.

Much later, in 1977, when she was working as a tour publicist for Peter, Paul & Mary, Itchie met Phil Ramone. Through him she encountered all kinds of artists and spent time hanging out in studio sessions, nursing thoughts about making a record herself. "When my sister met Karen she was a good performer, but she hadn't started her singing career, she was starting to evolve into that, singing back-up on a few sessions. I think Karen pushed her into becoming a singer," says Doug Ichiuji. His sister was a constant companion for Karen—after recording sessions, for instance, they would eat at Serendipity, a Manhattan restaurant with elaborate desserts, or they would spend time at the Bottom Line, a cool music club in Greenwich Village. At weekends she would sometimes get away and stay with her childhood pal Debbie Cuticello (née Vaiuso) at her home in Guilford, Connecticut. She enjoyed the escape, being anonymous for a while and being cared for with her old friend's well-cooked Italian meals.

*

Karen liked to encourage and support her friends' ambitions, maybe because she herself felt a sense of unexpressed potential. Even though she valiantly tried to stay chirpy during the sessions for her solo album, it was clear there was underlying tension and frustration—something that was conveyed in habitual behavior. Doug Ichiuji visited the studio a few times and noticed that Karen always had drumsticks in her hands. "She was playing with the drumsticks all the time. She'd be talking to Phil in the sound room and hitting the sticks on the table. I think it was a stress reliever, something that was second nature to her. It could have been a release or a distraction." As a drummer himself, Ichiuji could see her need for acknowledgment. "I don't think people gave her credit for being as good as she was. They thought she was a great singer who wanted to play the drums, but it could have been the other way round."

One day Karen walked into a session, sat at the drums and spontaneously started to play. "Okay, we know, you play really well and you really miss them," thought Liberty Devitto. He knew how important the instrument was to her. "Sitting behind the drums is like having a wall of protection. I've always felt that way about my drums, nobody can penetrate that wall. If someone took away my drums, I'd feel I got out of the shower and walked naked into the room and someone threw me a surprise party and hadn't got dressed yet," he says.

Karen's incessant drumming hinted at a nervousness about the project and whether it would work. There was a lot riding on the album. Ramone warned arranger Bob James in advance that his role was to be "a kind of substitute Richard," but Karen wanted to record something different from Richard's usual music direction. "I guess in some ways he was described as her dictator. My role was kinda scary and dangerous, not in my comfort zone," says James. "I loved the challenge that Phil was putting in front of me, with a firmly established superstar talent. It was a very big deal and flattering to be asked. But what could I possibly come up with? There was so much history and baggage. I knew we were setting out to do something that the Carpenters' fans didn't necessarily want."

A towering influence in jazz and fusion music, James is also one of the most sampled players in hip hop, with fragments from his songs "Nautilus" and "Take Me to the Mardi Gras" used as break beats by everyone from Run-DMC to Ghostface Killah and Slick Rick. After studying music at the University of Michigan, James's first big break came on the early 1960s' bebop scene when he was hired as a piano accompanist for jazz singer Sarah Vaughan. "I often refer to it as my second college education, because she was state of the art as a jazz vocalist. To land the job with her was a big deal for me and to make her happy was a challenge. Her influence on my piano-playing stays with me to this day. I understood that I could inspire her and make her sing better if my groove was good. Because she was an improvisor she sang differently depending on how she was being supported."

James took the same approach with Karen and was at first optimistic. "Karen had such an appreciation for drums and instrumental support. She had the jazz feel, no question." Two years previously she had sung a duet with Ella Fitzgerald for a Carpenters ABC TV special. Dressed in tailored trousers and a tuxedo jacket, looking almost androgynous, Karen delivered "Someone to Watch over Me" with a slow, sultry jazz undertow. One outtake from the filming shows them in rehearsal singing the song. Then at the end Karen says, "Okay?," and Fitzgerald, perched on a bar stool in a gauzy cocktail dress, answers shyly, "You be sounding like me." The camera crew make the pair do take after take in a way that is almost comical, like being over-casual with the Crown Jewels. Both Fitzgerald and Karen show forbearance toward this offhand treatment, going on to harmonize "My Funny Valentine" with deft call and response, creating a precious moment of pop history.

In New York, Karen could draw on her experience of singing with one of the great divas, but with James she seemed a little overawed and conversation was minimal. By then she had been back home on the visit to Los Angeles and her mother's under-whelming response to early recordings had triggered Karen's nerves. "I remember she was struggling, her health wasn't great and the sessions were kinda awkward and strained. Phil and I were there as her support system, to give her the opportunity to do her own thing, but we didn't necessarily know what her own thing would be," says James. He describes her solo album sessions as a fishing trip deal. "You don't know what you're looking for, so you try stuff and throw in a line. You might try a polka or a waltz, to see what bites. That's what I felt Karen and Phil were struggling with."

James had worked a lot with Quincy Jones and remembered a key piece of advice from the legendary producer—that if he tried to create "money music" or theorize about what would win a Grammy, he wouldn't be trusting his talent or instinct. "Most musicians undervalue their own talent, and Karen had some of that insecurity too, not believing or understanding what made her voice so magical," says James. "It was probably mysterious to her, 'Why am I such a big star?' I could feel [it] in the way that she sang and the way she was as a person, so honest and natural and innocent. The Carpenters' sound was a very specific over-dubbed choral thing. She wanted to be freed from that pressure to just sing."

James also got the impression that Richard had a silent psychological hold over the process. "Even though people perceived Karen as having the ultimate talent, the voice that people fell in love with, she yearned for more control over her art. That was a big part of the motivation to do her own album. I never saw Richard at the sessions and there was this feeling that he was not happy she was doing it." Karen had enormous respect for her brother and sometimes during her solo recording sessions was troubled about what Richard would think. Ramone, however, made it clear to Karen that she was the priority. "This is your record, not your brother's. It doesn't matter that much what he thinks."

As a way of putting a stamp on the record, Ramone encouraged Karen to record a cover of the Paul Simon song "Still Crazy After All These Years." Simon wasn't pleased with her version. According to Glenn Burger, a former engineer at Ramone's A&R Studios, Simon said in a voice "that combined derision, snobbishness, concern and alarm, 'Karen, what are you doing? This stuff is awful!' . . . His insensitivity was stunning."[21]

Despite Simon's verdict, many hear Karen's jazz-tinged version as a unique performance—world-weary, fragile, and deeply moving. Russell Javors argues that "Still Crazy" represents what Karen felt at the time, "without anybody putting restraints on her and saying 'You can't say that or we'll lose our popularity and our fanbase.' I think that's why Phil was so insistent on her doing that song." Rob Mounsey agrees, noting the song's air of melancholy reflection, as if Karen is watching the world pass her by. "The song resonated with her. She had very big ears, as we say. She could hear everything that was happening." Maybe the song meant so much to Karen because it touched a part of her that still longed for love and still yearned to find the person with whom she could share her life.

CHAPTER 15

1980

It's hard because we're constantly around the same circle of
people. We're always looking for somebody nice, somebody
that's real and has a way with 'em that's going to make me
happy for the rest of my life.[1]

By the time sessions for Karen's solo album finished early in
1980, the mood was jubilant. The album had been scheduled
for release by A&M, and everyone involved was very proud of
the project. Phil Ramone invited Russell Javors along to the
listening party in A&R Studios, where the album was played
to Derek Green, by then senior vice president of A&M internationally as well as managing director in the UK. He had flown
over specially for the occasion. Ramone and Karen eagerly
played the album, but even though Ramone claimed later that
the New York playback elicited a positive reaction with Champagne corks popping, Javors remembers it differently, picking
up on the underlying tension in the room.

"Phil was excited to get the reaction, as was Karen, but it was like an oil painting in there. It was brutal," says Javors. What about the Champagne popping? "All I know is, it was very tense. Somebody from A&M [Green] was sitting there stony-faced, not responding. Usually you'll hear 'Oh, that's great,' but there was nothing like that. You could just see the air go out of the room. My feeling was, it was already dead, the decision was already made."[2]

Shortly after that Ramone and Karen flew to Los Angeles to play the album to Richard, Herb Alpert, and Jerry Moss. The response there was even worse. Track after track was met with indifference and at the end of the playback Moss asserted that the album didn't have a hit song. Karen offered to record some new tracks, but the A&M team weren't keen to invest any more time or money in the project. Sensing the way things were going, Ramone remixed some songs and had another informal playback with Green at his friend Quincy Jones's house. Jones's enthusiasm didn't make any difference. Even though the A&M sales team were poised, artwork had been prepared, beautiful photographs done, a catalog number had been assigned, and Karen had invested $400,000 of her own money into the sessions, A&M decided to cancel the album. Later, Green told the writer Ray Coleman, "We knew we had a dog from a commercial sense . . . to everyone's credit the record was stopped."[3]

Green's dismissal of Karen's work was both disrespectful and devastating. "I gotta get my money back. Go in and get my money back," a panic-stricken Karen said to her lawyer, Werner Wolfen. Arguing that they had nothing to offset the solo record expense, A&M decided to charge the money against future Carpenters royalties. Karen was deeply hurt at this complete rejection.

She had made a female soul album, her first compelling statement as a solo artist. Listening to the record over forty years later, what comes through is Karen's own fresh, funky aesthetic. She sings in a higher register than on the Carpenters albums, weaving throughout her own intricate vocal arrangements. Her approach is intimate, light, and upbeat, a conscious departure from the low, lush overload of songs like "Solitaire" or "This Masquerade." She's responsive to the musicians, like sax player Michael Brecker who adds a jazz touch to "If I Had You" or bassist Louis Johnson from funk band the Brothers Johnson, whose relaxed, laid-back sound pulses through "Lovelines." This is an album of nimble, sophisticated soul; classy and smart like Teena Marie's *Lady T* or Patrice Rushen's *Pizzazz*.

Unfortunately the A&M executives could not get past the freight of the Carpenters' success and couldn't take a risk. Not only that (as Paul Simon's reaction shows), they did not understand it. The soul pop sound Karen was exploring was part of a female-driven scene featuring singers as diverse as Donna Summer, Linda Ronstadt, Diana Ross, and Melissa Manchester. Its release would have strengthened Karen's career as a solo performer and given the Carpenters a whole new audience. "I felt we were scratching the surface of what she could do. The Carpenters' records were Richard's vision and she was the soldier, but Karen wanted to make her own statement," says Javors. "The whole thing was so bitter-sweet, a rollercoaster of emotions. I felt bad for Karen, because she put her heart and soul into this. And her money. She liked it. So to have her opinions and desires squashed was very hard to watch."

At the heart of this story is a question of authorship and ownership. When it comes to recognition and royalties, the music industry is weighted in favor of male artists, and in the 1970s and '80s this attitude was even more pronounced. Olivia Newton-John said later that, when Karen first played her the solo tapes, Richard was present and he gasped, "You've stolen the Carpenters sound." But, Olivia demurred, "she *is* the Carpenters sound."[4] Since then Richard has said that at the beginning of the band's career he devised all the overdubs and tight harmonies and was unhappy when he heard overdubs on Karen's solo work. But this is at odds with the picture of Karen in New York working on her vocal arrangements, meticulously mapping her sound. She crafted her own ideas and deserves full credit for that.

Bob James notes that many major solo artists don't achieve a hit album with their debut. Billy Joel's first release was in 1971, but he didn't achieve global success until 1977 with his fifth album, *The Stranger*. Pressure to score a quick hit means that major labels often can't commit to the necessary artist development before a magical song or sound is found. "In Karen's case, it was even more difficult to follow up on the huge success she'd already had with the Carpenters' formula. To start over again must have felt like an impossible pressure. How could this one album project compete with what she had already done?" says

James. "Phil and Karen were searching for the perfect song that would express what was in her mind. Had her health been better, then she could have kept going and found something."

It is clear that Karen was at the start of a new phase, experimenting with a sound that was a more personal musical statement, but once the album was shelved she didn't have the strength and stamina to fight for her solo career. Liberty Devitto became aware of Karen's struggle with anorexia when they had almost finished recording and were doing overdubs. "Karen didn't drink. She didn't eat either. I remember hugging her and feeling, like, nothing but a sack of bones. I hate to say it that way because she was so beautiful."

One night after recording Ramone had a Christmas party to celebrate. He invited all the musicians but Karen decided not to come. The guys called her from the party and Devitto said, "If you're going to stay in your room at least order room service. Eat something."

"Oh, yeah, okay," mumbled Karen.

Devitto still remembers that exchange with sadness. "I didn't know anything about anorexia but someone explained to me what was going on with her. Us guys, we just ate all the time. Being Italian, from an Italian family, you eat all the time. Just the concept of somebody eating and then getting rid of it was like, *What? Are you from Rome?* Romans used to do that to eat some more. The concept of anorexia was so foreign to me. I was like, *Why? Why would you do that?*"

Doug Ichiuji remembers his sister caring for Karen that whole period she was in New York. "Anorexia is an addiction, right?

My sister was trying to keep Karen on the straight and narrow. The temptation was there and she had demons in her head saying 'You can do this.'" Karen worked hard to disguise her anorexia, but everyone around her saw there was an issue. "She was incredibly thin and you knew there was something going on," says Javors. One night his wife had dinner with her and Itchie, and Karen made a point of saying, "I'm going to finish everything on my plate." Then she excused herself and went to the ladies' room. "It was certainly noticeable," says Javors, "but it didn't impact on the sessions at all." Even though her health was deteriorating, Karen knew how to conserve enough energy to sing well in the studio. Resolutely professional during recording, she went to great lengths to keep her private anguish secret.

It's arguable that the recording sessions buoyed up Karen's mental health and her self-identity. The album could have been part of a recovery, a way for her to mature and find herself. Instead she felt deflated, and as soon as the sessions finished she missed the family energy of Ramone's studio, the supportive environment and the companionship. "I think she fell in love with the band and everything we were doing," says Devitto. One night while he and the band were touring the US for Billy Joel's *Glass Houses* album they called her from the road. "We were crazy, like any rock guys we drank a lot and did all kinds of things and we'd call her from our hotel rooms at night, wake her up and say things like, 'Hey, Karen, what are you wearing? D'you have those little bunny pajamas on with the feet?' She'd be laughing and laughing."

Karen's road humor came out in her appreciation of proto-punk garage rock band the Troggs and the legendary *Troggs*

Tapes, which were an influence on Peter Cook & Dudley Moore's obscene double act Derek & Clive and spoof metal film *Spinal Tap* and were a favorite with Ramone's musicians in New York. The tapes were left running in a 1970 session in which the Troggs swear profusely, trying to work out the hit song that will (never quite) revive their career. In response to their efforts producer Dennis Berger remarks, "I know that it needs strings, that I *do* know."

After Billy Joel's show in Los Angeles, Karen came backstage. The band were expecting her to praise them and to say how great the gig was, but the first thing she uttered was, "I'll tell ya one thing. It needs strings."

The guys collapsed with laughter. "She was so funny. I actually fell in love with her. If I wasn't married, I'd have asked her to marry me," says Devitto. "I thought she was a beautiful person—looks, voice, everything about her. The whole package."

*

After they shelved her album, A&M rallied around and coaxed Karen back into the studio with Richard, as if the solo outing had just been an embarrassing mistake. Her role in the Carpenters had always been clearly defined. "Karen is the star . . . she's the lead singer and the featured part of the act. I keep the public in mind and try to stay on top of all the successful products," Richard once said, and there was a sense of relief that she was returning to the fold.[5] Feeling a little bruised by the affair, Ramone noted ruefully, "Now it was time to get their business together and go back to work."

Karen's ex Tom Bahler was a good friend of Ramone's and thinks that her solo record was a pivotal point. "She could have done a number of records with Phil. I think she was beginning to free herself. But she was not free—she had one foot in the Carpenters and one foot in the new Karen Carpenter," he says. Because she was a drummer he said that she could "sing with a rhythmical drive and kick booty," whereas Richard was a classically trained pianist and "more of a ballad guy. Maybe he wasn't crazy about her record because it was so different."

It would have taken Karen a great deal of strength to resist her family and stand her ground as a solo artist. "Michael Jackson got slapped around and belted more than anybody else in the Jackson family, because he stood up to his father and wouldn't give in." Having worked with Barbra Streisand and Diana Ross, Bahler also understood what women had to overcome to reach their full potential as artists. "I love them for the strength of resisting all the men who told them to just shut up and sing," he says. "Quincy Jones was actually concerned about me and Karen getting so close, he felt that she was kind of a creative trap for me because I was so freewheeling. He said, 'There is no freewheeling to that family.' The Carpenters were absolutely warm and loving and so felt safe. And I think Karen felt unsafe when she went outside that." Bahler believes that she needed to rebel, that she had all kinds of possibilities available to her. "But I think in that family, she was swimming upstream. No . . . she was swimming up the waterfall."

When she was asked a year later by BBC Radio 2 presenter Ray Moore whether she felt tempted to launch a solo career, Karen said carefully, as if trying to convince herself: "It comes and goes. The real comfort is what we [the Carpenters] do together." She added that the offer of a solo career piqued her interest. "But it doesn't make any sense because the most comfortable is here . . . with Richard. He excels in what he does, I do what I do. It's a perfect combination. So it doesn't make any sense to go lookin' anywhere else."

Back in Los Angeles, with the solo album shelved, Karen had time to brood about her future. She told friends she was ready to find a husband and settle down. Thinking she might have been too peremptory in rejecting Terry Ellis, with Itchie's encouragement she phoned him and arranged to meet for lunch. Halfway through the meal she said, "I made a big mistake in ending our relationship. Can we get back together?" Ellis told her gently that he was engaged to be married, so there was no possibility of reuniting.

Karen's friend Carole Curb then invited her on a blind date. "Carole knew that I was still looking and she said, 'I think I've got somebody.' My normal reaction would be, *Yeah, sure gal!*" recalled Karen, but she decided to give it a try anyway.[6] The date was Tom Burris, aged thirty-nine, a man Curb had met through her brother Mike, who by then had moved from the music industry to politics. In 1980, Mike Curb was lieutenant governor of California and vice chairman of Ronald Reagan's presidential campaign. Burris was an eager Reagan supporter and a member of the Commission of California, which worked on relations with

Baja California. Burris had donated ambulances to some hospitals in the Mexican state and Carole Curb was impressed with his philanthropy. A high-school drop-out from Long Beach who had worked as a welder and steel contractor before setting up his own business in 1964 as a property developer, Burris was blond, suave, gallant, and seemingly successful.

The double date with Burris, Curb, and her then husband Tony Scotti took place on April 12, 1980. "Usually you open the door and go 'Urgh!'" Karen said later, but when she walked into Ma Maison in West Hollywood and saw Burris she was immediately attracted. There was only one problem, however. When asking her about her life, Burris claimed not to know who Karen was. She asked him incredulously, "Have you been under a rock for ten years?" It seems strange, given Mike Curb's music industry connections and the fact that Scotti was an actor and cofounder of teen-pop label Scotti Brothers Records, and that the Mike Curb Congregation was regularly on TV, that Burris had no awareness of the current pop industry. "He listens to classical and country," Karen explained later, "and now I've got him listening to everything."[7]

The other snag was that Burris was already married with an eighteen-year-old son, though he told Carole Curb that he and his wife had separated and were about to get a divorce. Shortly after meeting Karen, he disappeared for a few weeks and returned with renewed enthusiasm. There was speculation that he had gone and finalized a quickie divorce in Las Vegas. He was an ardent suitor, inveigling his way into her life, charming friends and family. Burris seemed engaging, but Itchie thought he was "overly manicured" with a plastic smile and Frenda Leffler dismissed him later as "a phony and a blowhard."[8]

Karen was happy, though, and after an exceedingly rapid two-month courtship, Burris proposed to her. Even at thirty years old she deferred to her mother, checking in with Agnes first to ask if she should get married. It's ironic that having been so controlling of Karen's former relationships, Agnes let her loose with this, shrugging shoulders and saying, "That's up to you . . . you're old enough to know what you're doing."[9] Karen waited for Burris's divorce to be finalized and then, on June 19, accepted his proposal. Having let Terry Ellis slip away, she wasn't going to make the same mistake again.

The original plan was for a year-long engagement, but this was drastically shortened to a couple of months when the couple announced they were going to be married in August. Friends were worried about the speed with which the courtship was progressing and that made them suspicious of Burris. "That's when everyone's antennas went up," said Itchie.[10] The family secretly hired a private investigator to check him out, but Karen was oblivious, entranced and at the same time determined to marry and move forward with her life. When Itchie carefully asked her if he knew about the anorexia, Karen said breezily that she was over it now because she was so happy.

Karen wanted a big Beverly Hills wedding, so Leffler helped her with the arrangements and organized a wedding shower. Over fifty women were invited to the event on August 3 at the ritzy Hillcrest Country Club, near to Karen's duplex at Century Towers. The Garden Terrace was decked out with lilies and orchids, and the theme was "Showering Karen with Love and Affection." Karen was a warm, loyal companion and loved by a huge sorority of female friends, most of whom were at the event. But even though she looked radiant in yellow organdie, some there sensed something was awry. Maria Galeazzi, Karen's former stylist, was shocked at how thin she was. And Petula Clark says, "I didn't much like it. I sensed it wasn't right for her, I was concerned. She was obviously happy, but I didn't have a good feeling. In the group there were nice people, mixed in with people I didn't know. I couldn't understand it then, but I felt she was with the wrong people. Knowing her fragility, she didn't fit in with that whole Hollywood glamour thing and I think that had something to do with her becoming anorexic. Mixing with the beautiful people, she didn't realize how special she was."[11]

In the 1970s, some commentators scoffed at Karen's fashion sense, but as a musician and drummer she had her own supreme sophistication and style. "Nobody could compete with Karen, she was unique in the way she looked and sang, she didn't care about that stuff. The problem was, she was starting to mix with people who *did* care about that." Clark believes that this fed into Karen's anxiety about achieving the perfect figure and social status.

Karen's ultimate marker of social success was the grand celebrity wedding. Maybe it was from feelings of insecurity, or consolation for the cancelation of her solo album, or a sense that she was running out of time, that Karen rushed into marriage. A date was set for August 31, 1980, but the ceremony very nearly didn't happen when Burris confessed to her, just three days beforehand, that he'd had a vasectomy. Karen was anxious to become a mother. She had always loved children—she was a doting godmother to Leffler's twins, Ashley and Andrew—and she was desperate for a child of her own. This news was devastating, not just because it wrecked her hopes of motherhood, but also because she felt deceived. What other information was Burris withholding? Suddenly, her fiancé could no longer be trusted. Karen went to her mother, feeling hysterical, saying she would have to call off the wedding. Agnes's response was detached and cruel. More concerned about the public shame and all the guests who'd been invited and the extended family who were traveling miles to attend and the camera crews that had been booked for the press conference, plus the photocall afterward, Agnes told her daughter that she had no choice but to go ahead and they would "fix it" afterward.

The wedding went ahead in grand style. Richard and John Bettis had written a special song for the occasion and flown Peter Knight over from London to arrange the orchestra. "Because We Are in Love" is swoony, schmaltzy, and over the top, like a song in the final fairytale scene of a 1940s Hollywood movie. Initially Richard wanted Karen to sing it live at the wedding, as a dedication to Burris. "I said, 'Are you out of your mind?' We couldn't quite picture that gorgeous gown and a microphone, it didn't fit. So we decided to [record and] play the song instead," Karen said later.[12] The song was recorded over two days with an eighty-piece orchestra and sixty-voice choir. Knight, who had just flown in from the UK and was jetlagged, hadn't quite bargained for the scale of the arrangement. He managed to get the job done, but the pressure was intense and frenzied. "Everybody was so crazed," said Karen, "and Peter's hair was standing on end."

She had also contacted Tom Bahler, asking him to assemble a choir for her wedding. He was happy to do so and later didn't miss the irony of the situation. "Karen was worried about my daughter coming after them for money. And that's exactly what she married. I remember meeting her husband and I thought, *Oh, ick*. I didn't say anything because I didn't want to do anything that would make her uncomfortable," he recalls.

On August 31, Karen put on a brave smiling face for the wedding, which became a highly mediated event. She and Burris were married in the Crystal Ballroom of the Beverly Hills Hotel with ten bridesmaids and over 450 wedding guests including Olivia Newton-John, Dionne Warwick, Burt Bacharach, and Herb Alpert. Richard played the piano while Peter Knight conducted the choir with Earl Dumler on oboe and Gayle Levant playing the harp. "I had the privilege of playing for her wedding. I had so much respect for Karen, I loved her like she were my sister," recalls Levant. "My God, the day of her wedding she was so beautiful in the way she was dressed and she had this gorgeous hat. She was like a vision."[13]

Gloriously extravagant in the style of ye olde English garden, the wedding venue was virtually buried in flowers. Every window and pillar in the room was covered with trellises bedecked with white orchids, gardenias, violets, and lemon leaves and giant baskets of orchids were suspended from the ceiling. "Because We Are in Love" was played over loudspeakers as Frenda Leffler, the maid of honor, and her three-year-old twins (Ashley as flower girl, Andrew as ring bearer) led down the aisle the brides-maids including Itchie, Carole Curb, Karen's cousin Mary Rudolph, hairdresser Sandy Holland, and New Haven pal Debbie Cuticello. And there was Karen, on the arm of her father Harold, wearing a white *mousseline de soie* gown modeled after an eighteenth-century riding ensemble, with a 15-yard train of iridescent seashells and sequins, cascading from a white chiffon picture hat. Her outfit was designed by Bill Belew, the creator of Elvis Presley's sequined Las Vegas jumpsuits and costume maker for many Carpenters TV performances.

Televangelist preacher Dr. Robert Schuller (best known for his regular *Hour of Power* broadcast) officiated over the ceremony. While Karen solemnly declared her vows, onlookers noted that Burris seemed less serious, mimicking Schuller when he said in an overly deep voice, "I do." Bahler was concerned. "To be blunt, it felt like bullshit. I didn't feel love from him to her. It seemed like it was [a] movie, that they were playing roles." After the ceremony the couple held a press conference and posed for photographs and the luncheon toast after the reception was proposed by Lieutenant Governor Mike Curb. Burris and Karen led off the first dance with the oddly egotistical choice of "We've Only Just Begun," before cutting a slice of the towering four-tiered wedding cake covered in white fondant icing.

After the occasion the Carpenters fan club newsletter featured an offer to buy wedding photos and gave a detailed description of where all the blooms came from in that profusion of flowers, including the "two thousand stems of orchids from Singapore . . . and one hundred dozen gardenias and pikaki from Hawaii."[14]

Afterward the newlyweds took the somewhat unusual step of inviting the extended family to their honeymoon in Bora Bora, including Karen's aunt Bernice. Most quietly declined, apart from Burris's brother and his wife. Their resort hotel had no radio or TV and Karen dubbed it "Boring Boring," cutting short the holiday in a rush to return to Los Angeles. Lounging around on a private island in French Polynesia would have been paradise for some, but Karen needed a distraction and was anxious to get back to a familiar environment. As soon as she could, Karen was reinstalled in the studio with Richard, working on sessions for their next album. Music was a way of anchoring herself in the world, the way she gained an equilibrium. When talking about Karen's expectations for married life, her friends frequently used the term "white picket fence," shorthand for a settled suburban middle-class life. This was always so at odds with her musical world of touring, recording, and collaborating with musicians. Even though she couldn't quite see it, that had become her real family, her community. The wedding in the Beverly Hills Hotel was like an elaborate showpiece executed to perfection, as if Karen was trying to convince herself that in getting this right, everything else would work out.

CHAPTER 16

1981

It was getting windy and choppy . . . which means "Get out while you can!" Going back, getting into a swell we hear "clunk." I'm trying to remain calm because we're supposed to know what we're doing. I go downstairs and Tom says we broke the drive shaft. Oh, terrific! We didn't have any steering and I was trying to figure out why I was nearly falling overboard.[1]

In November 1981, Karen and Oliva Newton-John were interviewed on *The Merv Griffin Show* and Karen talked animatedly about a recent boat trip they made with their partners to Catalina, a rocky island off the coast of southern California. After a night partying Tom Burris took them out on the water from Newport Beach. He and Newton-John's boyfriend Matt went diving while the women sipped drinks, chatted, and sunbathed on deck. Toward the end of the day, disaster struck when the drive shaft broke. "We didn't have any steering, so Tom had to steer back with the engine," recalled

Karen. By the time they got back to Catalina it was five o'clock and too late to fly out, so the couples booked the last two rooms in a grungy hotel. "Oh, it was a flashback to the early days of touring, we had a lot of cockroaches in the room," laughed Karen. Pictures from that night show Karen and Newton-John cozy in pyjamas on a bed in basic accommodation, camping out, and roughing it, but enjoying each other's company.

Karen's female friendships, it seems, were more enduring, relaxing, and rewarding than her romantic relationships with men. By then her marriage was in difficulties and the Catalina story highlighted the lack of communication between her and Burris. The fact that he hadn't told her about his vasectomy until just before the wedding meant that she could not fully trust him. After a while that eroded her self-confidence and led to a resurgence of anorexia. She still craved affection and wanted to be intimate with him, but he was put off by her emaciated body and was slow to respond, so they became more and more distant from each other. Outwardly Karen projected a calm professionalism to her friends and colleagues, though she was beginning to panic inside.

On *The Merv Griffin Show* the Carpenters performed "I Want You Back in My Life Again," from their new album, *Made in America*. The record was meant to mark the band's comeback, but instead it stalled in the US *Billboard* charts at number fifty-two. Their audience, it seemed, had moved on.

Made in America was recorded at the same time as President Reagan was elected, ushering in an era of Reaganomics, where tax and government regulation was reduced to foster a neoliberal free market "trickle-down economics" that ended up benefiting the wealthy. On Reagan's Inauguration Day, January 20, Karen came onto the A&M lot wearing a track-suit top emblazoned with the patriotic slogan "MADE IN AMERICA." Richard thought that would be a perfect title for the album. The Carpenters were not particularly political, but just as their White House performance for President Nixon in 1973 struck an odd note, this title seemed to echo Reagan's campaign slogan "Make America Great Again" (later used by President Trump in 2016). It would appeal to some of the Carpenters' older adult fanbase, but was maybe not the best move when aiming for a glorious comeback.

The Carpenters' tenth and final studio album has an off-center energy, as if striving to express too many things at once—with the swoony, orchestral wedding song "Because We Are in Love" set against more taut, ambiguous tracks like "Somebody's Been Lyin'" and "When It's Gone," where Karen sings in a spare, subdued style. Many 1970s bands were unmoored by the '80s, trying to find relevance in a music world being remolded by newly emerging sounds of electronic synth pop and hip hop. Previous Carpenters albums were always notable for their clarity, and here the music seems less defined. The strongest tracks on *Made in America* are those showing a through-line between them and Karen's solo work.

The rhythmic pop of the Skinner, Bell & Wallace song "Touch Me When We're Dancing," for instance, is in tune with the disco mood on Karen's solo album, while "I Believe You," first made a hit in 1977 by R&B singer Dorothy Moore, has a deep bluesy lilt. One of the album's standout songs is Phyllis Brown and Juanita Curiel's "Strength of a Woman." Here Karen expressed an emotional complexity that mirrored her personal life. In the song a woman decides to stand by her husband, even though she struggles with feeling like a victim. The call and response chorus with Stephanie Spruill, Carolyn Dennis, and Maxine Waters Willard expresses the sisterly support she can count on in her crisis.

"We have to go through it to get to it, right?" says Spruill. "We may be a victim but we are also victor in the end. That's how we realize our truth. I've been victimized as a woman in a past marriage, I understand that when you go through that you say, 'Enough is enough. I will survive this, because I am great.' So when a woman is going through that process you have empathy, give her some wise words."[2] One of the top session singers in the business, Spruill was born in South Central Los Angeles and in her teens won a scholarship to Eddy Cantor's Foundation of Creative Talent before becoming a percussionist, vocalist, and arranger, working with Giorgio Moroder, Donna Summer, Gloria Gaynor, and R&B artist David T. Walker. "I was like a triple threat—I could dance, play percussion and sing with a 5½-octave range," says Spruill.

Just before recording "Strength of a Woman" the singers gathered round the piano with Richard to work out their arrangements. "I want you guys to go to the church. You know what to do, Stephanie," he said. On the track Karen sings with bluesy conviction, buoyed up by the women's gospel vocals. Spruill remembers Karen gazing at them through the sound-booth glass. "She looked so beautiful, with an understated beauty. I was on the mic and I'm looking at Karen behind the glass as I'm singing. I believe she was going to another level spiritually, that's what I felt. Afterward she came out and thanked us." Spruill sensed a resilience in Karen. "She was soft and demure, but a tough cookie at the same time. Playing drums the way she did, she was a toughie! And that's the way women are, that's the way we survive, we wear both hats."

Not all the *Made in America* sessions were as joyful. One musician remembers a session he played where Karen just stood by, "looking really depressed. We never spoke." While mastering the album in late spring 1981, Carpenters engineer Bernie Grundman noticed her weight loss. By now, after mastering their albums for over ten years, he had seen Karen in many different moods and noticed how her weight had fluctuated wildly over time. "It was very inconsistent the way she looked. I saw her go through a lot of changes where she was not being good to her body," he says. "Karen was anorexic and bulimic and she would look pretty bad at times. That's so hard on your body. I don't know why she was always worried about her weight. But that's her misperception of what she was."[3]

Made in America was released on June 29, 1981 with a swanky launch party in the grounds of the luxury Hotel Bel-Air. During promotion for the album there was no more talk of Karen's solo project and she spoke to journalists about the telepathic thinking between herself and Richard, as if she was trying to erase any difference or any sense of family conflict. As she grew more fragile, it seemed to matter more than ever that their sibling connection was harmonious. "Luckily we think the same and our musical tastes are the same," she asserted. "I can look at him and know what he's thinking . . . We've always gotten along, always had the same interests—music and cars and racing and movies and television."[4]

Despite Karen's upbeat approach for interviews, she was privately negotiating slippery emotional terrain in her marriage. For a while after the wedding she had been happy, eating healthily, and appearing settled. But the man who had been duplicitous about his vasectomy before their wedding gradually became more demanding, asking Karen for financial loans for cars, condos, and yacht trips. After the hair-raising trip to Catalina Island, they had an anniversary vacation in August, hiking from Colorado to Vancouver in Burris's four-wheel drive—hardly a glamorous holiday. Karen had reservations about Burris that intensified the more he drained her finances, freely spending her money on luxury goods and his own projects for property development. On September 1 (the day after her appearance on *The Merv Griffin Show*), Karen sought legal counsel and revised her will, making sure that while Burris would inherit their Newport Beach house, everything else would go to Richard and her parents.

In October Richard and Karen embarked on a brief promotional tour, with dates in Europe. Used to hiding her anorexic condition, Karen was blindsided by a tense tabloid-style interview on BBC current affairs show *Nationwide*. The interview was prerecorded with the siblings sitting on the studio sofa and after just one minute the presenter, Sue Lawley, whose background was in news and politics, asked Karen directly, "There were rumours that you were suffering from the slimmer's disease anorexia nervosa. Is that right?"

"No, I was just pooped. I was tired out."

"You went down to about 6 stone in weight, I think, didn't you?"

"I have no idea what '6 stone in weight' is," said Karen, rolling her eyes, looking edgy and ill at ease.

"It's 84 pounds."

"No . . . no."

Lawley kept trying to probe, but Karen refused to open up. Richard then came to his sister's rescue. "I don't feel we should be talking about the weight loss . . . It's not what we're here for."

"I am just asking you the questions people want to know the answers to," responded Lawley.[5]

After a break in recording they started the interview again and this time Lawley left out the anorexia question. Karen found it hard enough to be honest about her eating disorder with close family and friends, so she would never have made herself vulnerable on prime-time TV. Lawley's intrusive style of questioning shows how little was really known about anorexia at the time. There was an insensitivity to Karen's struggle, no awareness about what it takes to tackle and recover from the disorder. Sometimes it is crucial for a sufferer to keep up a façade, to provide an "official" explanation for their weight loss, and in Karen's case this was down to "exhaustion" or "overwork" or "colitis."

Karen may have avoided direct questions on TV, but privately one of her best friends was able to express concern. Petula

Clark was starring as Maria in *The Sound of Music* at the London Palladium, so that week Karen went to see the show and paid Clark a visit in her dressing room backstage. Even though they lived thousands of miles apart, she and Karen still had a special friendship and had kept in touch regularly since the beginning of the Carpenters' career. "We had a chat and I gave her a hug. She was just skin and bone. I looked her in the eyes and said, 'Karen, whatever you're doing you've got to stop this.' She was so lovely and the whole thing was so tragic," recalls Clark. "That was the last time I saw her."

The Carpenters' promotional tour continued in November to Rio de Janeiro. Karen made a trip to a radio station, Radio Cidade, and wooed the hosts with her customary humor and enthusiasm for the music she was hearing in the barrios. Despite her engaging chat, the deleterious effects of the anorexic behavior were drastically affecting her appearance. There are photographs from this tour where she looks a little unkempt, with ill-fitting tracksuit bottoms and a creased, shiny tour jacket several sizes too big, her gaunt face and glassy eyes framed by a tight perm.

On November 9, a few days after their return from Brazil, Harold Carpenter had a family party for his birthday in a Downey restaurant. After the meal the family went back to Newville Avenue, but Burris and Karen disappeared upstairs where they had a stormy row. Burris then came hurtling down the stairs, announcing to her parents, "You can keep her," before flouncing out the door. Some accounts report that this was the last time he saw her, but Frenda Leffler recalled making a visit soon afterward to the couple's house in Bel Air, where she found them in the middle of a $20,000 upgrade. Karen was generous with gifts but frugal with her hard-earned money, so this raised alarm bells for Leffler.

Friends in Karen's close circle wondered if Burris was a gold digger and suspicions were realized when Karen phoned Leffler in hysterics to say that a fancy Rolls-Royce Corniche car he "gave" her as a present was going to be repossessed by a loan company. "I am *not* a bank," she shouted at him, before driving over to Leffler's and collapsing in a heap on her front doorstep. Karen was mortified—too embarrassed to go home to Downey and too embarrassed to admit to her parents that her marriage had failed, so she stayed with Leffler for a while, immobilized by a severe depression. The situation got so bad that Leffler's mother Melba would cradle her and sometimes Karen was so inert she had to be spoon-fed like a baby. The only thing that raised her spirits was bathtime with her god-children, when Karen would help Leffler splash water over little Anthony and Ashley.

Nicky Chinn observes that Karen's separation from Burris was the start of her unraveling. "When she finally did get married, she couldn't have made a bigger mistake. He was awful," he says. "That's probably because Karen reckoned he was the best she deserved. It's funny, isn't it, that he claimed never to have heard of the Carpenters when he first met her? Absolute bullshit. He was a shocker. In the end he let her down very badly." Chinn sees the paradox in Karen's situation, arguing that feeling insuf-ficient will always get in the way of having a relationship and finding love. "Because you don't deserve love, especially if you feel unlovable."

Karen wanted to find love again, but the divorce had a direct impact on her well-being and her weight was frighteningly low. She also wanted to record another Carpenters album but knew she had to get better first. Having recovered from his problems during his stint in rehab, Richard urged Karen to get therapy, too. He knew it was the only way their career could continue. She lunched with friends in Beverly Hills, asking them, "How do I get over this?" She reached out again to Cherry Boone O'Neill. Karen was able to be blunt and direct to her confidante, seemingly determined to beat her anorexia. "She had this way of talking—'I'm gonna beat this thing, I know I can do it. I'm gonna lick this thing,'" recalls O'Neill. "What surprised me about Karen was, she had this public persona of being feminine and frail-looking (except for when she got behind the drums). But she could talk like a truck driver, or a salty sailor. That was a surprise! She had this low voice and almost sounded like a guy. But she was very determined and very, very hopeful."

O'Neill knew what it took to recover from anorexia, that the process was long and difficult, so she suggested to Karen that she relocate to the northwest for a quiet life and seek treatment with Dr. Raymond Vath, a psychiatrist based in Seattle who had been of significant help. He had encouraged O'Neill to read Eric Berne, creator of the concept of transactional analysis and author of *Games People Play*. Berne believed that effective therapy examines functional and dysfunctional social relations as well as the individual. If you look at those social transactions and rewrite your life script, he argued, you can start the healing process.[6] O'Neill remembers how challenging that was. "When you try to rescript your life and let go of the identity that you've been hanging onto, as maladaptive as it might be, it's scary. You've not stepped into that new identity yet, it's not fleshed out," she says. "But it can also be exciting, because you're the one that gets to write the script, instead of trying to fit into a mold that other people have presented for you."

Transactional analysis is now frequently used as a tool in psychotherapy, but in the early 1980s it was still a relatively new concept. In order to get better, O'Neill had to rewrite her life script by moving away from Hollywood and showbusiness. "No rehearsals, no fittings, no pressure to look and be perfect, to pretend to be something I was not," she wrote in *Starving for Attention*. "The thought soothed me."[7] After spending months of therapy with Vath in Seattle, O'Neill moved with her husband Dan to the small Kona Village community in Hawaii and stayed there for two years. She knew the consequences of returning to Los Angeles and media pressure before she was ready—in 1978 for instance, the filming of Boone family TV specials on ABC led to a serious relapse. For a while O'Neill was also prescribed lithium, medication that stabilized her mood disorders.

To Karen the thought of moving to the northwest, far from family, friends, and the music scene she was familiar with, was too daunting. She remembered Steven Levenkron and in November 1981 asked Itchie to call him on her behalf. The therapist was irritated when Itchie rang him, talking in conspiratorial tones about an anonymous celebrity who was suffering anorexia. He already had a long list of clients that he treated with the utmost confidentiality and said, as before, that the "unnamed famous person" should call him direct.[8]

The next day Karen rang him with a purposeful approach, telling him that she had a plane ticket and could see him that Saturday for three hours. Levenkron refused, saying he didn't work at weekends and, besides, her problem was not something that could be fixed in three hours. At this, Karen crumbled and started to cry, but he stood firm, explaining that such a short trip would be the worst care possible and she needed to commit to a long-term plan for recovery. "You sit down and think about whether you really want to fight this thing or not," he said.

After the call a tearful Karen talked it through with Itchie and the latter suggested she move to New York for treatment. She could see Levenkron regularly and have a break from the stultifying round of recording schedules, dinners with her parents, and weekly trips to the bowling alley with Richard. Three hours after her initial call, Karen phoned Levenkron again and they agreed that she would move to New York and see him one hour a day, five days a week for a year.

Like O'Neill, Karen had to start rewriting her life script, and she knew that in order to do this she needed a break from her Los Angeles life and independence from her mother. New York and Levenkron seemed like the ideal and most discreet solution, but O'Neill was not convinced that was the best option. "I went from being in Los Angeles to a very rural area where there wasn't the hubbub of the city and reminders of the pressures. Karen went from Los Angeles to New York City, where she was still in the mayhem and chaos of a big city. I tried to encourage her to go someplace where she wasn't being reminded of that all the time. But she had set her sights on working with Steven Levenkron and being in New York and he was supposedly the big name, the expert at the time."

For Karen, though, being in New York meant she could spend time with people she loved and trusted, like Itchie and Phil Ramone. It's probable that she could have benefited from medication as well as talking therapy, but apart from hospital visits she had not been in treatment long enough for a diagnosis. Although she was suffering chronic anorexia and had been ill since her collapse in 1975, proper treatment for Karen hadn't yet begun.

She had delayed getting help, partly because she was aware of her status in the public eye and wary of media scrutiny. In the 1970s and early '80s it was hard for artists to admit to mental health problems, for fear it would jeopardize their career. Diagnosed with bipolar disorder in the 1960s, Nicky Chinn can understand Karen's predicament. "There were two issues. One, it was taboo. Two, it wasn't understood. If Karen had developed anorexia in the 1990s, she would still be alive, without a doubt. But back then people were kind of discovering mental illness. Anorexia they didn't understand, it was just someone who doesn't eat. Well, there is a hell of a lot more to anorexia than that. When I told Karen she was too thin, she would always say, 'I've been working too hard, that's why.' Working too hard was the basic excuse and we bought it because we didn't know any better. We didn't know what anorexia was, we didn't have a clue."

CHAPTER 17

1982

It's like being haunted. It's the worst thing in the world.[1]

Karen didn't open up to many people, but she knew her friend Carole Curb had also struggled with bouts of anorexia, so she felt able to confide in her about how much the illness had taken over her life. Anorexia had become a tyrannical force in her psyche, telling her that food was an enemy to be fought. Thoughts of food and the methods to eliminate it had become obsessive, dominating her day and disrupting her sleep. "It's like being haunted," she said. Research shows that sufferers and their close others experience the disease as an entity. As the disorder strengthens it develops a life of its own, habits become fixed and the sufferer needs high-intensity care.[2] The savage irony of the disease is that when it starts the victim may achieve their ideal weight quickly, but as the self-imposed superdieting regime takes hold their goal weight disappears and the thinner they get the fatter they feel.

Karen knew instinctively that she needed someone strong to help her fight the anorexia, someone who saw through her denial and her attempts to hide the illness. In his phone calls, Steven Levenkron had been firm and direct about the treatment he could offer, speaking in a no-nonsense way that reassured her. The psychotherapist had already been practicing for twelve years and was on a mission to develop effective treatment for the mystery disease. Later he was to document this journey in his book *The Anatomy of Anorexia*, explaining how, as it takes hold, the illness banishes self-doubt and creates an illusion of identity and purpose. "To recover from anorexia would mean to temporarily lose one's self, to lose everything achieved by the illness," he wrote.[3]

Describing himself as a "nurturant-authoritative" psychotherapist, Levenkron's approach was controversial. With his treatment, Karen would be dependent on him in order to override the authority of the disease, until she established her own separate identity. He would become a father figure, guiding and navigating her through the process. Suspicious of Levenkron, Karen's family thought she would have been better off being "fixed" by a Beverly Hills doctor—but that hadn't worked for her, and she was ready to try something more radical.

In January 1982, Karen flew to New York and moved into a two-bedroom suite in the City Regency Hotel near Central Park, taking along twenty-two suitcases of matching clothes and shoes. Karen Ichiuji moved into the second bedroom, as a source of support and companionship for the duration of her stay. Karen had invested a lot in this treatment—the suite was

$6,000 a month before food and phone bills—but, she argued, she needed to feel comfortable. Then she paid Levenkron $100 for each session, which totaled $2,000 a month. Karen's willingness to set aside the time and the money showed her initial level of commitment to the therapy.

In theory she was determined to beat her anorexia, but from the beginning she was undermining the treatment in surreptitious ways. Levenkron's office on East 79th Street was nineteen blocks away from the Regency Hotel, but instead of conserving energy by taking a limousine Karen would power-walk up Madison Avenue, burning calories as she did so. After breakfast with Itchie—bacon, two eggs over easy, and toast—she would visit the bathroom and ingest Dulcolax laxatives so she could purge. And in the suite she found it hard to relax, standing and continually moving about in order to lose weight.

Levenkron was used to his patients showing resistance to treatment, so he noticed immediately her restlessness and frequent trips to the bathroom. Her compulsive behaviors had developed over time, so he knew it would take a while to dislodge them. At one of their early sessions he discussed with Karen what she was taking to expel food and she owned up, saying she could ingest more than ninety Dulcolax at once. Under his supervision the aim was for her to cut down and eventually stop. He then asked her if she had taken anything else and she admitted to taking ten pills a day of Synthroid, a thyroid medication, which would have the effect of speeding up her metabolism. Levenkron was horrified. Overdosage of thyroid medication could lead to coma, convulsions, and heart attacks. "Give me the bottle," he said.

Karen handed it over and he locked it in his desk drawer. The date of the prescription was August 17, 1981, just three months before she had contacted him about therapy. Oddly enough, he kept the bottle in his office long after their sessions, as a reminder and a gruesome relic.

Over the next three months during intensive therapy sessions Karen began to disentangle the way anorexia had become her security, her way of coping with the world. Levenkron noticed that she was not used to having her needs met and was unaccustomed to receiving care. During one pivotal session he said that she needed to accept his care before they could make any progress.

"I don't need any care," she said. "I'm successful like this."

"But you do need care because you are incompetent . . . because you can't keep yourself alive."[4]

She looked at him in shock. This was a turning point for Karen, when she recognized how much she had been an attentive friend and daughter, skilled at nurturing other people but unable to nurture herself. She agreed with Levenkron that she would stop taking laxatives.

Karen kept in touch with her family by phone and in April 1982 went home for a two-week visit, halfway through her treatment. Friends were concerned that despite her therapy Karen still looked emaciated and was yet to put on weight. She seemed purposeful, however, talking about a schedule for recovery, firmly believing that she could conquer her illness within the time-frame allocated and still honor recording commitments for the next album. It was during this fortnight that Karen went into

A&M's Studio D with Richard and began work on new demos. The first work vocal was on "You're Enough," a fresh Richard and John Bettis composition. The title is poignant and an example of how in his lyrics Bettis intuited whatever Karen was going through at the time. Self-acceptance is a key part of recovery and here he telegraphs to her that "good enough" is enough, that perfection lies in accepting imperfection.

A few days later she and Richard laid down the vocal for "Now," a Roger Nichols and Dean Pitchford song. On one level it is about the supportive power of romantic love, but it could be heard another way as an "end of days" spiritual transformation. On both these tracks Karen's voice is a little nasal and below par, but there is a new emotional openness in her delivery that suggests although she was physically still very unwell, she was maturing and developing self-awareness. "Now" was to be her last recording.

*

After returning to New York, Karen took up more power walking, striding through Central Park to Levenkron's office in a compulsive effort to keep her weight down. Karen was still painfully thin, rarely weighing above 78 pounds, so Levenkron suspected she was taking laxatives again. Concerned that they should be making more progress at this stage, Levenkron contacted Itchie and asked if she could check if there were pills hidden in the bathroom or under the mattress in her bedroom. Itchie was panicking about her friend, so she agreed and of course found laxatives concealed all over the suite.

When Levenkron confronted Karen about this during therapy she was deeply upset with Itchie, telling her she felt betrayed. Itchie was mortified at losing her friend's trust, but she didn't know what to do. Doug Ichiuji says that Itchie's attention on Karen was constant. "My sister was trying to keep her on track. She would find all Karen's secret stashes and flush them down the toilet and keep her focused. I guess my sister was Karen's support."[5] Even though Karen found it hard to control her compulsive behavior, the sessions with Levenkron helped give her a perspective on her anorexia, some kind of mental framework to begin dealing with it. "My understanding was that she was getting better," says Ichiuji. "You're never 'cured' for the most part, but I think she understood her issue and was starting to eat a little more."

Although it was upsetting, the confrontation with Itchie meant that Karen had to be more honest with herself, and that awareness led Levenkron to think she was ready to be honest with her family. Treatment of anorexia sufferers involves the whole family, but often they are uncertain about what to do and may collude with the eating disorder behaviors by ignoring them and covering them up or, in Agnes's case, dismissing the anorexia as just dieting gone too far. Or they may do the opposite and show extreme distress and anger, like Richard, who railed at Karen to eat. Anorexia can trap everyone into spirals of confusion.

Levenkron argues that "the anorexic is emotionally closer to her disease than she is to her family . . . the disease is attacking the family system."[6] Treatment for anorexia needs to happen with a collaborative approach, so the victim feels supported and allied with their family in beating the disease. Karen had made some progress with Levenkron, opening up about her condition, but with minimal family involvement in her therapy there was a limit to how far she could progress. Richard and her parents were wary about being drawn in, seeing the therapy very much as Karen's process. Eventually, however, they were persuaded to fly to New York for a group therapy session in Levenkron's office. Agnes in particular was resistant to therapy, viewing psychoanalysis as self-indulgent, and was suspicious about what could be achieved.

Once everyone was in the room Karen began sobbing, telling her parents how sorry she was for ruining their lives. She told them that she felt so bad, so degraded, and ashamed of how the disease had nearly wrecked her career and chances of a happy marriage and children. She was laying herself bare. As they watched her, Levenkron said, "I think Karen really needs to hear that you love her."

"Of course I love you," said Richard.

Agnes was silent. Levenkron nudged her foot with his shoe. Saying she preferred to be addressed as Mrs. Carpenter, Agnes just retorted, "We don't do things that way." Agnes found it impossible to tell her daughter how much she was loved; she was from a proud family who didn't demonstrate love for their children through physical affection. According to Levenkron, however, she stood up, went over to Karen and embraced her. That was an important moment. "We got the hug for Karen," he said.[7]

It is clear that Karen craved her mother's nurture, and in many accounts Agnes has been blamed for not showing her daughter enough love and being too domineering. However, it could also be argued that she was protective of a daughter she knew to be vulnerable. Deep down, maybe she was afraid that, left on her own, Karen would always struggle with her well-being.

And there was something missing on the father's side, too. Where was Harold's voice in this meeting; where was his hug? Maybe it went unrecorded; maybe no one thought it was worth recording—but there is a lack, an absence. Rebecca Segal, who traveled on the road with the Carpenters for months on end, recalls: "I met her father several times but I couldn't tell you a thing about him. I don't remember anything about how he felt at all. But I can remember Agnes and what she felt. I always got the sense it was her relationship, her marriage, her kids."

In her book *The Absent Father Effect on Daughters*, therapist Susan Schwartz argues that the presence of a father is important for the development of a girl's sense of self and her place in the world. Without it she is lost, "she has no bearings, she can be disconnected from her body."[8] A father can be emotionally absent even if he is physically present, a blank space that cannot reflect to her a separate, individual self. Friends say that Harold doted on his daughter, but he rarely gave her a hug or a kiss, and every time she rang home he would just hand the phone to Agnes. He didn't see how urgent it was to communicate directly with Karen. A disrupted, unsettled childhood in China, England, and America, where he had spent long periods of time away from his parents, had obviously taken its toll.

Harold was nineteen years old, living with his aunt and uncle in Maryland, when tragedy struck. His mother, Nellie, had left the family and returned to England to try and rebuild her life with his father, George. But soon after she arrived they separated and she died of pleurisy in a house in Shepherd's Bush, west London, on March 27, 1927. She was only forty-four years old. Harold was a stoic character, but the death of his mother so far away left a residual sadness. Later in life he was taciturn and slow to speak, as though he had become used to passively watching the world around him.

Agnes's personality dominated the household, leaving the children to search out their father's influence. Tom Bahler remembers Agnes as "the conductor of the train. Harold wasn't subservient, I would say they had a balanced love. It's just that he wasn't a forceful guy. The mom meant well, she wasn't the evil mom, but she was overprotective."[9]

Richard once described in an interview what he had inherited from Harold: "My love of cars and music, my draggy voice and the way I will hold things inside me all come from my father." Karen, too, mirrored her father's tendency to hold things inside, making it hard for people to get close and to help her. It is notable that she often looked for father figures in her life, like her choir teacher Frank Pooler, her boss Herb Alpert, or her managers. There is a sense of intense loneliness in Karen, that she was ricocheting around from an unnurturing mother to a wounded absent father and Richard, whom Agnes spoiled and lionized. As Susie Orbach wrote, when "the mother is unable to provide a reasonably nurturing environment . . . defences arise to fill the gap where a sense of self is lacking."[10] What Karen desperately needed from both her parents was openness and positive attachment, not ambivalence.

*

After the meeting in Levenkron's office the family stayed away. He said that they never once rang him, but then Richard claimed Levenkron didn't call them either. He was distinctly unimpressed with the therapist, particularly after Levenkron suggested that when she was through treatment Karen might not want to sing any more. Even though Karen loved to sing and connect with a crowd, ultimately it was the need to perform and dutifully meet everybody's expectations that made her sick. Like Cherry Boone O'Neill, whose anorexia worsened when she went back to recording with her family, one of Karen's most self-destructive traits was perfectionism. "We spend an awful lot of time trying to achieve perfection," she once said of the Carpenters. "It's a full-time job and it's by far the foremost thing on both our minds."[11]

By the summer of 1982, Karen seemed to be making headway in mentally understanding her condition, but the compulsive behaviors were entrenched and she still wasn't putting on weight. A concerned Itchie rang Levenkron, saying that Karen was losing energy and getting thinner and she wondered when this thing was going to turn around. "She's not responding as quickly as I'd hoped," he said, and decided to try something a little more confrontational. The next day he got Karen to change into a bikini, stand in front of a long mirror and look at her emaciated body. She didn't see anything wrong; in fact she told him she was gaining some weight.[12]

Karen may have thought she was doing fine, but at this time anyone who ran into her was shocked, like Harold Childs, who was in New York to attend promotional meetings. "I was in a taxi on Park Avenue and I saw someone standing on a corner. It took me a while to realize that it was Karen, because she had lost so much weight," he says. Word got round that she had an eating disorder, and many people wanted to help but didn't know how. The photographer Ed Caraeff was living in New York by then and had started working as a gourmet chef, with his own restaurant. "I was cooking healthy food and I wanted to feed her, nurture her, make her healthy. I don't think that would have been enough. I didn't act on it, I didn't understand it." Caraeff saw her lifestyle as a problem that may have fueled the disorder. "The Carpenters were a money-making machine with all these people depending on her. There was pressure to keep making money, do another album, do another tour. Maybe Karen should've moved to Vermont and grown potatoes."

Stephanie Spruill, who sang with Karen on the sessions for "Strength of a Woman," has a particularly poignant memory. In August 1982 she was performing with Olivia Newton-John on her Physical tour and had a date at Forest Hills, the New York stadium that hosted the US Open tennis tournament until 1977. "We were rehearsing 'Let's Get Physical,' a song where I had to be full-throttle. Olivia had us doing aerobics and then she'd speed it up real fast. We'd run across the stage and do aerobics at the same time. Honey, I was in super shape!" As they exercised, Spruill turned round and noticed a woman in a suit behind them. "I said, 'Ah, there's a lady here exercising with us.' But she was exceptionally thin and not doing it full out."

Later that night after the show all the singers and musicians went into Manhattan to go clubbing. "The club owner had closed down the club—Olivia had it like that, she was so popular! She treated us so well, she gave us inscribed Rolex watches and mine said 'Thank you Stephanie for this tour,'" recalls Spruill. Karen came along to the club and sat next to Newton-John and Spruill recognized her from the aerobics workout earlier in the day. "I was eating all the food—caviar, lobster—but I didn't see Karen eat that much." At one point Karen's head was sagging and she was clearly exhausted, finding it hard to engage with everyone around her. Spruill was perplexed, aware that something was very wrong. "Before the tour started there were plans for Karen to drum on a few shows, but that was dropped because of her deteriorating health."

By the autumn, Karen was getting dangerously close to collapse. Levenkron was alarmed one day when she came into his office saying, "My heart is beating funny." She also said that she felt dizzy and couldn't walk. Realizing that she needed immediate medical attention, Levenkron got in touch with his friend Dr. Gerald Bernstein and on September 20 she was admitted to Lenox Hill, an intensive-care hospital on the Upper East Side. Karen weighed 77 pounds and was severely dehydrated with a blood potassium level of 1.8. Potassium is critical to the functioning of heart muscle cells and the normal healthy level is 3.6–5.2

millimoles per liter. Anything less than 2.5 is life-threatening. Also Karen's digestive tract was so damaged she had to be fed by intravenous drip. The doctors accidentally punctured her lung while inserting the tube, so for a while she also had excruciating chest pain before the wound healed up.

Even though she had resisted gaining weight for a long time, once she was in hospital Karen allowed herself to be cared for. Research shows that anorexic patients can sometimes accept high-calorie fluids through an IV, because they feel they are receiving treatment instead of "putting on weight." The large drip-infusion bag offers reassuring proof that they are genuinely ill.[13] For Karen, the IV enabled her to regain some strength and she tried hard to stay positive. Over the next seven weeks she gained 20 pounds, first from intravenous nutrition and then through eating small meals. "The extent of her bravery has to be stressed," said Dr. Bernstein. Many anorexic patients suffer from strong phobias of weight gain and resist or sabotage treatment once they start eating solid food again, but Karen fought the fear. "I'll just have to keep remembering that they're supposed to look like this," she said to Levenkron, when her arms began to look less spindly. Determined to get better and gain enough weight to continue working on the album she and Richard had started, Karen kept going with her treatment. She also nourished the spark with continuous drumming in her hospital room, tapping on table tops between all the cards, gifts, and Mickey Mouse toys that had been given to her by friends and well-wishers. She finally got round to reading Cherry Boone O'Neill's book *Starving for Attention*, taking inspiration from her friend's story of recovery.

Richard paid a visit on October 25 and was saddened by her emaciation, despite her upbeat conviction that she was growing stronger. "Diet for Karen became an obsession. She's a very tough ... resilient and persistent personality ... the strength of her personality kept driving her on, saying 'I can do it, I can do it,'" he had said in 1975, at the time of her first hospitalization.[14] But that single-mindedness was no longer serving her, to the point that she needed drastic intervention. Richard was furious that she hadn't been given inpatient treatment sooner, denouncing Levenkron as ineffective. Levenkron argues that when he first began working with Karen he wanted to admit her to inpatient care, a center like Menninger's, but she point-blank refused. Karen's therapy came too late, when her compulsive behavior had already done its damage and, as he admits himself, the "less-than-perfect modality" was the only treatment that she accepted. Friends were dismayed that Karen's anorexia became chronic and that she reached such a critical condition, even while she was undergoing therapy. However, Levenkron specialized in one area, psychotherapy, and that is what he provided. Anorexia treatment in the 1970s was still in its early stages, with a lack of consistent, joined-up thinking between psychotherapy, psychiatry, and clinical medicine—the necessary network of care that is involved in treating eating disorders today.

Now she was getting stronger, Karen began making plans for the next phase of her life, and on October 28 in her hospital room she signed a petition for divorce. This was her statement of independence. Karen then discharged herself from hospital on November 8, stubbornly committed to keeping to her own schedule of being "well" by Thanksgiving. She went back to the Regency Hotel with a personal nurse, under strict instructions not to speed-walk to Levenkron's office. After two weeks Karen felt bored and homesick. Declaring, "I'm cured," she got Agnes and Harold to fly over and take her back home to Los Angeles. During her last therapy appointment on November 16, she gave Levenkron a framed needlepoint canvas she had stitched in her hotel suite. Emblazoned with the phrase "YOU WIN—I GAIN," the canvas communicated with Karen's customary wordplay that, to her at least, the goal had been achieved. Levenkron told Karen she was leaving him too soon, that treatment would take at least three years, but she waved away his concern, promising to follow up with him on the phone. "I guess she had gotten some very good help. She was her own person," recalls Gayle Levant. "No matter what I would have said, or Richard or her parents or family or close friends, she was still going to go by what was in her head."

There was a sense of Karen taking care of her affairs and reaching out to people. At this point, for instance, she called Tom Bahler, who by then had got married to someone else. "I know you're married. I'm not calling to hit on you, I just wanted to apologize to you," she said.

"Karen, that means a lot."

"Well, I've been seeing a psychotherapist and learned a lot about myself since then. And I just wanted to say that I'm sorry, you know?"

"Thank you. I will always love you no matter what form it takes. I loved you the moment you walked into the studio, you're an extraordinary human being."

For Bahler that phone call was a resolution. He had no idea that within three months she would be gone.

Even though Karen read O'Neill's book while she was in hospital, she was in denial about the process necessary for recovery. "She was in such a difficult position being the hub of the big wheel that was the Carpenters. She had so many people depending on her to be functional and present," recalls O'Neill. "I tried to encourage her to have a more open-ended approach to recovery. She was very optimistic and very upbeat and she approached her recovery the way she approached a lot of other things, like, 'I'll roll up my sleeves and dig in and do it.' But you can't approach the recovery process that way. It has to be a process and that takes time. You can't just say, 'Okay, after a month I'm going to call it good and throw myself back into the pressures of the same environment that had caused the problem in the first place.'"

Karen made it home to Thanksgiving, weighing just over 100 pounds. She ate ostentatiously on Thanksgiving Day and rang Itchie that night to tell her about everything she had eaten. Those around her felt relief and delight at what seemed to be progress, that she was keeping busy and was well enough to honor social engagements. On December 17, for instance, she serenaded Frenda Leffler's children and their classmates with a pre-Christmas celebration at their school in Sherman Oaks. She bundled up her thin frame in bulky sweaters and tracksuit bottoms, giving the illusion of being fit and healthy, but in reality she ate little and slept a lot. Agnes was troubled by all the pills that Karen had been prescribed by her doctor and which she took regularly, including the antimigraine barbiturate butalbital. Karen was still fragile and still had a long way to go.

CHAPTER 18

1983

I'm gonna beat this thing. I know I can do it.[1]

Dionne Warwick remembers joking with Karen at a photo session for the twenty-fifth anniversary of the Grammy Awards, on January 11, 1983. They were in a group portrait with other previous winners including Quincy Jones, Gladys Knight, and Glen Campbell. "She had discovered what was going on and was trying to get her life back together," says Warwick. After the group photo Karen walked over to her and said, "Hey you!"

"Yeah, whaddya want?"

"Look at my ass. I've got an ass."

"Wh-a-at?"

"Yeah. I've been eating my ass off!"

"That's wonderful, baby, I'm so happy for you."

"I'll never have one as big as yours!"

That was the last time Warwick saw her.[2]

In January 1983, Karen was living her life as if she was back on track, shopping and socializing. She bounded into Herb Alpert's office on New Year's Day saying, "Look at me!," and he agreed that she looked better. She told him she couldn't wait to get back into the studio and also get a group together and start performing again. She met with Richard and their college friend Dennis Heath on January 14, but halfway through dinner she looked stricken, excused herself and went to the ladies. When Karen returned to the table she said she was fine and they went to the nearby A&M studios to listen to playback of the tracks recorded the previous April.

Richard knew that she wasn't fine, however, and told their lawyer Werner Wolfen that he was worried. Word got back to Karen, and she angrily confronted Richard, asking for a meeting with Wolfen in his office. There she chided Richard for what she saw as disloyalty, saying that she had stuck by him and not said anything to friends or family when he came back from rehab and was "acting strange." She was better, she said, "and now you're gonna have to stick by me." But, Richard retorted, "I was in good health. I was cured. You are not in good health. I'm only telling you this because I love you."[3]

On January 27, Karen's housekeeper Florine Elie found her lying on the floor of the wardrobe in her Century City apartment. Karen was groggy and barely awake, so Elie helped her into bed and got on with her cleaning. By the time she finished, Karen was sitting up, saying she felt better. Elie was troubled, though, and rang to check on her the next morning.

On February 1, Karen dined with Richard at Scandia on Sunset Boulevard and they were joined by their stage producer,

Joe Layton, to discuss plans for touring. On February 2, Karen drove to Wolfen's office to look again at her divorce papers and they made an appointment to sign the documents on February 4 at 3 p.m. In these moments, Karen was industrious and elated, keen to rebuild her life. She rang Itchie, who at that point was nine months pregnant with her and Phil Ramone's first child. Karen talked about her plans to go to New York and be there for the birth.

On February 3, she drove from Century City to Downey, where she met her mother. Karen wanted to buy a new washer-drier for her condominium and, being a good Downey girl, she decided to get it over the counter at Gemco hypermarket. When she couldn't find what she wanted that afternoon, she decided to sleep over at her parents' house and continue the search in the morning. She, Harold, and Agnes then went out to Big Boy to eat, and Karen had a shrimp salad. She was still hungry when they left the restaurant, so she stopped for a taco on the way home.

That evening she made two phone calls. The first was to Phil Ramone, to discuss travel plans for her trip to New York. "Can I use the f-word?" she asked him.

"You're a grown woman. Say whatever you want."

"Well, I think we made a fucking great album."[4]

The next call was to Frenda Leffler, telling her to get some red nail polish for their midday manicure the following day. Karen was determined to sign her divorce papers in style. Then she said, "I feel like my chest is tired." Sometime after the call ended, Leffler rang Agnes, asking her to check on her daughter. Karen was sleeping peacefully in bed.

On the morning of February 4, Karen awoke, padded down to the kitchen, turned on the coffee pot and went back upstairs. At 8:45 a.m. Agnes heard the wardrobe doors slide open in the room above. "Karen's up," she said to Harold, before going down to the kitchen. When the coffee was ready she called the bedroom phone, but Karen didn't answer. Agnes went to the foot of the stairs and called again but there was no response, so she went up to the bedroom. She found Karen lying unclothed and motionless on the wardrobe floor. Clutching her close, she screamed to Harold to call for help.

Florine Elie also worked for Harold and Agnes. On that morning she arrived just before nine o'clock to find Agnes desperately trying to resuscitate her daughter. Elie was followed by three firemen from Downey Fire Department and paramedics from Adams Ambulance Service. The paramedics found a faint pulse and began performing CPR, while Agnes rang Richard in hysterics, barely able to get her words out. After driving in a panic from Lubec Street, Richard arrived at Newville Avenue in time to see the paramedics taking Karen out of the house on a stretcher. As the ambulance took off with a siren and flashing lights he broke down, aware, with a terrible sense of inevitability, that his sister was dying.

Karen was admitted to Downey Community Hospital at 9:23 a.m., having gone into full cardiac arrest. An assistant to the anaesthetist was a family friend who recognized Karen and was distraught. When she told the registered nurse, Pat Tomlin, who their patient was, she realized that the hospital would need to be prepared for a press avalanche and sent one of the staff to inform the hospital manager. Dr. Irv Edwards and his ER team spent twenty-eight minutes trying to revive Karen, but at 9:51 she was pronounced dead. Agnes and Harold were distraught. "Can't you bring her back?" they wailed, but Edwards gently explained there was nothing more they could do. Richard, meanwhile, sat there feeling numb and hopeless, trying to process the fact that his sister, his lifelong musical partner, was dead at thirty-two years old. The family stayed for a while at the hospital before they were given a police escort back to the house. By then, news had broken and press and TV crews were gathered behind a cordon at the end of Newville Avenue.

As reports of Karen's death spread through the music industry there was collective shock and disbelief. The A&M compound was usually a hive of activity, with musicians, producers, and label personnel working in the studios or hanging out in the car park, but on that day the place went quiet. Alan Oken remembers, "There was a pall over the studio lot. It was deadly silent. In most active hours of the day there was usually a constant buzz, but that day it was dead. No one was walking around. Nobody. People were stunned. It felt like the lot was stunned." Harold Childs remembers radio stations calling them all day. "We knew she was sick, but didn't realize how sick she was. It was a shock to the whole country. She'd become America's sweetheart. Her sound reached so many people, so many loved to hear her voice."

Stephanie Spruill was in South Africa on a world tour with Julio Iglesias when she heard the news. "I was going to my room with my luggage and the radio was on. The announcer said, 'Breaking news: sad to announce that Karen Carpenter passed away because of anorexia.' I had never heard of that word before in my life, I didn't know what that was. I just fell to the floor and started crying, a guttural cry. I couldn't believe it. Karen, no longer here, with us? How? I loved her and I imagine how Olivia felt, because they were real good buddies."

Doug Ichiuji called his brother-in-law, but Phil Ramone and Itchie had not yet heard the news. "I said, 'You need to tell [Itchie], someone needs to tell her.' He told her and she just went bonkers. It was bad. She was about to have a baby. I went up to New York to help her calm down and help her get through it. A lot of friends came to her aid, we knew how close she was to Karen."

In his diary, Karen's teacher and mentor Frank Pooler wrote, "Karen Carpenter died at 10 a.m. this morning from heart failure. She was only 32. I had known her since she was 16. An old dear, dear friend has gone and I grieve for Richard and her parents. I delivered a note to Rich informing him that the choir was at his disposal. A cop guarding the parents' home said he would give it to Richard. I feel down. So many fine memories of the fun and music we shared over so many years. She will be missed by millions."[5]

Investigations took place into the cause of Karen's death. On the afternoon of February 4, the Los Angeles County medical examiner, Dr. Ronald Kornblum, carried out a two-hour autopsy and, pending further results from laboratory tests, deferred his decision. Meanwhile the Downey Police Department went to Karen's Century City apartment and searched for anything suspicious. They took away some medication including Ativan pills, which are usually prescribed for anxiety disorder. The final autopsy report came on March 11, with cause of death recorded as "emetine cardiotoxicity due to or as a consequence of anorexia." Traces of ipecac syrup were present in the liver. Taken in high quantities, it can cause potassium deficiency, which leads to heart arrhythmia and slowly dissolves the heart muscle.

Steven Levenkron was appalled to hear about the emetine— during his phone calls after she returned to Los Angeles, she had assured him she was no longer taking laxatives. Typically, Karen was being selective with the truth, not admitting to Levenkron that she was using ipecac instead. Karen didn't like to make herself vomit, but according to Itchie the use of ipecac started while Karen was with Tom Burris, though it was not constant. She recalled the phone conversation after Thanksgiving when Karen sounded hoarse, saying she had been ill because she had eaten too much. Now Itchie could see that Karen probably ingested ipecac that night, adopting bulimic behavior that she felt enabled her to eat without gaining weight. "I talked to the coroner myself and he said it was only a matter of time," Itchie said. "She had just starved her organs for so long."[6]

Cherry Boone O'Neill says that news of Karen's death took her breath away. "It hadn't been that long since I had spoken with her. When I heard the news and even to this day, if I hear her voice singing I feel so sad." She believes that Karen's descent was rapid because she had left treatment in New York so abruptly and gone home. "She went to the same doctors who prescribed diuretics and she was back in that pressure-cooker environment. So she went back to the old familiar behaviors that she had always fallen into before. Karen wasn't an exerciser and with her bulimia she opted for using ipecac, so internally there was a lot of stress and strain. It was too much for her heart and her body."

After her death Karen's body was dressed in a rose-colored suit and laid out in a white coffin surrounded by red and white roses. Family and friends came to visit and pay their respects, including the disgraced Burris, who barely acknowledged any-one as he strode in and threw his wedding ring into the coffin with Karen's body. People in the room showed little response to this dramatic gesture. "I feel totally guilty, like I'd like to reverse everything," he later told *People* magazine. He maintained that while they were married he had tried to find a doctor, but Karen "wouldn't admit she had an eating problem."[7] Since then Burris has never spoken out. Although Karen had not signed her divorce papers (she was due to do so on the day she died), her updated will had been finalized, leaving the marital home to Burris and the $6 million fortune to her family. After Karen's death he reached a settlement with the Carpenter family, part of which was not to give interviews or to discuss their marriage.

With Karen's passing, tributes poured in from around the world—from musicians, artists, fans, and politicians. Her voice and her music had resonated with so many people, on such a profound level. "People loved Karen, she was held in the high-est regard. I didn't know too much about Richard, he seemed an unusual guy. She was the real superstar," Alan Oken says. "Karen was such an important figure, it was awe-inspiring to be around her."

THE STORY OF KAREN CARPENTER

On February 6, Petula Clark was doing a show with the London Philharmonic Orchestra at the Royal Albert Hall. For the finale she sat at the piano and began telling a story, about how she had been asked to sing "For All We Know" at the 1971 Academy Awards show. The song was recorded by the Carpenters for the film *Lovers and Other Strangers* and had been a US number-three hit for the band—it also won an Academy Award. "It was a very glittering occasion with as many stars in the audience as there were on stage, very Hollywood. I was a little jumpy," said Clark. "I received a telegram before I went on which made me feel a lot better; it was from the lady who had made this song a hit . . . She became a very dear friend of mine. She said, 'Hi Petula, sing the song pretty for me tonight.' Her name was Karen, Karen Carpenter." The audience burst into heartfelt applause. Clark added, "Karen, my sister, my friend, it's hard to believe this strange, tragic end. You were funny and nice . . . a little naive . . . and you lived for your music. And now, for you, I grieve."[8]

There was silence as Clark sang the song with a simple, unadorned piano accompaniment. Remembering that tribute forty years later, she says, "It was really off the cuff. Her death happened suddenly and I didn't know what to do. I'd never played that song before and it was a challenge, at the Royal Albert Hall. There was always a chance I might slip up with the words. But everybody knew that song and I just wanted to pay homage."

In 2000, Clark said in a TV documentary that Karen's death "bothered" her and it still bothers her now.[9] "That illness is such a mystery. They never found out what caused it, some underlying unhappiness. Her family life was difficult and she felt under too much pressure, wanting to be a beautiful person, the same old silly thing. She didn't need to prove that to anyone. She was so lovely, the whole thing was so tragic."

On February 7, Frank Pooler went to the chapel at Forest Lawn Cypress memorial park to rehearse the choir for Karen's memorial service. They ran through "Adoramus te, Christe," a flowing sacred motet by Giuseppe Corsi da Celano, the spiritual "Give Me Jesus" and the Bach–Gounod version of "Ave Maria." Upon hearing "Give Me Jesus," David Alley, who was part of the choir and who had been in love with Karen, burst into tears. "So did most of us. I remember that day very well," Pooler wrote in his diary.

Karen's funeral was on February 8, at 1 p.m. in Downey United Methodist Church. Police held back crowds who had lined the street as limousines filed through. At the service were numerous close friends, such as Olivia Newton-John, Dionne Warwick, Burt Bacharach, and Carole Curb. Karen's childhood minister Reverend Charles Neal gave the eulogy, a familiar figure from her days in the Methodist youth ministry. Pallbearers including David Alley, Herb Alpert, John Bettis, Ed Leffler, Gary Sims, Ed Sulzer, and Werner Wolfen carried Karen into the church, while Frank Pooler led the choir from Cal State, which included his friend and student Stan DeWitt. Soloist Dennis Heath performed the "Ave Maria," the same setting that Karen had sung so powerfully for their 1978 *Christmas Portrait* album.

"It was an impressive service, Karen would have been pleased. It was packed," says de Witt. "We were in the balcony in the back. It was very emotional, very somber. I remember feeling a sense of kind of being part of history in a way; we were witnessing something that millions of people probably would have loved to have been part of. It felt important, that we were kind of honoring her with our singing." It seemed fitting that Karen's old teacher and mentor was there at the end. "I get the impression that the mother and father found it difficult to show love, yet she was someone who needed a lot of love and affection. And it seems that Frank was a very warm person, maybe took a fatherly role," says DeWitt.[10]

After the funeral there was a private ceremony at Forest Lawn Cypress for a small group of family and friends. Karen never wanted to be buried underground, so her body was entombed in a marble crypt at the Sanctuary of Compassion in Forest Lawn's Ascension Mausoleum. Above her tomb was a mosaic reproduction of the *Madonna and Child with St Martina and St Agnes* by El Greco and a gold epitaph with the inscription "A star on earth—a star in heaven."

The spiritual ceremony around Karen's death and her gilded entombment had the air of sacred worship usually attached to a martyr or a saint. But in the months after her death, many voiced a sense of troubled disquiet at her passing. Tommy Morgan, for instance, whose harmonica graced their hit song "Rainy Days and Mondays," says, "The sense of loss was so big, it affected everyone. This business can eat people alive."

Karen's friend Nicky Chinn feels that she was a down-to-earth Downey girl who achieved a superstardom that she was never really able to handle. "Karen was very lovable. She didn't think so, but she was a very sweet, funny person. I've known a lot of stars in my time and she wasn't like most of them," he says, convinced that all her inner turmoil was expressed in the Carpenters' songs. "The tone was staggering, the feeling, the pain. There never has been a singer like her. There have been some who can belt out a song and do it wonderfully well, like Celine Dion or Whitney Houston. But Karen *understated* herself and the emotion. She never went for the big notes, because she knew that wasn't her."

Dionne Warwick sees an entertainment industry that puts unrealistic pressure on performers to be slim and beautiful. "I think that's the silliest thing in the world. Why would you want to be slim and beautiful? When people say, 'I'm going to get a facelift, get my eyes done, get my chin done, get my neck done,' my first question to them is: 'What makes you think you can improve on what God made perfect?' You can't. Once you start trying to change it, that's when it gets worse and worse and worse." She still feels the loss of her friend. "I miss her terribly. We would talk at least two or three times a week and I knew her family very well. Karen was a dream. What happened to her is sad, that she passed from anorexia, but her life was not sad. She was a hoot. She loved to laugh, she was fun to be around."

For Russell Javors, the overall feeling was one of waste and the question of whether the tragedy could have been avoided. "It's not like people weren't trying to help her. Phil and Karen [Itchie] were very much aware and tried to help every way they could," he says. "I know it was an area of concern and one that didn't get swept under the rug. There was such overwhelming sadness when she died."

For Doug Ichiuji, one memory stands out—how Itchie gave birth to a son, BJ, two days after Karen died. The experience was bitter-sweet, a bloom of new life in the midst of devastation. When his first daughter was born, he received an unexpected gift from Agnes Carpenter, who sent him Karen's baby blanket, and he appreciated her friendliness. For a while, Itchie continued to develop her singing career as Karen Kamon and had some mainstream success, performing the song "Manhunt" on the soundtrack to the movie *Flashdance*. In 1984, she also had a hi-NRG pop hit with "Loverboy" and a bit part in the US TV police drama *T. J. Hooker*. Itchie had New York club style and a dynamic pop voice, but her career never really gathered momentum.

Karen's death left a huge void at the center of the music industry and seemed to impact on those around her for a long time. "I don't think my sister ever recovered; she went into a tailspin," says Ichiuji. "Her health started to go down not long after Karen passed away and just snowballed." Itchie became ill with lupus and struggled with her health for many years until she died in 2020, at the age of sixty-eight. Though she was often in pain, Itchie rarely complained. She was always happy to share recollections of Karen; it was important to her to keep her memory alive. "They were kindred spirits, like sisters. So close and connected," says Ichiuji.

Harpist Gayle Levant couldn't believe that the friend she had made music with for so many years had gone. She is convinced that toward the end of her life Karen had turned a corner and seemed to be back on track. "Then her heart couldn't take it and she didn't make it—like her mind and emotions were starting to deal with it, but her body by then had given up. I just wish she was still with us," she says. "I'm hoping that the way she phrased, the way she sang, will resonate forever. Karen's legacy is the gift that she gave to us through her art, the voice in her heart. She didn't just sing the words; she lived them. She told the story."

The photographer Ed Caraeff sums it up simply, remembering the pensive girl he shot for the *Horizon* album cover as the sun went down over Coldwater Canyon. "She lived her life the way she wanted to. She was not being looked at any more."

And finally, drummer Liberty Devitto, who shared those special solo sessions with Karen in New York: "There's no ending to Karen Carpenter. It's like she was there, she was beautiful, she had a wonderful voice, she entertained so many, she was funny, we all loved her and then she was gone."

EPILOGUE

Karen's passing was mourned throughout the world and then, after she was laid to rest, there was a period of quiet. No one could have anticipated, however, that within three years her story would re-emerge in a way that was huge, troubling, and luminescent, and that entailed a complete re-evaluation of the Carpenters' legacy.

A month after Karen's death, Richard returned to the studio and listened to "Now" and "You're Enough," the two tracks they had been working on during their last recording session. He added arrangements and combined them with outtakes and previously unreleased material to create a new compilation, called *Voice of the Heart*. The album included a beefed-up version of "Make Believe It's Your First Time" from her solo album. "I know she would have wanted it this way," Richard said. It's debatable whether Karen would really have wanted the addition on her solo work of elaborate harmony vocals, so this decision was more in tune with Richard's taste. Released in October 1983, the album sold a modest 300,000 copies in the US and garnered respectable reviews.

At the same time as *Voice of the Heart* was released, the Carpenters were given a star on the Hollywood Walk of Fame. Richard then worked on a posthumous compilation of unreleased tracks from the 1977–78 *Christmas Portrait* sessions and recorded a few new ones at Abbey Road Studios in London, to create the 1984 compilation *An Old-Fashioned Christmas*. That year Richard also settled down in his personal life. On May 19, 1984, in Downey United Methodist Church, he married his cousin Mary Rudolph, the woman he had been dating on and off for the previous eight years.

By 1986, three years after Karen's death, Richard was ready to work on his first solo album. He began to refashion songs originally reserved for Karen—like "Something in Your Eyes," which featured Dusty Springfield on lead vocals. Although before the recording session Springfield was plagued with self-doubt and in awe of Karen's legacy, she delivered a husky, soulful, authoritative performance. When Richard's album *Time* was released in October 1987, this track was released as the first single. Springfield was miffed that she was not shown on the record's picture sleeve and she only had a tiny credit under Richard's name—even though two months before she'd had a US *Billboard* number one with the Pet Shop Boys and the song "What Have I Done to Deserve This?" The lead single from *Time* received radio airplay and reached number twelve in the US adult contemporary charts, showing that there was some interest in Richard, but the public was missing Karen.

Dionne Warwick, the other guest female vocalist on his album, expressed that sense of loss in the raw vocal on the Carpenter–Bettis song "In Love Alone." She said afterward that this was one of the hardest recording sessions she had ever done. Originally Richard planned to play it for Karen during a Christmas party he was hosting in 1982, but because of bad weather she decided not to attend and then she never got to hear it. The song, like several tracks on the album, became a tribute to Karen. While Richard is expressive in his piano-playing, he can be less effective as a lead vocalist, sometimes struggling to get the tone right. On the track "When Time Was All We Had," for instance, which is dedicated to his sister, the sentiment is slightly compromised by an odd, jaunty feel.

There's a sense on this album that Richard was going in two different directions—situating himself as both a "blue-eyed soul" act like Hall & Oates or Dan Hartman and also a string ballad maestro mourning his sibling—and these elements weren't an easy mix. The romantic ballads seemed too sugary, missing the way Karen's voice would bring a depth and clarity that counter-balanced anything overembellished. In their partnership, she was very much the yin to Richard's yang.

At first it seemed that the impact of Karen's work and the Carpenters' legacy would slowly unfold with astutely put-to-gether compilations and Christmas treats, but then a student film emerged in 1987 that challenged A&M's carefully constructed picture of the Carpenters—Todd Haynes's animated horror *Superstar: The Karen Carpenter Story*. Haynes went on to make major features including *Velvet Goldmine* and *Far from Heaven*, but when he shot *Superstar* he was a graduate student at Bard College in upstate New York. He and cowriter Cynthia Schneider were involved with AIDS activism in New York City. They also shared a love of female artists like Joni Mitchell and Dionne Warwick, they had been reading women's studies literature such as Susie Orbach's groundbreaking psychoanalytical work *Fat Is a Feminist Issue*, and they were both Carpenters fans. For Haynes, who was born in 1961, their music reminded him of his southern California childhood, a period in the early 1970s that "felt like the last moment of pure popular-culture fantasy and fakeness that I shared with my parents, when we were still united in this image of happy American family-hood."[1]

Drawing on these influences, *Superstar* tells Karen's story through dolls, some assembled from repurposed Barbies and others picked up in flea markets and vintage stores. It was shot on 16mm and Super8 with a homemade aesthetic, on miniature sets that recreated locations such as Downey, the A&M offices, Karen's Century City condo, a hospital room, and a Las Vegas stage. It is highly stylized, like the scene featuring a split-screen phone conversation Karen has with Cherry Boone O'Neill. The 43-minute film parodies the TV biopic genre, telling Karen's story using a schlock horror style and a montage of clips from news footage—the Vietnam War, the Kent State massacre, and Watergate—disaster movie *The Poseidon Adventure*, and saccharine 1970s TV shows *The Brady Bunch* and *The Partridge Family*. Most controversial of all is the use of Holocaust footage, suggesting there is a link between self-starvation and the "fascism" of anorexia.

Karen is portrayed in a sympathetic light, as the victim of an overcontrolling family and a music industry obsessed with money and celebrity. There is also the suggestion that Richard is a repressed homosexual and that Karen, in her awkward tomboyish manner, has an ambiguous sexual identity. *Superstar* set the framework for an alternative reading of the Carpenters. The tag line of *The Poseidon Adventure* was "Hell, Upside Down" and *Superstar* was one of the first cultural interpretations of the Carpenters that turned their story upside down to explore the shadow side— in the same way that TV series like *Twin Peaks* and *Stranger Things* did in the 1990s and 2010s.

Although some critics said the film was done in "bad taste," Haynes has always been adamant that it was respectful of Karen. Aware of the sarcasm and dismissive attitude around the Carpenters at the time, Haynes said, "I felt she deserved to be redeemed." Because he made it as a student film, Haynes didn't clear music rights with the Carpenters' estate and at first many venues who saw this as a legal problem rejected *Superstar*. As a result, the film premiered in three downtown locations—at Film Charas, a squatted Latino community center, the Millennium arts center and the Pyramid club, the epicenter of the gay drag punk scene.

The film was reviewed favorably in the *Village Voice* and by Barbara Kruger in *Artforum* and soon caught on, being shown in venues across the US and at film festivals including the Utah Film Festival (later renamed Sundance). Not everyone enjoyed it—during the discussion after a showing at the Toronto Film Festival in 1988 a female audience member shouted at Haynes,

"This film degrades women and anorexics and offers no gender analysis. I want you to explain this piece of SHIT!"[2]

Superstar was adopted by teachers and as an educational aid by eating disorder clinics and even though the film was premiered in 1987 it was some time before there was a legal challenge. In 1988, Mattel sent a cease-and-desist letter saying, "You are associating our product [Barbie] with death." However, Haynes argued that the brand wasn't mentioned in any of their publicity and the dolls in the film weren't clearly Barbie product— many of the heads and bodies had been changed and mixed with other dolls and the dolls had been painted with enamel and scratched beyond recognition. "We had a little factory of separate, exchangeable body parts," he said. And for Karen, the doll he used had full, round cheeks, so for later scenes he tried carving them down. "It made these huge sort of gashes in her face. So we ended up using pancake make-up to fill in the gashes and it created a very kind of otherworldly effect."[3]

Mattel dropped their challenge, but a more serious one arrived in October 1989 when Haynes and Schneider received more cease-and-desist letters: from Richard's music publisher, Almo Music Corporation, from A&M, and from the estate of Karen Carpenter, saying, "You are using without our permission the Carpenters' logo, images, life story and music." This showed a desire to protect not just the Carpenters' music, but also their image. *Superstar* had to be removed from circulation. The film disappeared from the art house circuit, but since then bootleg copies have exchanged hands and VHS transfers have been shown at secret screenings. As a result, *Superstar* has become an underground cult classic, and in 2003 *Entertainment Weekly* rated the film number forty-five on its list of "Top 50 Cult Movies."

After Karen's death, the family tried to steer the way the Carpenters' story was mediated. In 1984, they had approved a proposal for a biopic about Karen's life, and Jerry Weintraub approached Barry Morrow, the award-winning screenwriter of *Rain Man*, to write the script. Morrow was not a big fan of the Carpenters, but after listening closely to their music he became captivated by the sadness and sorrow in Karen's voice and signed up to the project. When he went to Downey and met Agnes, however, he was disconcerted by her prickly demeanour. Before he walked in the door, the first thing she said to him was, "I want you to know I did not kill my daughter."[4] From the initial stages of development to filming in the autumn of 1988, there was tension over how the family would be represented. Because he had an executive producer role, Richard closely followed filming and was a constant presence on set. The former *Fame* star Cynthia Gibb played Karen, and Richard spent time intensively working with her on lip-synching and drum parts, for instance. As part of researching Karen's character she also spoke to Agnes and Harold.

"We shot some scenes in the family home in Downey and I found it terribly difficult at first to talk to her mother and father," she said. Gibb found it an eerie experience going through Karen's clothes that were stored in a trunk in Downey, trying on for the part her dresses, blouses, shoes, and even her wedding gown. "The first day I opened the trunk there was a ghost in the room, an energy about the clothes that was very real . . . I felt Karen's spirit there among all her possessions. It's something I will never forget as long as I live. Karen was the hardest character to let go of when the film was finished."[5]

Josh Cruze, the actor who played Herb Alpert, remembers that the actors and production team handled the subject matter with sensitivity. The film had an experienced director in Joseph Sargent, who had worked with Gregory Peck in the 1977 film *MacArthur*. "It was a very kind, warm set, very giving with a lot of love, especially the tough scenes, like when Cynthia was singing her last song in the studio where Karen recorded her vocal," recalls Cruze. Many scenes were shot on the A&M lot, and Alpert came down to introduce himself to Cruze. A musician who has his own group, Bandidos de Amor, Cruze was "tickled pink" to be playing Alpert. "We chatted—he was a very nice gentleman, a wonderful man. Nice spirit. I was a teenager growing up with all that music and Tijuana Brass was a band that I liked. For many years, I thought that they were all Hispanic and came from Tijuana. I didn't know that Herb wasn't Hispanic!"[6]

On January 1, 1989, *The Karen Carpenter Story* was aired on CBS and broke viewing records, becoming the highest-rated TV movie of the year. It also started a fevered cultural conversation about eating disorders and anorexia and the potentially corrosive effects of the media scrutiny that comes with fame. Although Richard had been involved with the film at every stage, he was unhappy with the outcome, later dismissing it as "ninety minutes of creative licence that give biopics in general a dubious tone." Gibb countered this, saying that the final movie was "whitewashed," with the image of Agnes Carpenter toned down and certain unflattering scenes removed. Barry Morrow had been required to redraft his script four times, and when he was asked to write a fifth draft in December 1988 he refused and another writer, Cynthia Cherbak, was brought in to soften the edges of Agnes's character.

However, the family pressures on Karen are still evident. "When I saw the film I said, 'Oh my gosh, those parents were very possessive, they look like showbusiness parents,'" says Cruze. For him, the film is painful to watch but raises important issues. "We all go into this field as artists, because we want to express ourselves and we want to be regarded. But there's so many issues that affect us, where we try to fit in—whether it's weight gain, whether it's parents, whether it's social class. I think that this film has held up because it deals with anorexia . . . it shows that you can be very successful, but personal issues and demons surface when you're alone. Karen was a great singer, but she didn't focus on how great she sang, or that they had hit songs, but the insecurity she had regarding her weight."

Agnes and Harold may have been in denial about the extent of Karen's illness, but after her death their own health suffered. In 1988, Harold died of heart failure on Richard's birthday, October 15, at the age of seventy-nine. Agnes died eight years later on November 10, 1996, following triple-bypass heart surgery, and both parents joined Karen in the family crypt at Forest Lawn Cypress. They stayed there until 2003, when Richard had the bodies exhumed and reinterred in a new family mausoleum in the Tranquillity Gardens at Valley Oaks Memorial

Park in Westlake, just a few minutes' drive from his home in Thousand Oaks.

*

As the decade turned, the Carpenters' music was appreciated in a different context. Experimental art rock band Sonic Youth anticipated the dismantling of popular culture that came with 1990s grunge, first with their 1988 Ciccone Youth project and reinterpretation of Madonna songs. Then for their 1990 album *Goo* they recorded "Tunic," a song dedicated to Karen, suggesting in bald, dramatic tones that in her passive resistance to being the perfect good girl, she made herself disappear.

Directly inspired by a bootleg version of Todd Haynes's *Superstar,* Sonic Youth bassist Kim Gordon was personally moved by Karen's story. "She was an extreme version of what a lot of women suffer from—a lack of control over things other than their bodies, which turns the female body into a tool for power," wrote Gordon in her memoir *Girl in a Band.* The song was titled "Tunic" because Karen was so thin "her clothes hung on her bones like flowing biblical robes. She couldn't make peace with her own body's curves."[7] With its droning, taut guitars and Gordon's deadpan vocals, this six-minute epic is devastating in its simplicity. "Tunic" paints a chilling picture of Karen looking down from heaven, talking to her mother and her brother and saying goodbye. Gordon wrote the song as a reflection on self-esteem and body image and developed this idea further in an open fan letter to Karen, published in the book *Sonic Youth: Sensational*

Fix. "I must ask you, Karen, who were your role models? Was it yr mother? What kind of books did you like to read? Did anyone ever ask you that question—what's it like being a girl in music? What were yr dreams?" she wrote.[8]

Gordon's song reverberated with alternative rock fans, creating the space for a new visioning of the Carpenters. In the 1990s, Generation X was coming of age, children of divorce and single-parent households who were critiquing consumerism, societal pressures, and the American dream. The Carpenters' track "Rainy Days and Mondays" summed up the zeitgeist. "This was an important song for many Gen X-ers whose parents got divorced and played this song on repeat," says Beth Sather, a grunge fan from Portland whose mother played the Carpenters.[9] In contrast to baby boomers who equated the Carpenters with "white bread" conservatism, a younger audience heard the pain and implicit soulfulness in their music.

"Tunic" paved the way for an important tribute album, 1994's *If I Were a Carpenter*. Released by A&M, the compilation was the brainchild of Matt Wallace, producer for the Replacements and Faith No More. For this fourteen-track collection, a raft of Carpenters songs were reimagined by acts as varied as Sheryl Crow, the Cranberries, Grant Lee Buffalo, and Babes in Toyland. Sonic Youth contributed an eerie version of "Superstar," while Dutch indie rock band Bettie Serveert interpreted "For All We Know."

"Karen was awkward, a misfit, insecure like us," says Bettie Serveert's lead singer and guitarist, Carol van Dijk.[10] While recording their second album for Matador the band were invited to join the project on the recommendation of Sonic Youth, so

319

they jumped at the chance. They had long been Carpenters fans, especially drummer Berend Dubbe, who describes the music as "out of this world. The slick production, it's insane and beautiful and almost too smooth so you feel a little weird when you listen. It's really extreme music, not easy listening at all, because it's very involved."

Van Dijk loved the fact that Karen was a drummer. "I thought that was so cool. She felt more comfortable singing behind the drums, it's like a barrier. I totally got that. I'm an introvert and extremely shy, not an obvious front person in the spotlight. I understood why she felt safe behind the drum kit." When Bettie Serveert recorded "For All We Know" in their Amsterdam studio, Van Dijk had to sing in a low register so she lay flat on the floor with the microphone just above her face and the guys in the band placed flickering candles around her. This adds to the distorted, hauntingly poignant interpretation of the song. "I focused on trying to live the song, picture it inside me," says Van Dijk. "I don't do a lot of covers, I have to feel it in my heart. That's why we chose this one."

On this compilation there is a feeling of solidarity with Karen, particularly from the female musicians. The Carpenters had been superstars in Japan, so it was fitting that Japanese all-girl punk band Shonen Knife showed their appreciation by recording a Ramones-style version of "Top of the World." "For me it's the most POP song in all the Carpenters' songs. I knew I couldn't sing it well like Karen, but I thought I could express it my way, so I arranged it as a rock and punk version," says singer and guitarist Naoko Yamano.[11] She was a young teenager into hard rock when the Carpenters toured Japan in the 1970s and didn't much care for their music. But after Yamano started Shonen Knife she listened to them afresh and grew to love the arrangements. "Their music is well thought out, they have craftsmanship like a carpenter," she says.

Richard Carpenter was pleasantly surprised with the compilation, grateful that a new generation were plugging into their music. With the appreciation of a whole new audience, there was pressure from fans for A&M to release Karen's forgotten solo album. Four tracks had appeared, remixed by Richard, on the Carpenters' 1989 collection *Lovelines*—but finally, sixteen years after it had been completed, Karen's album was released as it was originally recorded. Richard endorsed its release, writing in the liner notes, "Karen was with us precious little time. She was a great artist. This album reflects a certain period and change of approach in her career. As such it deserves to be heard . . ." Even though it received mixed reviews (and still does), producer Phil Ramone was happy. "I don't apologize for any of it. I know how she felt about it and I know how I feel. I still feel good about it. Some of the songs on there are definitely mature works—and worthy of Karen Carpenter," he said.[12]

Many reviewers still adopted a disparaging tone, unable to get past the received notion of Karen as just the lustrous unworldly voice of the Carpenters. *New York Times* critic Rob Hoerburger wrote, "The last of America's great virginal sweethearts was even, in her own polite way, singing about the joys of sex and finally catching up to women's liberation." He went on to describe Richard as "part Pygmalion . . . the master carver of her sound." Karen was still represented as hopelessly naive, a woman without agency.

Richard continued to curate Carpenters material into the 2000s and by then fans were getting irritated by the constant reframing of her voice. The 2004 compilation *Time Goes By* featured unreleased demos, live shows, and TV performances between 1967 and 1980, including Karen's famous medley with Ella Fitzgerald. Released in their original form, these rarities would have captured living moments from Carpenters history. But Richard couldn't resist remixing elements or adding sugary strings and background singers. "Perhaps he just has too much free time, perhaps he is an obsessive tinkerer," wrote Allmusic.com reviewer Tim Sendra. "Whatever the excuse, the archival value of the songs has been tampered with and that makes the songs less valuable somehow."[13]

Remixing and keeping Karen's voice before the public is an enduring tribute from Richard to the sister he grieves for, but it allows less space for Karen to be discovered on her own terms, as a musician and artist in her own right. Gradually, however, appreciation of her work has deepened year by year and the Carpenters, once ridiculed by writer Nick Kent as having "WASP-ish neutroid charm," are now seen as iconic innovators. Karen's influence has been far-reaching. In 2016, for instance, My Chemical Romance frontman Gerard Way shared an intense cover of "Superstar" from the recording sessions for their *Black Parade* album. "This track was a warm-up," he wrote on Twitter. "Because I used to warm up to the Carpenters. It was a pleasure to sing. I <3 u Karen Carpenter." Then, in 2022, transgender female artist Ethel Cain released *Preacher's Daughter*, a ground-breaking album of ethereal dream pop and southern Gothic, that dealt with themes of nostalgia, poverty, substance abuse, and transgenerational trauma. One of Cain's earliest and most important musical influences was Karen Carpenter. Listening to her voice, alongside classical music, "lent itself to the melodrama that permeates my life."[14]

The impact of Karen's story is also felt in the music business and the way female artists are treated. Her death marked the beginning of greater awareness about eating disorders and mental health. "The first thing that people learned was the seriousness of an eating disorder, that it wasn't just something to joke about," says Cherry Boone O'Neill. In 1984, she saw *Splash*, a romantic comedy starring Daryl Hannah as a mermaid who becomes human and goes shopping in a department store in New York. "In the scene a saleswoman says, 'Oh, you'd look good in anything. You're like my daughter, she can wear anything. She's anorexic.' The line was meant to be funny, but that wasn't funny to me," recalls O'Neill. "It's one thing to read a statistic like with anorexia there's a 10 percent mortality rate. But, when somebody as prominently and publicly known as Karen Carpenter becomes one of those 10 percent, that makes everybody stop and think, *Oh, this is a very serious thing, this isn't something to be joked about.*"

In the years after Karen's death, a number of celebrities decided to go public about their eating disorders, among them Diana, Princess of Wales, and singer Lena Zavaroni (who sadly died in 1999 from pneumonia, already weakened by years battling anorexia). There was scant knowledge of anorexia nervosa and bulimia prior to Karen's death, making eating disorders difficult to identify and treat. Her family started the Karen A. Carpenter Memorial Foundation, which raised money for research on anorexia nervosa and eating disorders. Today it is the Carpenter Family Foundation and in addition to eating disorders, the foundation funds the arts, entertainment, and education.

It is worth asking how much has changed in the last forty years, particularly for women in entertainment. The idealization of thinness continued into the 1990s with supermodel Kate Moss saying, "Nothing tastes as good as skinny feels," and in the 2000s and 2010s the impact of the internet, social media, and digital streaming put pressure on performers to be constantly available, glossy and airbrushed. "Perfect is a tricky word. It makes you sick," says pop artist Kesha. "What the fuck is perfect? And who gets to decide?"[15]

More recently the willingness of artists to speak out has helped to destigmatize eating disorders so that sufferers can get support. Taylor Swift, for instance, talked in her 2020 documentary *Miss Americana* about how the constant scrutiny of her appearance caused her to stop eating. "It's not good for me to see pictures of myself every day," she says. A younger generation have been frank about these issues in song—from Fiona Apple's "Paper Bag" ("Hunger hurts, but starving works, when it cost too much to love") to Rilo Kiley's "Jenny You're Barely Alive," Lana Del Rey's "Boarding School" and Halsey's "Devil in Me."

This is all part of a cultural conversation that makes the music industry accountable and conscious of what it is communicating to female artists about success. Ironically, many performers' problems worsen when they achieve global fame. In the film *Amy*, interviewees disclose that during the recording of her hit album *Back to Black*, Amy Winehouse's struggle with bulimia sharply intensified. Shirley Manson, lead singer with industrial rock band Garbage, said that she had self-harmed as a teenager when she was in a toxic relationship and managed to stop it when she met someone who was "loving and respectful." However, the huge success of their 1998 album *Version 2.0* led to her becoming the "media 'It' girl" and the re-emergence of a drive to self-harm. The glare of the media attention gave her a self-consciousness she hadn't felt since puberty. "I was suffering from extreme 'imposter syndrome,' constantly measuring myself against my peers, sincerely believing that they had gotten everything right and I had gotten everything so very wrong," she said in 2018.[16]

It's arguable that Karen suffered a form of imposter syndrome. Living in the shadow of her brother, she didn't realize how talented she was, doubting that she deserved accolades. As Nicky Chinn said, she couldn't believe it when John Lennon stopped her and said, "I just gotta tell you, love, I think you've got the most fabulous voice."

Richard Carpenter has commented that, "when it came to running into . . . Lennon or Streisand, she seemed sometimes like a teenager aspiring to greatness, whereas in fact she was recognized not only as great but world famous."[17] This self-doubt, combined with the relentless pressure of touring and living in the media spotlight, had a damaging effect on Karen's mental health and sense of resilience. It seems that the achievement of success was also Karen's most vulnerable moment. Judging by the experiences of 2020s stars like Demi Lovato, Taylor Swift, Sam Smith, and Greyson Chance, there are still lessons to be learned.

In an industry accelerated by the effects of digital media and streaming and the constant need for new commercial product, the higher the stakes, the higher the stress. As Adele said, "Fame is toxic and touring is lonely."[18] There is a high prevalence of eating disorders in female musicians, particularly among those on international tours. According to neuroscientists Kapsetaki and Easmon, solo singers have more eating disorders than instrumentalists, suggesting "that [singers have] an ambivalent association with their primary instrument, i.e. it is one's body that makes music."[19] It's not surprising, therefore, that Karen's anxiety increased when she was persuaded to abandon the drums and become the lead singer at the front of the stage.

The risk factors for female performers are a combination of perfectionism, anxiety, stress, and the expectation that they should strive to attain (and maintain) that elusive size eight. One singer interviewed for Can Music Make You Sick?, a survey conducted by the charity Help Musicians UK, was measured monthly by her record company and if she was slightly over size eight, they would say, "I'm not sure how serious you are about your career."[20]

Karen kept her battle secret, but many younger female singers—like Taylor Swift, Kesha, Halsey, and Lady Gaga—

are critiquing that cultural idealisation of thinness. What contributed to Karen Carpenter's isolation was the belief that anorexia was shameful and taboo. Younger women, emboldened by Third Wave and MeToo feminism, are calling for more support. "I thought I wasn't supposed to eat food," says Kesha. "Then, if I ever did, I felt ashamed. I was slowly starving myself and the sicker I got the more people around me were saying, 'You look so beautiful. So stunning.' I'm so anxious I feel I'm going to explode from the secrets."[21] Halsey felt so strongly about the issue that in December 2020 she posted on Instagram a picture of her malnourished body without a trigger warning. She has since apologized to her fans, but is still vocal about the need for the music industry to take better care of its artists.

There are signs that the industry is changing. Music managers are given better training in how to recognize mental health and addiction issues and organizations such as Help Musicians and Music Support offer guidance on early intervention and prevention. There is greater awareness of language and the words we use and the toxic impact for artists of hypersexualisation and body shaming. After her stint as Carpenters tour manager Rebecca Segal went on to become a very successful executive for Sky Entertainment and Networks and she has seen a significant shift in attitude across TV, film, and music. "That we can even talk about these things is wonderful," she says, "but there is still stigma and still more work to be done. Mental illness is like having an invisible disability. You constantly have a persona, you constantly have a mask on, never fully authentic.

Living anyone's life other than your own—your mother's, your brother's, your fame—that's a painful life for anybody."

Record companies now have workplace policies to protect the mental health of their artists and employees. In 2022, for instance, Warner Music Group launched their groundbreaking Environmental Social Governance report, which has clauses on diversity, inclusion, and climate change—and a key section on mental health programs for its creative community. Many artists are prioritizing their well-being, even if it means canceling a tour, postponing an album, or quitting the pressures of the business altogether. "It's easier to say with hindsight, looking back, what if everybody just could have given Karen an indefinite timeout?" says Cherry Boone O'Neill. For her, relinquishing control was the hardest thing to do, because for so long her identity was bound up in obsession with her body weight, calorie intake and a grueling exercise schedule. To give that up meant losing her security and her identity, without having a replacement. "That's the scary part. It's like deciding to voluntarily fall off a cliff and being afraid to let go because you can't see the safety net, you don't know if you're gonna survive. But what you don't realize is that there's a very soft place to land if you allow the process to unfold."

Strides are being made, too, in terms of greater gender equality. Universal Music has connected with USC Annenberg's Inclusion Initiative to address the ways women are excluded from areas like songwriting and production and as instrumentalists. Compared to when Karen started out in the 1970s, female artists today have so much more support and freedom to realize their full potential. "Hopefully we don't just look back at Karen's life with sadness," says Segal. "She left an extraordinary musical legacy. She has one of the most distinctive, beautiful voices ever. You put on a record and you have no question who it is—that's a real rarity. More and more people will discover her. Some people burn brighter because they may not burn as long."

Imagine a scenario. A young Karen Carpenter singing and playing drums, developing her innovative technique as a central part of the act, and building her production skills in the studio. If she has periods struggling with her mental health, early intervention and treatment is there to help her rest, take care of herself and build resilience. Longevity is the goal, rather than short-term success—a long, rich career in which she plays glorious music with her brother in the pop band and she also creates solo projects, exploring other genres, indulging her wild side, the outer reaches of her creativity. She may collaborate with other artists, she may hold drum workshops, she may produce young female musicians, she may become a key figure in the industry. It would be nice to think this is possible now.

Karen's untimely death has dominated her story, but what also endures is the transformative power of her voice, her expertise as a drummer and who she was as a person. Across fan sites and social media, YouTube reaction videos and TikTok, people enthuse about Karen as a singer and a drummer. As Twitter user @Taige42 wrote in May 2021, "Go youtube, search 'Karen Carpenter on drums' and prepare to have your mind blown."

Karen carved out her own path, with a sound that encapsulated sweet sadness, a sensitive soul and a deep understanding of song. Once she was asked how she wanted the Carpenters to be remembered. "For our contribution to music. Because that is the main thing in our lives, what comes from within us through music. We've tried to maintain an even keel over the years. This business has a tendency to shake egos, but I hope we haven't changed that much." She just wanted to be remembered as a musician and a "nice person."[22]

It was as profound and simple as that.

BENEDICTION

I went to Los Angeles to find her. The first time I encounter her, I'm walking down Avenue of the Stars towards Fox Studios in the bright sunshine and she enters my head saying, "I had such fun in that apartment, twenty-two floors up." What's not to love? Twenty-six years old, she was at the top of her game. Garrett the Uber driver is playing Kodak Black's "Super Gremlin" in the car and I get a sense that Karen would have loved hip hop—the wordplay, the camaraderie, the clothes and playful conspicuous consumption. In the same way she joked with Billy Joel's boys in the New York studio, she was a drummer at heart, driven by words and rhythm, and hip hop would have appealed to her tomboy side.

I spend the next day in Downey. I go to Downey High School—a wide square building with a vast slab of concrete out front—built in 1950s style in a time of expansion. The school had to be sizable to accommodate all those children growing up in the suburbs during the California boom time. I walk round the corner to 5th Street, where Karen and Richard had their apartments, "Close to You" on one side of the road, "Only Just Begun" on the other. It's a street with neat green lawns and sweet-smelling rose bushes; white, pink, and red blooms, pretty in the sunshine. I turn left and head along Downey Avenue, a long, straight road that becomes less appealing the further I walk down. The cars are rushing past, there's nondescript housing, car spares shops, cheap malls, and, as I get nearer to 22020, the apartment building where the Carpenter family lived when they first moved to Los Angeles, the thought flies into my head, "This is where the depression started, this is where the eating disorder started." Karen was thirteen, uprooted and dispatched from the haven of New Haven to this place where she didn't know anyone. This part of Downey feels empty and soulless, intersected by roads and a railway track.

I can't get Wi-Fi and feel cut off, so make my way round to Downey Library, where they have free Wi-Fi, and order another Uber. I am drained and dispirited. Is this what she felt like? This driver, Eli, plays KROQ on the radio and doesn't know who the Carpenters were. Downey is very spread out, with wide, utilitarian streets. Eli drives to a slightly wealthier neighborhood and we turn into Newville Avenue and he parks outside number 9828 so I can take a photo. Here it is, the house that was on the cover of the Now & Then *album. It's smaller than I expected, pristine and perfect ranch style, well maintained. It stands four-square and indefatigable on this suburban street. This is where the family lived, even after Richard and Karen were famous. This is what Karen came back to after world tours and after they'd been in the studio all day in Hollywood. This place. I can't get rid of the feeling of emptiness. It drains me for the rest of the day; it's discouraging and sad. I get no sense from Downey of nourishment, of something creative thriving there.*

The next day I feel revived. It's a beautiful warm spring day. Maybe I'll find Karen again. I'm invited to my friend Wendy's house for Passover. We go to Sherman Oaks and break matzo. It's my first Passover celebration—I'm a Catholic, but the matzo reminds me of the Communion host and I still feel moved by the spiritual message of unity and endurance and the sense of liberation from slavery. The slavery could be on a wide political scale, the suffering of peoples, or it could be in the quiet, closed suffering of the heart.

After Passover we drive back down the freeway to Hollywood. It's dark now and the night before the full moon, so the moon is glowing. We turn into Henson Recording Studios and the old A&M building. Faryal Ganjehei, head of studio operations, takes us to Studio A, the large room with a grand piano, and then we walk down the corridor to Studio B.

In the room candles are burning. There are Persian rugs on the floor and tapestries draped over the baffles. An old black baby grand piano stands there and fixed on the wall is an enormous crystal shaped like a heart. The engineers say, "This is Karen's heart and this is her room." The place is suffused with a feminine energy, a presence. Joe, the engineer, tells me that musicians love this studio. "There's always a song here," one of them said after a particularly good session. The engineers say it feels like someone's living space. Every night when they go to lock up the lounge area above Studio B they say, "Goodnight, Karen."

Joe plays a few Carpenters tracks into the studio and I sit on the sofa. It's pleasant, warm, womblike, a place of good vibes, and I don't want to leave. Then I hear Karen singing "Song for You" and I'm alert. It's uncanny hearing a song that was recorded in the same room—it's like an echo of an echo. A record is a sonic imprint, it captures so much information, spatial and acoustic detail that connects with emotion and memory. It's like Karen is singing in the room, and then she is—singing quietly, not belting it out, but knowing with surety the power of her voice, because she knows with surety the power of the words she is communicating. See? *she seems to be saying.* This is a song for you.

This studio is her happy place; this room is the motherlode. This is where the music was made and this, she says, is her gift to the world.

CARPENTERS: SELECT DISCOGRAPHY

Key US releases from 1966 to 1996, all issued on A&M unless otherwise indicated.

Singles

1966

"Looking for Love"/"I'll Be Yours" (Magic Lamp; credited only to Karen Carpenter)

1969

"Ticket to Ride"/"Your Wonderful Parade"

1970

"(They Long to Be) Close to You"/"I Kept On Loving You"
"We've Only Just Begun"/"All of My Life"
"Merry Christmas, Darling"/"Mr. Guder"

THE STORY OF KAREN CARPENTER

1971
"For All We Know"/"Don't Be Afraid"
"Rainy Days and Mondays"/"Saturday"
"Superstar"/"Bless the Beasts and Children"

1972
"Hurting Each Other"/"Maybe It's You"
"It's Going to Take Some Time"/"Flat Baroque"
"Goodbye to Love"/"Crystal Lullaby"

1973
"Sing"/"Druscilla Penny"
"Yesterday Once More"/"Road Ode"
"Top of the World"/"Heather"

1974
"Jambalaya (On the Bayou)"/"Mr. Guder"
"I Won't Last a Day Without You"/"One Love"
"Santa Claus Is Comin' to Town"/"Merry Christmas, Darling"
"Please Mr. Postman"/"This Masquerade"

1975
"Only Yesterday"/"Happy"
"Solitaire"/"Love Me for What I Am"

1976
"There's a Kind of Hush"/"I'm Caught Between Goodbye and
I Love You"

"I Need to Be in Love"/"Sandy"
"Goofus"/"Boat to Sail"
"Breaking Up Is Hard to Do"/"I Have You"

1977
"All You Get from Love Is a Love Song"/"I Have You"
"Calling Occupants of Interplanetary Craft"/"Can't Smile Without You"

1978
"Sweet, Sweet Smile"/"I Have You"
"I Believe You"/"B'wana She No Home"

1981
"Touch Me When We're Dancing"/"Because We Are in Love (The Wedding Song)"
"(Want You) Back in My Life Again"/"Somebody's Been Lyin'"
"Those Good Old Dreams"/"When It's Gone (It's Just Gone)"

1982
"Beechwood 4-5789"/"Two Sides"

Albums

1969
Ticket to Ride (first released under the title *Offering*): "Invocation," "Your Wonderful Parade," "Someday," "Get Together," "All of My Life," Turn Away," "Ticket to Ride," "Don't Be

Afraid," "What's the Use," "All I Can Do," "Eve," "Nowadays Clancy Can't Even Sing," "Benediction"

1970

Close to You: "We've Only Just Begun," "Love Is Surrender," "Maybe It's You," "Reason to Believe," "Help," "(They Long to Be) Close to You," "Baby It's You," "I'll Never Fall in Love Again," "Crescent Noon," "Mr. Guder," "I Kept On Loving You," "Another Song"

1971

Carpenters: "Rainy Days and Mondays," "Saturday," "Let Me Be the One," "(A Place to) Hideaway," "For All We Know," "Superstar," "Druscilla Penny," "One Love," "Knowing When to Leave"/"(There's) Always Something There to Remind Me"/"I'll Never Fall in Love Again"/"Walk On By"/"Do You Know the Way to San Jose," "Sometimes"

1972

A Song for You: "A Song for You," "Top of the World," "Hurting Each Other," "It's Going to Take Some Time," "Goodbye to Love," "Intermission," "Bless the Beasts and Children," "Flat Baroque," "Piano Picker," "I Won't Last a Day Without You," "Crystal Lullaby," "Road Ode," "A Song for You" (Reprise)

1973

Now & Then: "Sing," "This Masquerade," "Heather," "Jambalaya (On the Bayou)," "I Can't Make Music," "Yesterday Once

More," "Fun, Fun, Fun"/"The End of the World"/"Da Doo Ron Ron (When He Walked Me Home)"/"Dead Man's Curve"/ "Johnny Angel"/"The Night Has a Thousand Eyes"/"Our Day Will Come"/"One Fine Day," "Yesterday Once More" (Reprise) *The Singles: 1969–1973*: "We've Only Just Begun," "Top of the World," "Ticket to Ride," "Superstar," "Rainy Days and Mondays," "Goodbye to Love," "Yesterday Once More," "It's Going to Take Some Time," "Sing," "For All We Know," "Hurting Each Other," "(They Long to Be) Close to You"

1975

Horizon: "Aurora," "Only Yesterday," "Desperado," "Please Mr. Postman," "I Can Dream, Can't I?," "Solitaire," "Happy," "(I'm Caught Between) Goodbye and I Love You," "Love Me for What I Am," "Eventide"

1976

A Kind of Hush: "There's a Kind of Hush," "You," "Sandy," "Goofus," "Can't Smile Without You," "I Need to Be in Love," "One More Time," "Boat to Sail," "I Have You," "Breaking Up Is Hard to Do"

1977

Passage: "B'wana She No Home," "All You Get from Love Is a Love Song," "I Just Fall in Love Again," "On the Balcony of the Casa Rosada"/"Don't Cry for Me Argentina," "Sweet, Sweet Smile," "Two Sides," "Man Smart, Woman Smarter," "Calling Occupants of Interplanetary Craft"

1978

Christmas Portrait: "O Come, O Come, Emmanuel," "Overture" ["Deck the Halls (With Boughs of Holly)"/"I Saw Three Ships"/"Have Yourself a Merry Little Christmas"/"God Rest Ye Merry Gentlemen"/"Away in a Manger (Luther's Cradle Hymn)"/"What Child Is This? (Greensleeves)"/"Carol of the Bells"/"O Come All Ye Faithful"], "Christmas Waltz," "Sleigh Ride," "It's Christmas Time"/"Sleep Well, Little Children," "Have Yourself a Merry Little Christmas," "Santa Claus Is Comin' to Town," "Christmas Song (Chestnuts Roasting on an Open Fire)," "Silent Night," "Jingle Bells," "First Snowfall"/"Let It Snow! Let It Snow! Let It Snow!," "Carol of the Bells," "Merry Christmas, Darling," "I'll Be Home for Christmas," "Christ Is Born," "Winter Wonderland"/"Silver Bells"/"White Christmas," "Ave Maria"

The Singles: 1974–1978: "Sweet, Sweet Smile," "Jambalaya (On the Bayou)," "Can't Smile Without You," "I Won't Last a Day Without You," "All You Get from Love Is a Love Song," "Only Yesterday," "Solitaire," "Please Mr. Postman," "I Need to Be in Love," "Happy," "There's a Kind of Hush," "Calling Occupants of Interplanetary Craft"

1981

Made in America: "Those Good Old Dreams," "Strength of a Woman," "(Want You) Back in My Life Again," "When You've Got What It Takes," "Somebody's Been Lyin'," "I Believe You," "Touch Me When We're Dancing," "When It's Gone (It's Just Gone)," "Beechwood 4-5789," "Because We Are in Love (The Wedding Song)"

1983

Voice of the Heart: "Now," "Sailing on the Tide," "You're Enough," "Make Believe It's Your First Time," "Two Lives," "At the End of a Song," "Ordinary Fool," "Prime Time Love," "Your Baby Doesn't Love You Anymore," "Look to Your Dreams"

1996

Karen Carpenter (solo album): "Lovelines," "All Because of You," "If I Had You," "Making Love in the Afternoon" (with Peter Cetera), "If We Try," "Remember When Lovin'" Took All Night," "Still in Love with You," "My Body Keeps Changing My Mind," "Make Believe It's Your First Time," "Guess I Just Lost My Head," "Still Crazy After All These Years," "Last One Singin' the Blues"

ACKNOWLEDGMENTS

I want to thank Karen's friends and fellow musicians who contributed to this book, generously giving up their time to share such vivid memories—Cherry Boone O'Neill, Tom Bahler, Clare Baren, Ed Caraeff, Harold Childs, Nicky Chinn, Petula Clark, Jay Dee Maness, Liberty Devitto, Jeff Dexter, Stan DeWitt, Jay Graydon, Bernie Grundman, Doug Ichiuji, Bob James, Russell Javors, Gayle Levant, Thad Maxwell, Tommy Morgan, Rob Mounsey, Cubby O'Brien, Alan Oken, Alan Osmond, Rebecca Segal, Stephanie Spruill, Dionne Warwick.

Thank you also to Bettie Serveert, Miki Berenyi, Chris Briggs, Len Brown, Chris Charlesworth, Cathy Capozzi, Joshua Cruz, Glyn Davis, Faryngel at Henson Recording Studios, Wendy Fonarow, Lisa Gee, Harlie Axford, Kristina Kelman, Naomi Kooker, Ann Munday, Keigo Oyamada (Cornelius), Andy Prevezer, Bruce Ravid, Shonen Knife, Julian Spear, Jon Wozencroft for their thoughts and perspectives on the cultural impact of the Carpenters and A&M Records in the 1970s and beyond.

Thanks to London College of Music, University of West London, for access to very helpful research on music, mental health, and well-being, plus recent work on addiction and eating disorders. Also, a special mention to researchers Polly Hancock and Ruth Miller from punkgirldiaries.com for their excellent detective work and insight. And thanks to Carpenters fans and Carpenterologists who have contributed so much valuable research to the field and kept the fires burning.

Thanks to Malcolm, Erran and Maya, and all my family and friends, for your love and support . . .

And thank you, Karen, for your gift to the world.

NOTES AND SOURCES

Invocation

1. Baudrillard, J. (1988) *America*. Verso.

1 1950–1963

1. Coleman, R. (1994) *The Carpenters: The Untold Story*. Boxtree.
2. Tuna, C. (1976) "Karen Carpenter: Nothing to Hide Behind" radio interview, in Schmidt, R. (ed.) (2012) *Yesterday Once More: The Carpenters Reader*. Chicago Review Press.
3. Coleman, R. (1994) *The Carpenters: The Untold Story*. Boxtree.
4. BBC Radio 2 (1983) Ray Moore interview with the Carpenters.
5. Author interview with Cathy Capozzi, March 2022.
6. BBC Radio 2 (1983) Ray Moore interview with the Carpenters.
7. Renzoni, T. (2022) *Historic Connecticut Music Venues*. History Press.
8. Zappa, F. with Occhiogrosso, P. (1989) *The Real Frank Zappa Book*. Simon & Schuster.
9. Coleman, R. (1994) *The Carpenters: The Untold Story*. Boxtree.
10. Tuna, C. (1976) "Karen Carpenter: Nothing to Hide Behind" radio interview.
11. Gautschy, D. (1971) "The Carpenters: They've Only Just Begun." *TV Record Mirror*.

2 1963–1966

1. Coleman, R. (1994) *The Carpenters: The Untold Story*. Boxtree.

2. Haynie, L., South, S., Bose, S. (2006) "The Company You Keep: Adolescent Mobility and Peer Behavior." *Sociological Inquiry* 76 (3).

3. Schmidt, R. (2010) *Little Girl Blue: The Life of Karen Carpenter*. Omnibus Press.

4. Nagourney, A. (2015) "Brown's Arid California, Thanks Partly to His Father." Available at nytimes.com/2015/05/17/us/jerry-browns-arid-california-thanks-partly-to-his-father.html. Accessed April 2022.

5. Didion, J. (2003) *Where I Was From*. Knopf.

6. Nolan, T. (1974) "Up from Downey." Available at rocksbackpages.com/Library/Article/the-carpenters-up-from-downey. Accessed June 2021.

7. Tuna, C. (1976) "Karen Carpenter: Nothing to Hide Behind" radio interview.

8. Author interview with Naomi Kooker, September 2022.

9. Tuna, C. (1976) "Karen Carpenter: Nothing to Hide Behind" radio interview.

10. Gautschy, D. (1971) "The Carpenters: They've Only Just Begun." *TV Record Mirror*.

11. Hardwick, N. (1973) "Karen Carpenter: When I Was 16." *Star*.

12. Tuna, C. (1976) "Karen Carpenter: Nothing to Hide Behind" radio interview.

13. KNXT LA TV (1972) "Jerry Dunphy Visits the Carpenters." Available at youtube.com/watch?v=_BzaAh1T-Q4. Accessed July 2021.

14. Helmore, E. (2020) "Viola Smith, pioneering swing and big band drummer, dies aged 107." Available at theguardian.com/music/2020/oct/24/viola-smith-swing-big-band-drummer-dies-aged-107?fbclid=IwAR1n E5WAY-4Yb1zntKIsEz9lLuQ-IBkpnbPqEA4KZTvEuKX8JDJAzFD9eFc. Accessed June 2022.

15. Author interview with Amie McBye, February 2022.

16. Gautschy, D. (1971) "The Carpenters: They've Only Just Begun." *TV Record Mirror*.

17. Cerra, S. (2019) "Roy Harte and Drum City: 'Drummers Are Like Hockey Goalies . . .'" jazzprofiles.blogspot.com/2019/04/roy-harte-and-drum-city-drummers-are.html. Accessed May 2022.

18. Beale, L. (2010) "Drum pioneer snares a big chunk of the market." Available at latimes.com/archives/la-xpm-2010-apr-04-la-fi-himi-belli4-2010apr04-story.html. Accessed May 2022.

19. Downey High School yearbook, 1967.

20. Author communication with Corey Christensen's stepson Artie O'Daly, December 2022.

21.   Gautschy, D. (1971) "The Carpenters: They've Only Just Begun." *TV Record Mirror*.

22.   Steinbeck, J. (1955) "Like Captured Fireflies." San Francisco, CTA Journal, 1952–1969.

23.   Author interview with Stan de Witt, April 2022.

24.   Pooler, F. (1973) "The Choral Sound of the Carpenters." *The Choral Journal*.

25.   May, C. (2014) "Hal Blaine & Joe Osborn interview 2013." Available at youtube.com/watch?v=G--Y9FxVI0k&t=1462s. Accessed January 2022.

26.   Nolan, T. (1974) "Up from Downey." Available at rocksbackpages.com/Library/Article/the-carpenters-up-from-downey. Accessed June 2021.

3 1967–1968

1.   O'Reilly, B. (2014) "The Carpenters with Fred Napoli." CKFM Radio Toronto interview. Available at youtube.com/watch?v=HLbkCYEYndc. Accessed May 2021.

2.   Tennessean. (2014) "The Story Behind the Song: 'Yesterday Once More.'" Available at youtube.com/watch?v=xsE4EGyZQJs&t=6s. Accessed June 2022.

3.   Ibid.

4.   Coleman, R. (1994) *The Carpenters: The Untold Story*. Boxtree.

5.   O'Reilly, B. (2014) "The Carpenters with Fred Napoli." CKFM Radio Toronto interview. Available at youtube.com/watch?v=HLbkCYEYndc. Accessed May 2021.

6.   WCFL Radio (1970) Dick Biondi interview with the Carpenters.

7.   Cidoni Lennox, M., May, C. & Carpenter, R. (2021) *Carpenters: The Musical Legacy*. Princeton Architectural Press.

8.   Hunger, J. (2018). "Weight Labeling and Disordered Eating Among Adolescent Girls." *Journal of Adolescent Health* 63 (3). Available at pubmed.ncbi.nlm.nih.gov/29705495. Accessed May 2022.

9.   Cartner-Morley, J. (2009) "Twiggy at 60: 'It's amazing I didn't go stark raving bonkers.'" Available at theguardian.com/lifeandstyle/2009/sep/19/twiggy-at-60-interview. Accessed May 2022.

10.   Coleman, R. (1994) *The Carpenters: The Untold Story*. Boxtree.

11.   Ibid.

12. Suntorypop (2010) "Carpenters 'Your All American College Show' 12/01/69." Available at youtube.com/watch?v=OKa_4hkNjPE. Accessed April 2021.

13. Author interview with Tom Bahler, October 2022.

4 1969

1. Rockduo (1978) "Carl Goldman Interviews Karen Carpenter for FM100 Los Angeles Radio." Available at youtube.com/watch?v=dMYqhu7oQ0g. Accessed May 2021.

2. Coleman, R. (1994) *The Carpenters: The Untold Story*. Boxtree.

3. Billy Rees (2020) "Herb Alpert—Signing the Carpenters to A&M" (from 2010 BBC Four documentary *Herb Alpert, Tijuana Brass and Other Delights*). Available at: youtube.com/watch?v=T0rNeiy65tE. Accessed June 2021.

4. Author interview with Thad Maxwell, February 2022.

5. O'Reilly, B. (2014) "The Carpenters with Fred Napoli." CKFM Radio Toronto interview. Available at youtube.com/watch?v=HLbkCYEYndc. Accessed May 2021.

6. Author interview with Petula Clark, February 2022.

7. Rockduo (1978) "Carl Goldman Interviews Karen Carpenter for FM100 Los Angeles Radio." Available at youtube.com/watch?v=dMYqhu7oQ0g. Accessed May 2021.

8. May, C. (2014) "Hal Blaine & Joe Osborn interview 2013." Available at youtube.com/watch?v=G--Y9FxVI0k&t=1462s. Accessed January 2022.

5 1970

1. Rockduo (1978) "Carl Goldman Interviews Karen Carpenter for FM100 Los Angeles Radio." Available at youtube.com/watch?v=dMYqhu7oQ0g. Accessed May 2021.

2. May, C. (2014) "Hal Blaine & Joe Osborn interview 2013." Available at youtube.com/watch?v=G--Y9FxVI0k&t=1462s. Accessed January 2022.

3. Carpenters Collector (2020) "Carpenters 'Chuck Findley interview.'" Available at youtube.com/watch?v=cYIolL8KVWg. Accessed June 2022.

4. Rockduo (1978) "Carl Goldman Interviews Karen Carpenter for FM100 Los Angeles Radio. Available at youtube.com/watch?v=dMYqhu7oQ0g. Accessed May 2021.

5. Leslie, P. (2020) "Roger Nichols Interview on the Paul Leslie Hour." Available at youtube.com/watch?v=w3xd74CvWWU. Accessed June 2022.

6. Nashville High (2012) "Paul Williams, We've Only Just Begun." Available at youtube.com/watch?v=kuFTZu2n9gY. Accessed June 2022.

7. Author interview with Dionne Warwick, February 2022.

8. Coleman, R. (1994) *The Carpenters: The Untold Story*. Boxtree.

9. Rockduo (1978) "Carl Goldman Interviews Karen Carpenter for FM100 Los Angeles Radio." Available at youtube.com/watch?v=dMYqhu7oQ0g. Accessed May 2021.

10. Weatherford, M. (1995) "Elvis Presley, Who Would Have Turned 60 in 1995, Once Reigned in Las Vegas. Some Say He Still Does." Available at nevadamagazine.com/issue/february-1995/6994. Accessed June 2022.

11. Author interview with Petula Clark, February 2022.

12. Ten-Q Radio Los Angeles (1977) "Passage—the radio interview."

13. Simpson, G. (2022) "Elvis Presley's wild Las Vegas years: From hair dye on walls to moment it all went wrong." Available at express.co.uk/entertainment/music/1627273/Elvis-Presley-Las-Vegas-years-Elvis-decline. Accessed June 2022.

14. Ten-Q Radio Los Angeles (1977) "Passage—the radio interview."

15. Cidoni Lennox, M., May, C., & Carpenter, R. (2021) *Carpenters: The Musical Legacy*. Princeton Architectural Press.

6 1971

1. BBC Radio 2 (1981) Ray Moore interview with the Carpenters.

2. Author interview with Tommy Morgan, March 2022.

3. Cidoni Lennox, M., May, C., & Carpenter, R. (2021) *Carpenters: The Musical Legacy*. Princeton Architectural Press.

4. Author interview with Jon Wozencroft, June 2022.

5. MacDougall, F. (1971) "The Carpenters: Nailing Down Success." *Teen*.

6. Coleman, R. (1975) "Carpenters—Good, Clean, All-American Aggro!" *Melody Maker*.

7. Amendola, B. (no date) "An Interview with Hal Blaine." Available at moderndrummer.com/2005/07/hal-blaine-2 December 2022.

8. Coleman, R. (1994) *The Carpenters: The Untold Story*. Boxtree.

9. Ibid.

10. Coleman, R. (1975) "Carpenters—Good, Clean, All-American Aggro!" *Melody Maker*.

11. McKay, G. (2018) "Skinny Blues: Karen Carpenter, Anorexia Nervosa and Popular Music." *Popular Music* 37 (1).

12. Tuna, C. (1976) "Karen Carpenter: Nothing to Hide Behind" radio interview.

13. Coleman, R. (1975) "Carpenters—Good, Clean, All-American Aggro!" *Melody Maker*.

14. Author communication with Martin Slattery, July 2021.

15. Author interview with Amie McBye, February 2022.

16. Author interview with Wendy Fonarow, September 2021.

17. MacDougall, F. (1971) "The Carpenters: Nailing Down Success." *Teen*.

18. Michaels, K. "Rainy Days and Carpenters Always Get Me Down." *Chicago Tribune Magazine*.

19. MacDougall, F. (1971) "The Carpenters: Nailing Down Success." *Teen*.

20. Walsh, J. (2014) "Sex, Tipsy Tories & Elizabeth David: Fifty Years of the West End's Infamous Nightclub Annabel's." Available at independent.co.uk/arts-enter tainment/films/features/sex-tipsy-tories-elizabeth-david-fifty-years-of-the-west -end-s-infamous-nightclub-annabel-s-9846626.html. Accessed August 2022.

21. Schmidt, R. (2010) *Little Girl Blue: The Life of Karen Carpenter*. Omnibus Press.

7 1972

1. BBC Radio 2 (1981) Ray Moore interview with the Carpenters.

2. Author interview with Harold Childs, November 2021.

3. Coleman, R. (1975) "Carpenters—Good, Clean, All-American Aggro!" *Melody Maker*.

4. Author interview with Gayle Levant, April 2022

5. Armstrong, D. (1971) "Why They're on Top?" *Southeast News*.

6. MPI Home Video (1998) *Close to You: Remembering the Carpenters*.

7. Hoyle, B. (2018) "Richard Carpenter: 'The Cultural Impact of the Carpenters Would Make a Great Doctoral Thesis,'" Available at thetimes.co.uk/article/ richard-carpenter-the-cultural-impact-of-the-carpenters-would-make-a-great -doctoral-thesis-qzkvvbxcz. Accessed May 2022.

8 1973

1. Carpenters Collector (2020) "Carpenters Interview 1971 Grammies." Available at youtube.com/watch?v=gRa9fkqk8pM. Accessed April 2021.

2. Arnett, J. (2000) "Emerging Adulthood: A Theory of Development from the Late Teens Through the Twenties." *American Psychologist.*

3. Coleman, R. (1975) "Carpenters—Good, Clean, All-American Aggro!" *Melody Maker.*

4. Carpenters Collector (2020) "Carpenters Interview 1971 Grammies." Available at youtube.com/watch?v=gRa9fkqk8pM. Accessed April 2021.

5. Coleman, R. (1976) "Carpenters Uber Alles!" *Melody Maker.*

6. Author interview with Cubby O'Brien, September 2021.

7. Carpenters Collector (2020) "Carpenters Interview with Wink Martindale 1970." Available at youtube.com/watch?v=1TGt3cBFIac. Accessed April 2021.

8. Suntorypop (2010) "Karen Carpenter—Tony Peluso Tribute." Available at youtube.com/watch?v=85hv6MS0tX4. Accessed May 2021.

9. Coleman, R. (1975) "Carpenters—Good, Clean, All-American Aggro!" *Melody Maker.*

10. Tuna, C. (1976) "Karen Carpenter: Nothing to Hide Behind" radio interview.

11. Wolfe, T. (1968) *The Pump House Gang.* Bantam [1999 edition].

12. Adams, S. (2018) "Smiley Smile." Available at designobserver.com/feature /smiley-smile/39740. Accessed July 2022.

13. Author interview with JayDee Maness, October 2021

14. Author interview with Clare Baren, September 2021.

15. Author interview with Bruce Ravid, November 2021.

9 1974

1. MacDougall, F. (1971) "The Carpenters: Nailing Down Success." *Teen.*

2. Author interview with Chris Charlesworth, May 2022.

3. Author communication with Alan Osmond, September 2022.

4. Tuna, C. (1976) "Karen Carpenter: Nothing to Hide Behind" radio interview.

5. A&M Press Release (1971). "Karen in the Kitchen: Who Says a Young Female Superstar Can't Be a Top-Notch Cook?"

6. Schmidt, R. (2010) *Little Girl Blue: The Life of Karen Carpenter.* Omnibus Press.

7. Dave's Osmond Videos (2020) "Being the Osmonds (2003 UK Documentary Featuring the Osmond Brothers)." Available at youtube.com/watch?v=X2VmdtLTuCk. Accessed June 2022.

8. Ibid.

9. Author interview with Cherry Boone O'Neill, October 2022.

10. Author interview with Lisa Gee, July 2022.

11. Coleman, R. (1975) "Carpenters—Good, Clean, All-American Aggro!" *Melody Maker*.

12. Coleman, R. (1994) *The Carpenters: The Untold Story*. Boxtree.

13. Author interview with Cubby O'Brien, September 2021.

14. Haber, J. (1974) "Carpenters Nail Down a Spot in Pop Pantheon." *Los Angeles Times*.

15. Schmidt, R. (2010) *Little Girl Blue: The Life of Karen Carpenter*. Omnibus Press.

16. Nolan, T. (1974) "Up from Downey." Available at rocksbackpages.com/Library/Article/the-carpenters-up-from-downey. Accessed June 2021.

17. Author interview with Nicky Chinn, March 2022.

18. Author interview with Gayle Levant, April 2022.

19. Author interview with Clare Baren, September 2021.

20. Coleman, R. (1975) "Carpenters—Good, Clean, All-American Aggro!" *Melody Maker*.

21. Author interview with Jeff Dexter, February 2022.

22. Author interview with Rebecca Segal, October 2022.

23. Karen's Condo (2010) "The Carpenters Karen & Richard—Tonight Show 1978." Available at youtube.com/watch?v=XxwARLDFGYs. Accessed May 2021.

24. Tong Hop (2015) "The Man Who Called THE BEATLES! Tatsushi Nagashima Behind the Scenes in Japan." Available at youtube.com/watch?v=j45CnC1pTpk. Accessed October 2022.

25. Author communication with Miki Berenyi, October 2022.

26. Author communication with Cornelius, October 2022.

27. Coleman, R. (1976) "Carpenters Uber Alles!" *Melody Maker*.

28. A&M Compendium (1975) "The Carpenters: An Interview," in Schmidt, R. (ed.) (2012). *Yesterday Once More: The Carpenters Reader*. Chicago Review Press.

29. Author interview with Thad Maxwell, February 2022.

30. Author interview with Bernie Grundman, March 2022.

10 1975

1. Nolan, T. (1974) "Up from Downey." Available at rocksbackpages.com/Library /Article/the-carpenters-up-from-downey. Accessed June 2021.

2. KNXT LA TV (1972) "Jerry Dunphy Visits the Carpenters." Available at youtube.com/watch?v=_BzaAh1T-Q4. Accessed July 2021.

3. Nolan, T. (1974) "Up from Downey." Available at rocksbackpages.com/Library /Article/the-carpenters-up-from-downey. Accessed June 2021.

4. Ibid.

5. Coleman, R. (1975) "Carpenters—Good, Clean, All-American Aggro!" *Melody Maker.*

6. Author interview with Clare Baren, September 2021.

7. Author interview with Ed Caraeff, July 2022.

8. Ten-Q Radio Los Angeles (1977) "Passage—The Radio Interview."

9. Carpenters Collector (2020) "Carpenters 'Chuck Findley interview.'" Available at youtube.com/watch?v=cYIolL8KVWg. Accessed June 2022.

10. Neil Sedaka press conference, Las Vegas, August 1975.

11. Coleman, R. (1975) "Carpenters—Good, Clean, All-American Aggro!" *Melody Maker.*

12. Ibid.

11 1976

1. Carpenters Collector (2020) "Carpenters Interview with Wink Martindale 1970." Available at youtube.com/watch?v=1TGt3cBFIac. Accessed April 2021.

2. Tuna, C. (1976) "Karen Carpenter: Nothing to Hide Behind" radio interview.

3. Schmidt, R. (2010) *Little Girl Blue: The Life of Karen Carpenter.* Omnibus Press.

4. Freidwald, W. (1995) *Sinatra! The Song Is You: A Singer's Art.* Simon & Schuster.

5. Author interview with Gayle Levant, April 2022.

6. Coleman, R. (1994) *The Carpenters: The Untold Story.* Boxtree.

7. Tuna, C. (1976) "Karen Carpenter: Nothing to Hide Behind" radio interview.

8. Author interview with Rebecca Segal, October 2022.

9. Schmidt, R. (2010) *Little Girl Blue: The Life of Karen Carpenter.* Omnibus Press.

12 1977

1. Ten-Q Radio Los Angeles (1977) "Passage—The Radio Interview."
2. On A&M Records (no date) "Sex Pistols." Available at onamrecords.com /artists/sex-pistols. Accessed July 2022.
3. Author interview with Chris Briggs, August 2021.
4. Richard And Karen Carpenter.com (no date) "Passage." Available at richardandkarencarpenter.com/Album_Passage.htm. Accessed August 2021.
5. Author interview with Jay Graydon, February 2022.
6. Author communication with Michael Boyle, April 2022.
7. Moran, B. (1978) "If Somebody Would Let Us Know What the Problem Is . . ." *Claude Hall's International Radio Report.*
8. Author interview with Jon Wozencroft, June 2022.
9. Author interview with Harold Childs, November 2021.
10. Rockduo (1978) "Carl Goldman Interviews Karen Carpenter for FM100 Los Angeles Radio." Available at youtube.com/watch?v=dMYqhu7oQ0g. Accessed May 2021.
11. Bangs, L. (1973) "Carpenters: Now and Then." Available at rocksbackpages .com/Library/Article/carpenters-inow-and-theni. Accessed June 2021.
12. Kent, N. (1973) "The Carpenters: Summer Sweethearts." Available at rocksback pages.com/Library/Article/the-carpenters-summer-sweethearts. Accessed June 2021.
13. Author interview with Bruce Ravid, November 2021.
14. Author interview with Wendy Fonarow, September 2021.

13 1978

1. BBC Radio 2 (1981) Ray Moore interview with the Carpenters.
2. Author interview with Chris Briggs, August 2021.
3. Godier, L., & Park, R. (2015) "Does Compulsive Behavior in Anorexia Nervosa Resemble an Addiction? A Qualitative Investigation." *Frontiers in Psychology.* Available at ncbi.nlm.nih.gov/pmc/articles/PMC4611244. Accessed July 2021.
4. Ibid.
5. Coleman, R. (1994) *The Carpenters: The Untold Story.* Boxtree.

6. Schmidt, R. (ed.) (2012) *Yesterday Once More: The Carpenters Reader*. Chicago Review Press.

7. Author interview with Cherry Boone O'Neill, October 2022.

8. Eli, K. (2018) "Striving for Liminality: Eating Disorders and Social Suffering." *Transcultural Psychiatry* 55 (4).

9. Author interview, anonymous, June 2021.

10. Author interview with Tom Bahler, October 2022.

11. Plath, S. (1965) "The Munich Mannequins" in *Aerial*. Faber.

12. Naglin, N. (1978) "The Carpenters Go Country?" *Country Music*.

13. Coleman, R. (1994) *The Carpenters: The Untold Story*. Boxtree.

14. Carpenters Collector (2020) "Karen Carpenter Interview Dec. 1978 Capital Radio UK." Available at youtube.com/watch?v=NWMqB9_jsZI. Accessed June 2021.

15. Liu, A. (2007) "Making up for Lost Time: The Path to Maturity Following Eating Disorders." Available at huffpost.com/entry/making-up-for-lost-time-t_b_40977. Accessed August 2022.

16. Coleman, R. (1994) *The Carpenters: The Untold Story*. Boxtree.

17. Carpenters Collector (2020) "Karen Carpenter Interview Dec. 1978 Capital Radio UK." Available at youtube.com/watch?v=NWMqB9_jsZI. Accessed June 2021.

14 1979

1. Moran, B. (1978) "If Somebody Would Let Us Know What the Problem Is . . ." *Claude Hall's International Radio Report*.

2. Coleman, R. (1994) *The Carpenters: The Untold Story*. Boxtree.

3. Grein, P. (1981) "Carpenters: Building on Experience." *Los Angeles Times*.

4. Author interview with Alan Oken, October 2021.

5. Moran, B. (1978) "If Somebody Would Let Us Know What the Problem Is . . ." *Claude Hall's International Radio Report*.

6. Boone O'Neill, C. (1982) *Starving for Attention*. Continuum.

7. Orbach, S. (1986) *Hunger Strike*. Faber.

8. Coleman, R. (1994) *The Carpenters: The Untold Story*. Boxtree.

9. Ibid.

10. Ibid.

11. Schmidt, R. (2010) *Little Girl Blue: The Life of Karen Carpenter*. Omnibus Press.

12. Shapiro, P. (2005) *Turn the Beat Around: The Secret History of Disco*. Faber.

13. Author interview with Stephanie Spruill, January 2022.

14. Grein, P. (1981) "Carpenters: Building on Experience." *Los Angeles Times*.

15. Author interview with Rob Mounsey, December 2021.

16. Rockduo (1978) "Carl Goldman Interviews Karen Carpenter for FM100 Los Angeles Radio." Available at youtube.com/watch?v=dMYqhu7oQ0g. Accessed May 2021.

17. Author interview with Liberty Devitto, December 2021.

18. Author interview with Russell Javors, December 2021.

19. Author interview with Bob James, November 2021.

20. Author interview with Doug Ichiuji, December 2021.

21. Berger, G. (2016) *Never Say No to a Rock Star: In the Studio with Dylan, Sinatra, Jagger and More . . .* Schaffner Press.

15 1980

1. Tuna, C. (1976) "Karen Carpenter: Nothing to Hide Behind" radio interview.

2. Author interview with Russell Javors, December 2021.

3. Coleman, R. (1994) *The Carpenters: The Untold Story*. Boxtree.

4. Ibid.

5. Lieberman, F. (1974) "The Carpenters: Soft Rock and 14 Gold Records." *Saturday Evening Post*, Indianapolis.

6. BBC Radio 2 (1981) Ray Moore interview with the Carpenters.

7. Ibid.

8. Schmidt, R. (2010) *Little Girl Blue: The Life of Karen Carpenter*. Omnibus Press.

9. Coleman, R. (1994) *The Carpenters: The Untold Story*. Boxtree.

10. Schmidt, R. (2010) *Little Girl Blue: The Life of Karen Carpenter*. Omnibus Press.

11. Author interview with Petula Clark, February 2022.

12. BBC Radio 2 (1981) Ray Moore interview with the Carpenters.

13. Author interview with Gayle Levant, April 2022.

14. A&M Corner (2003) "Karen Sings The Wedding Song at Her Wedding." Available at forum.amcorner.com/threads/karen-sings-the-wedding-song-at-her-wedding.1618. Accessed July 2022.

16 1981

1. Laura Branigan Forever—RunAndPlay (2014) "Karen and Olivia Talking about Catalina—Nov 2 1981." Available at youtube.com/watch?v=Tvtb63u96xY&list=RDUG1xrYhMUFs&index=3. Accessed June 2021.
2. Author interview with Stephanie Spruill, January 2022.
3. Author interview with Bernie Grundman, February 2022.
4. BBC Radio 2 (1981) Ray Moore interview with the Carpenters.
5. Dailymotion (2017) "The Carpenters Interview 1981 Anorexia." Available at dailymotion.com/video/x5w3qr0. Accessed October 2022.
6. Berne, E. (1964) *Games People Play: The Psychology of Human Relationships.* Grove Press [2016 Penguin Life edition].
7. Boone O'Neill, C. (1982) *Starving for Attention.* Continuum.
8. Coleman, R. (1994) *The Carpenters: The Untold Story.* Boxtree.

17 1982

1. Coleman, R. (1994) *The Carpenters: The Untold Story.* Boxtree.
2. Treasure et al. (2020) "Cognitive Interpersonal Model for Anorexia Nervosa Revisited: The Perpetuating Factors that Contribute to the Development of the Severe and Enduring Illness." *Journal of Clinical Medicine* 9 (3).
3. Levenkron, S. (2001) *Anatomy of Anorexia.* W. W. Norton & Company [Kindle edition].
4. Coleman, R. (1994) *The Carpenters: The Untold Story.* Boxtree.
5. Author interview with Doug Ichiuji, December 2021.
6. Levenkron, S. (2001) *Anatomy of Anorexia.* W. W. Norton & Company [Kindle edition].
7. Coleman, R. (1994) *The Carpenters: The Untold Story.* Boxtree.
8. Schwartz, S. (2021) *The Absent Father Effect on Daughters: Father Desire, Father Wounds.* Routledge.
9. Author interview with Tom Bahler, October 2022.

10. Orbach, S. (1986) *Hunger Strike*. Faber.

11. Tuna, C. (1976) "Karen Carpenter: Nothing to Hide Behind" radio interview.

12. Coleman, R. (1994) *The Carpenters: The Untold Story*. Boxtree.

13. Tonoike et al. (2004) "Treatment with Intravenous Hyperalimentation for Severely Anorectic Patients and Its Outcome." *Psychiatry and Clinical Neurosciences Journal* 58 (3).

14. Coleman, R. (1975) "Carpenters—Good, Clean, All-American Aggro!" *Melody Maker*.

18 1983

1. Author interview with Cherry Boone O'Neill, quoting conversation with Karen, October 2022.

2. Author interview with Dionne Warwick, February 2022.

3. Coleman, R. (1994) *The Carpenters: The Untold Story*. Boxtree.

4. Hoerburger, R. (1996) "Karen Carpenter's Second Life." Available at nytimes.com/1996/10/06/magazine/karen-carpenter-s-second-life.html. Accessed August 2022.

5. Frank Pooler's diary (1983), courtesy of Stan de Witt, April 2022.

6. Hoerburger, R. (1996) "Karen Carpenter's Second Life." Available at nytimes.com/1996/10/06/magazine/karen-carpenter-s-second-life.html. Accessed August 2022.

7. People Staff (2020) "A Sweet Surface Hid a Troubled Soul in the Late Karen Carpenter, Who Would Have Been 70 Today." Available at people.com /music/karen-carpenter-70th-birthday. Accessed October 2022.

8. 8969DEINZE (2020) "Petula Clark Remembers Karen Carpenter." Available at youtube.com/watch?v=EV-KPl9Y0JY. Accessed August 2021.

9. UK ITV (2002) *Close to You: The Story of the Carpenters*.

10. Author interview with Stan de Witt, April 2022.

Epilogue

1. Stephens, C. (1995) "Gentlemen Prefer Haynes." *Film Comment* 31 (4).

2. Davis, G. (2008) *Superstar: The Karen Carpenter Story*. Wallflower Press.

3. Ibid.

4. Schmidt, R. (2010) *Little Girl Blue: The Life of Karen Carpenter*. Omnibus Press.

5. Scott, V. (1988) "Actress Finds Karen Carpenter Role 'eerie.'" Available at upi.com/Archives/1988/05/25/Actress-finds-Karen-Carpenter-role-eerie /4075588300063. Accessed July 2022.

6. Author interview with Josh Cruze, April 2022.

7. Gordon, K. (2015) *Girl in a Band*. Faber.

8. Golsen, T. (2022) "The Tragic Song Sonic Youth wrote about Karen Carpenter." Available at faroutmagazine.co.uk/the-song-sonic-youth-wrote-about -karen-carpenter. Accessed August 2022.

9. Author communication with Beth Sather, August 2021.

10. Author interview with Carol van Dijk and Berend Dubbe (Bettie Serveert), October 2021.

11. Author interview with Naoko Yamano (Shonen Knife), October 2021.

12. Crowe, J. (1996) "Karen Carpenter's 'Lost' LP." Available at latimes.com /archives/la-xpm-1996-08-31-ca-39226-story.html. Accessed September 2022.

13. Sendra, T. (no date) "As Time Goes by Review." Available at allmusic.com /album/as-time-goes-by-mw0000697538. Accessed September 2022.

14. Wally, M. (2022) "Ethel Cain's America." Available at web.archive.org /web/20220808203352/https://www.wmagazine.com/culture/ethel-cain -preachers-daughter-album-interview. Accessed October 2022.

15. Hyatt, B. (2017) "The Liberation of Kesha." Available at rollingstone.com /music/music-features/the-liberation-of-kesha-123984. Accessed May 2021.

16. Daly, R. (2018) "Garbage's Shirley Manson Opens Up about Self-harm and Suffering from 'imposter syndrome.' . ." Available at nme.com/news/music /garbages-shirley-manson-opens-self-harm-suffering-imposter-syndrome-new -op-ed-2349430. Accessed May 2021.

17. Coleman, R. (1994) *The Carpenters: The Untold Story*. Boxtree.

18. Bletchly, R. (2015) "Fame is Toxic and Touring Is Lonely." Available at mirror. co.uk/3am/celebrity-news/adele-fame-toxic-touring-lonelypeople-6693239. Accessed June 2021.

19. Kapsetaki, M. & Easmon, C. (2017) "Eating Disorders in Musicians: A Survey Investigating Self-Reported Eating Disorders of Musicians." *Eating and Weight Disorders*. Available at link.springer.com/article/10.1007/s40519-017-0414-9. Accessed May 2021.

357

20. Gross, S., & Musgrave, G. (2020) *Can Music Make You Sick? Measuring the Price of Musical Ambition.* University of Westminster Press.

21. Hyatt, B. (2017) "The Liberation of Kesha." Available at rollingstone.com /music/music-features/the-liberation-of-kesha-123984. Accessed May 2021.

22. Rockduo (1978) "Carl Goldman Interviews Karen Carpenter for FM100 Los Angeles Radio." Available at youtube.com/watch?v=dMYqhu7oQ0g. Accessed May 2021.